Nature's Museums

Nature's Museums

Victorian Science and the Architecture of Display

CARLA YANNI

The Johns Hopkins University Press
Baltimore, Maryland

First published in the United States of America in 1999 by
The Johns Hopkins University Press
2715 North Charles Street
Baltimore, MD 21218-4363
www.press.jhu.edu

Library of Congress Cataloging-in-Publication Data
Yanni, Carla.
Nature's museums : Victorian science and the architecture of
display / Carla Yanni.
p. cm.
Includes bibliographical references.
ISBN 0–8018–6326–0 (alk. paper)
1. Natural history musuems – History – 19th century.   2. Museum
architecture – History – 19th century.   3. Architecture, Victorian.   I.
Title.
QH70.A1 Y25 2000
508′.074 – dc21
99–34204
CIP

A catalog record for this book is available from the British Library

Typeset by RefineCatch Ltd, Bungay, Suffolk
Printed and bound in Great Britain
1 3 5 7 9 10 8 6 4 2

For my parents, Joan and Joseph Yanni,
and my sisters and brothers,
Cathy, Barbara, Palma, Mark, Philip and Lisa

Contents

List of Illustrations

Acknowledgments

First I thank David B. Brownlee, Professor of the History of Art at the University of Pennsylvania, for lending his unflagging support to this book, which was originally my dissertation at Penn. Professor Brownlee fosters an atmosphere of profound respect among his PhD students, and he has thus gathered together a group of knowledgeable and helpful historians who have aided my work more than they know. My undergraduate adviser at Wesleyan University, Joseph M. Siry, played a pivotal role in my education by introducing me to architectural history. I thank him for that and for his continued interest in my research.

Many archivists helped me with my research, including Elizabeth Leedham-Green, Simon Bailey, Tina Craig and Alison Lindsay. Most especially, John Thackray, Archivist of the Natural History Museum in London and a scholar of Victorian geology, supported this project from its beginning. His early death is a loss for the history of science, but his dedication to the field remains manifest in countless scholarly works like this one.

I would like to thank the staffs of the following archives and libraries: the Cambridge University Library, the Cambridge University Archives, the Royal Institute of British Architects Drawings Collection, the British Architectural Library of the Royal Institute of British Architects (RIBA), the Trinity College Library at Cambridge, the Oxford University Archives, the archives of the Royal Museum of Scotland, the Scottish Record Office, the Public Record Office (UK), the British Library, the Library of Congress, and the libraries at the University of New Mexico and Rutgers University. Sarah Timmins de Gregory, a student at Rutgers, cheerfully ordered photographs and permissions, and helped prepare the manuscipt. My mother read this document when it was in a state that only a mother could read, let alone love. For her expert writing advice, I offer my warmest gratitude.

The University of Pennsylvania generously funded my graduate school education through its William Penn Fellowship program. The University of New Mexico's Research Allocations Committee and the Research Council of Rutgers, the State University of New Jersey, also contributed to the success of this project. The Rutgers Art History Department and Dean's Office (Faculty of Arts and Sciences) aided in the production of the book. And I was the first and last recipient of the Barbara Yanni Dissertation Fellowship, a fund established by my sister for architectural historians in her immediate family.

Several friends and colleagues read portions of the manuscript, helped prepare illustrations, or lent scholarly criticism; for their gracious help I would like to thank Nicholas Adams, Geoffrey Batchen, Paula Young Lee, Christopher C. Mead, Curtis Breslin, Dietrich Neumann and Kramer Woodard. I owe a great intellectual debt to the science historians James A. Secord and Sophie Forgan, neither of whom had any reason to be so nice when I arrived in England seven years ago with more enthusiasm than erudition. They freely shared their knowledge of Victorian natural history and challenged me to complete a book that was truly interdisciplinary. Of course, all errors are my own. Finally, I was fortunate to work with the editor Tristan Palmer, who instinctively understood the potential of this project in its early stages and supported its publication at every step.

Photography credits
For permission to reproduce photographs and drawings, I would like to thank the following: the Director of the British Geological Survey, the Trustees of the British Library, the Trustees of the British Museum, the Conway Library, the Detroit Institute of the Arts (Founders Society Purchase, Director's Discretionary Fund), the Museum of Jurassic Technology, the Natural History Museum Picture Library, the New York Public Library, the President and Council of the Royal College of Surgeons of England, the Royal Institute of British Architects (British Architectural Library), the Royal Museum of Scotland, the Scottish Record Office, the Syndics of Cambridge University, the Trustees of Sir John Soane's Museum, and the Victoria & Albert Museum.

Introduction

In November 1849, the rhinoceros at London's Regent's Park zoo died. Caroline Clift Owen, wife of the renowned anatomist and museum director Richard Owen, remarked in her diary that it was 'a natural consequence' of the beast's death that she now had 'a quantity of rhinoceros (defunct) on the premises.'[1] This macabre deposit came as no surprise to her, for she and her husband lived within the Royal College of Surgeons' compound, where Richard was keeper of that institution's museum. (He no doubt set about dissecting the animal at his earliest opportunity.) Mrs Owen's nonchalance may surprise us today, since dead rhinos hardly ever find their way into ladies' diaries, let alone their houses. But at the end of the eighteenth century and for the first few decades of the nineteenth, the pursuit of natural knowledge took place in gentlemen's houses, and this respectable locality reinforced the credence of the scientific principles founded there. It took until the end of the nineteenth century, and the efforts of men like T. H. Huxley, to make science a paid profession, conducted in universities and state-funded institutions. Some voyagers studied nature in the field, and other naturalists conducted experiments; but many men of science did their work in buildings we now easily recognize as natural history museums. Such buildings had not existed a century before. This book examines the history of that transition and its architectural manifestations. The universities, fellowships, government grants and museums that now pay for the work of science are often taken for granted, and that is why today it seems obvious that the natural history museum is the place for a dead rhino.

In the nineteenth century, museums produced natural knowledge, and were themselves architectural spectacles. As such, they comprised a rich cultural site suggestive of interdisciplinary historical study. Piled high with bones and stuffed animals, natural history museums were the primary places of interaction between natural science and its diverse publics. Studies of the natural world (what we now think of as biology and geology) were changing and conflicting disciplines, and thus no single vision of nature emerged in the Victorian period. Consequently, architects could not devise any one distinctive building type for natural history museums. British Victorian naturalists, politicians and architects agreed on the cultural worth of museums, but they disagreed on the proper presentation of natural science to the public. There exists a wide variety of museum buildings, and each is historically meaningful in its own way. *Nature's Museums* analyzes how the architecture of selected natural history museums in Britain contributed to the legitimization of knowledge.

Behind such technical concerns as site selection, lighting, and display techniques lay questions of the deepest concern to Victorians: what *was* nature? And how could nature best be presented to diverse audiences? How can long-lasting or monumental architecture respond to the needs of the scientific enterprise, which gains legitimacy from currency? Is it possible for museum architecture to articulate the nature of nature? These were the questions debated and given built form in display spaces for British natural history in the nineteenth century. *Nature's Museums* will suggest that socially contingent knowledge is indeed produced in local, carefully designed, highly specific places.

Nature's Museums consists of several case studies – the Hunterian Museum of the Royal College of Surgeons (1813; 1834–37), the Cambridge University Library (1829–1837), the Museum of Practical Geology (1847–52), the Oxford University Museum (1855–60), the Edinburgh Museum of Science and Art (1854–61), and the Natural History Museum, London (1865–81) and chapters which frame these case studies by placing them in earlier (eighteenth-century) and later (twentieth-century) contexts. Chapter 1 traces the general shift from natural history practiced in private homes to buildings designed specifically for scientific institutions. 'The integrity of gentlemen and their social relations served as a practical voucher of the reliability of the knowledge issuing from their houses,'[2] while museum buildings presented natural history to a large and diverse public. Both gentlemen's houses and public museums worked to legitimize knowledge, but in different ways. Chapter 2 examines several buildings in early nineteenth-century Britain, including the Cambridge University Library; the Hunterian Museum of the Royal College of Surgeons, the first purpose-built medical museum; and the Museum of Practical Geology, an explicitly public museum aimed at miners and artisans. Critics and historians acclaim Oxford for its architecture; the Edinburgh Museum – today the Royal Museum of Scotland – exemplified the influence of the Crystal Palace; and London's Natural History Museum was the best-funded, largest display of its kind in the British Empire. The buildings were mechanisms for defining natural knowledge, and tools for presenting nature to tourists, students and naturalists. The display strategies of these museums, and of several others along the way, reveal a range of socially determined meanings of nature – from divine Creation to natural resource.

Natural history was part of a complex social practice; it was not a single set of ideas.[3] It became a discipline at the end of the eighteenth century, when naturalists like Buffon and Linnaeus styled themselves as a new generation of thinkers, reviving a practice that had been lost since Pliny.[4] The study of natural history encompassed the fields we would now call geology and biology; its boundaries were not always clear, but for the most part Victorians used the term to describe the study of objects found in the natural world, including micro-organisms, plants, animals, rocks and fossils. Naturalists examined animals, vegetables and minerals for their physical characteristics, origins, inter-relationships and distribution. The modern word 'science' was sometimes used in the Victorian period to refer to natural history *and* chemistry, astronomy and physics (previously, natural philosophy); 'science' was an umbrella term meaning systematic and formulated knowledge.[5] The term 'natural knowledge' covered much the same ground as the modern word 'science.' For example, the full name of the Royal Society, the powerful organization of physicians and gentlemen of science, was 'The Royal Society of London for Improving

Natural Knowledge,' and when statues of famous scientists were installed in the Oxford Museum, the subjects were called 'Founders and Improvers of Natural Knowledge.'[6] But since natural history focussed on objects, it was the branch of science most easily presented in museums. Furthermore, collecting actually contributed to the development and legitimization of the discipline, because Enlightenment thinkers could present their collections systematically, and thus distinguish themselves from the courtiers who compiled supposedly disorderly 'curiosity cabinets' in Renaissance and Baroque Europe. Taxonomy, one of the essential practices of natural history, was made manifest in the museum. The various natural history museums differed from one another, but all displayed carefully organized collections of stuffed animals, as well as animals preserved in spirits, bones, fossils and rocks, or some combination of the above objects. In most museum buildings, lighting and circulation were the central architectural challenges. *Nature's Museums* attempts to show how the physical form of buildings differed, depending on the definitions of nature held by museum founders, even though at times the architecture was interpreted in ways unexpected by the museum officials.

The method used here is only one example of how architectural historians might enter a larger area of study: the relationship of architecture to the social construction of knowledge. It is my hope that further studies will illuminate the important ways in which architecture manipulates the public perception of truth, and the way in which architecture participates in the social construction of scientific knowledge. The case studies in this book cannot possibly capture all of the issues that link architecture to science, nor can a few institutions represent the hundreds of provincial museums built in the nineteenth century. Since my intent is to study divergent meanings of nature, I have emphasized displays of natural specimens rather than exhibitions of man-made machines and technological feats, although these were common in the nineteenth century, especially at world's fairs.[7]

The following chapters do not fit easily into existing frameworks for architectural history: they do not follow the careers of individual architects, and they do not celebrate architects' artistic abilities. On the other hand, this book is typical of many architectural historical studies, in that it 'reads' the buildings in order to construct an argument about social and intellectual history. The argument is that architecture contributed to the construction of knowledge, and it proceeds by looking closely at a few buildings – examples of what historian Sophie Forgan has called 'the architecture of display' – in order to suggest that architecture plays a significant role in the social production of local knowledge.[8] This method of interrogation has led me to examine in detail the discussions leading up to construction, since the completed building is only one answer to a complex question, and, at the time, not necessarily the most obvious answer, and to investigate the scientific theories held by the patrons of these buildings. Most of these buildings were the architectural products of multifarious committees, and as a result the buildings communicate ambiguously or ineffectually. I did not attempt to create a definitive catalogue of museums, but I hope that the methods and recurring themes here will provide tools for others who wish to study the architecture of museums, or architecture for science. *Nature's Museums* examines crucial issues – including display, nature and reception – with an emphasis on the broad cultural values that science has projected in western society since the nineteenth century.

Although this is, above all, an architectural history book, it is meant to be an interdisciplinary study that takes some of its methods from cultural history and the sociology of science. One group of currently practicing historians of science argues that science is not a fixed body of knowledge, but a complex set of conventions devised by a specialized community of academic practitioners.[9] As summarized by Jan Golinski, social constructivist philosophers and historians posit that 'Scientific knowledge is a human creation, made with available material and cultural resources, rather than simply the revelation of a natural order that is pre-given and independent of human action.'[10] In the following essays on natural history museums, I follow these scholars and attempt to support the position that natural knowledge was guided by human action and locally situated practices. But the architecture of the museums could not always act to legitimize one particular theory; in most cases, ideas about science or nature were in conflict, and the architecture therefore responded to that conflict. While each case study is, in part, self-contained, there are themes that link them together – lighting, the use of iron and glass, patronage, public accessibility, the scope of the collections, and style. While glass-ceilinged halls at first seemed to offer a direction for museum builders, when the form was co-opted by popular exhibitions, its usefulness for 'serious' science waned. Although the Natural History Museum in London was the wealthiest and most central, it was considered by many to be obsolete by the time it was completed, and therefore could not serve as a model for other museums.

CHANGING DEFINITIONS OF NATURE

The secular scientists who emerged at the end of the nineteenth century founded ideas about nature and the representation of nature that we still hold today. This is one good reason to study nineteenth-century science and architecture. And yet definitions of nature always were, and still are, in flux. Today, the controversy over cloning is an obvious example: is the cloned sheep Dolly a product of nature or culture? Some would argue that science is the study of nature, humans are part of nature, and thus when a human scientist produces a cloned sheep, the sheep is natural. But Dolly's opponents object to her specifically because she is born of an unnatural process. Americans, more than other national group, also must contend with the ongoing struggle between evolutionists and creationists. This struggle was *not* as polarized in Victorian Britain as it is today, a fact which confuses many non-specialists. Natural history museums in the United States present evolution as fact, completely disregarding any possibility of dissent. Similarly, natural history museums present western science as non-cultural and value-free, yet these same museums exhibit the cultural artifacts of non-western societies.[11] It is commonly remarked today that nature is under threat from unnatural forces, like suburban sprawl, genetic engineering, and managed wilderness (to name a few). This remark is implicitly founded on a contemporary definition of nature, and the perception of its fragility. While this book does not directly engage these contemporary issues, it attempts to reveal their historical origins.

BRITISH VICTORIAN ARCHITECTURE AND NATURAL HISTORY

The British Victorian period is celebrated both for its science and its grand public architecture, thus it seemed logical to focus this book on specifically British natural history displays. More generally, nature holds a central position in architectural theory, from the earliest speculations on caves as the first 'natural' architecture, to the association of the classical orders with the human figure, to the manipulation of nature itself in landscape gardens. Even so, 'nature' is a surprisingly under-theorized concept in architectural history, and the word is often used imprecisely. Of course, 'natural history' and 'nature' are not coterminous; neither are 'nature' and 'science.' I am merely proposing that the study of 'natural history' is one way to examine meanings of nature in the Victorian world – meanings that did influence architecture. Concepts of nature were crucial in the Victorian era, when professional scholars and others witnessed a transformation in the understanding of the span of history, the pace of natural change, and the value of close observation. Charles Darwin's theory of evolution caused many to contemplate the mechanism of natural trans-mutation, and taxonomists discovered and classified thousands of previously unknown plants and animals. In a general sense, science shifted from its status as a serious vocation, practiced by wealthy men, to a paid profession. At the start of Victoria's reign, the word 'scientist' was a recently coined academic term, but by the 1880s the word was widely used. We inherited the word, and so much else, from the Victorians.

In addition to academic shifts, natural history became a popular pursuit in the Victorian era, and consequently the exploration of the wonders of the earth and her creatures reached the broadest audience in history. Middle and upper-class parlors commonly displayed an aquarium, terrarium, or shell collection. In some private houses, shallow, glass-fronted boxes were hung on the walls to exhibit ornamental taxidermy, often a collection of birds, some exotic and others local.[12] Hunting trophies (the heads of big-racked deer, especially) presided over many an upper-crust Victorian parlor. During the height of the Romantic movement at the end of the eighteenth century, humankind's relationship with nature changed dramatically. Gentlemen and ladies developed a taste for walks in the woods, bird-watching and collecting shells. (Agricultural workers, who normally spent all day outside, were understandably less enthusiastic about strenuous outdoor activities on their days off.) Although every claim was made that the Romantic walkers were appreciating unspoiled natural beauty, there were countless mediations through which people viewed nature. One thinks of the obvious example of the Claude glass, the amber-tinted mirror through which eighteenth-century nature-lovers framed a view of the countryside in order to produce an effect like a varnished painting. Popular sentiment (and academic judgment) suggested that an appreciation of nature brought one closer to God, and this spiritual association certainly helped make natural history a common pastime. The British enthusiasm for bird-watching began in this period, as did the desire to protect animals against cruelty. Natural history field clubs were organized all over Britain. Offering a socially acceptable means to fraternize, drink, and roam the countryside, these clubs numbered in the hundreds.[13] These organizations were the seeds from which grew the conservation movement in Britain, and it is ironic that this same impulse – toward conservation – makes the vast collections of the Victorian museums appear today to be an indecent hoard. (And it is even more ironic that these very museums use conservation as an excuse to exist today, when many have questioned their usefulness.) Mining and other technological advances demanded the use (or exploitation, depending on one's point of view) of nature for capitalization by the empire. In publicly funded museums, nature became a medium through which to represent the state. London was the capital city, the center of the British Empire, and her museums were a source of imperial authority. The collections were material evidence of the vastness, wealth and potential of the empire.

Before a traveller went abroad, he might visit a museum to learn about his next post. And many sojourning Britons sent back specimens to the center of the empire for naming and analysis.

Three more specific reasons suggested a concentration on Britain: the pre-eminence of Darwin, the architectural importance of the Oxford Museum, and the significance of the Great Exhibition of 1851. T. H. Huxley (nicknamed 'Darwin's Bulldog' because he fought for the acceptance of Darwin's theories while the older, ailing naturalist stayed home) was the most powerful figure in the promotion of evolution. Darwin's theory of evolution was considered by Huxley to be the height of rationality and good sense, an advance that cast aside superstition and religious motivation. He promoted science as a secular undertaking that benefitted British society by encouraging reason, the competitive spirit and progressive values. Huxley thus invented the image of secular science that we take for granted today. (In fact, Huxley's self-promotional tactics diminished the serious work of the religious natur-alists who came before him, and he unfairly portrayed them as hobbyists.) Charles Darwin, T. H. Huxley and Richard Owen lived and worked in Britain, and although recent biographies describe the places where their science was produced, these places are mentioned briefly and seldom illustrated. Owen was one of the most powerful naturalists working in the nineteenth century, and he dedicated most of his career to curatorship: the architecture of the museums in which he worked deserves scholarly attention. Second, the Oxford University Museum, one of the most famous and beloved Victorian buildings, appears here in the company of other natural his-tory museums. Finally, the Great Exhibition housed in the Crystal Palace was a watershed for architectural design, ferrovitreous technology, display techniques, popular edification and public entertainment. While these issues influenced some museums' histories more than others, the Crystal Palace sets the stage for any discussion of grand display after 1851.

The themes and methods developed in *Nature's Museums* could certainly be extended to topics beyond Britain. The vast and important subject of French museum architecture and theory deserves detailed study; art historian Paula Young Lee has completed outstanding work in that area.[14] Scholars have also conducted research on museums in the United States. Donna Haraway's reading of the Africa Hall and the Teddy Roosevelt entrance at the American Museum of Natural History in New York offered a thought-provoking interpretation of institutionalized patri-archy and racism; historian Mary Winsor provided a thorough history of Louis Agassiz's Museum of Comparative Zoology in Cambridge, Massachusetts. Most recently, Steven Conn cleverly analyzed the role of museums in establishing the object-based epistemology that was central to nineteenth-century American intellectual life.[15] And while this is the first book-length study of British museums, my work is indebted to the careful scholarship of Sophie Forgan, who has set a high standard for research into the relationship between architecture and science.

STYLE AND MEANING IN THE ARCHITECTURE OF DISPLAY

To this day, style remains an enigma in eighteenth- and nineteenth-century archi-tectural studies: the range of historical models available to architects and the press coverage of 'the Battle of the Styles' throughout the Victorian period encouraged historians to believe there were distinct armies of partisan stylists, and discrete meanings for different styles. And certainly cases like Jefferson's Virginia State

Capitol (Roman republicanism as the antecedent for the new American republic) or Barry and Pugin's Houses of Parliament (a nationalistic use of the Gothic) promoted exact meanings through their respective historical references. But these were exceptions in nineteenth-century history, not typical situations. There was no single style associated with natural history museums, although there was a typically Victorian historicism in all the following buildings: the Hunterian Museum had a classical portico; the Cambridge University Library competition guidelines asked for a 'Grecian' building (although many of the entries were Roman); the Museum of Practical Geology looked like a Pall Mall gentlemen's club, the Oxford University Museum competition brief did not ask for any particular style (although historians have taken the Gothic winner to be an inevitable choice); Francis Fowke designed two museums in the late Renaissance style; and Waterhouse chose the uncommon (to say the least) neo-Lombard Romanesque for the Natural History Museum in London. Press coverage of the two competitions (Oxford, 1854) and the Natural History Museum (London, 1864) indicate that entrants submitted designs in the following styles: Greek, Greco-Romanesque, Byzantine-Romanesque, Romanesque, thirteenth-century Gothic, fourteenth-century Gothic, Venetian Gothic, Palladian, Venetian Renaissance, Brunelleschian Renaissance, and Bramantesque Renaissance. For the Oxford competition, E. M. Barry submitted one floor plan with three different facades (one Gothic and two Renaissance). Given the stylistic freedom of the Victorian period, it is often impossible to assign particular meanings to particular styles.

The most one can argue is that there was no simple correspondence between styles and meanings, because buildings carry meaning in different ways, and multiple meanings can easily co-exist in architecture. This is not to suggest that historians should give up on meaning: instead, we can look for intended meaning in studies of clients' requests, competition instructions, and the architects' own commentary. Furthermore, we can study unintended additional meanings in the architectural press, newspapers, and other contemporary reception. Neil Levine, architectural historian, describes the problem of communication as met by French architects:

> Meaningful expression was the real issue facing the nineteenth-century architect. The question of style was only a subset of that problem. With an apparently unlimited variety of forms available, the dilemma was how to ascribe meaning to any one, how to ensure its comprehension.[16]

British architects also aimed to achieve such 'meaningful expression' and to 'ensure its comprehension.' In the case of natural history museums, it is not only the exterior which communicated, but also the arrangement of interior displays. Different visitors comprehended the buildings and displays from different vantage points. One Victorian visitor might see the mammoth as a perfect example of the slow process of adaptation and extinction, while another might think it simply too big to fit on the Ark. The dozen or more architects mentioned in this book could not ensure the comprehension of their designs: there were too many co-existent definitions of nature, and too broad an audience. Often architects designed an envelope for the displays, while the curators arranged the collections and explained precisely what type of ground plan they wanted. In some cases, architects might have limited the curators by forcing them to place collections into a linear sequence of rooms, or they might allow more choice for the visitor, suggesting simultaneity of events or equal importance of different parts of the collection. Architects could not always control the interpretation of the audience (as the reception study in Chapter 4 proves); but they can influence audiences. I agree with Levine that architects' attempts to instill meaning – whether effective, spurious or ambiguous – are still the real issues in nineteenth-century architecture, and the following chapters will suggest that museum architecture was seen as representative of its content, especially by well-educated and articulate visitors.

MUSEUMS AND POWER

The French historian-philosopher Michel Foucault casts a long shadow over the history of visuality, museum studies, and even that most elusive of concepts, 'space.' Since many readers are familiar with his theories, their relationship to museum architecture requires only a brief summary. His most important writings for science and display can be found in *The Order of Things*, 'The Eye of Power,' in *Power/Knowledge*, and 'Of Other Spaces,' in *Diacritics*.[17] In *Power/Knowledge: Selected Interviews and Other Writings, 1972–1977*, Foucault argued that 'A whole history remains to be written of *spaces* – which would at the same time be a history of *powers* [both these terms in the plural] – from the great strategies of geopolitics to the little tactics of the habitat, institutional architecture from the classroom to the design of hospitals, passing via economic and political installations.'[18] For Foucault, power is a field of dynamic forces that contains resistance within it, a set of relationships including both pleasure and repression. Foucault called into question the boundaries of disciplines and emphasized the dependent relationship of knowledge and power; his work is therefore all the more important in the study of science museums. *The Order of Things* encouraged later writers to consider classification systems in western natural history as inherently hierarchical; 'The Eye of Power' clarified the important theme of visuality. His influence was valuable in museum studies, for it caused museum scholars to consider the high political stakes of exhibitions, especially exhibitions that claim an internal logic based on supposed neutrality. Describing the Foucauldian theoretical position, Sherman and Rogoff write: 'This model illuminates the ways museums both sustain and construct cultural master narratives that achieve an internal unity by imposing one cultural tendency as the prominent manifestation of any historical period.'[19] Sherman and Rogoff are skeptical about the internal unity presented by any museum, because it is only an illusion of unity. Some museums might present a single master narrative, but I argue that this is rare, and even if such a master narrative exists in one moment, it changes over time. There are usually several co-existing theories, rather than one master narrative, and the displays and architecture (if studied in precise historical detail) turn out to be surprisingly resistant to Foucauldian analysis. Take, for example, the monkeys carved in the main arch of the entrance to the Natural History Museum in London: to some visitors they symbolize the relationship between humankind and ancient apes, but these playful climbing animals certainly did not carry that meaning for Richard Owen, the museum's chief patron and one of evolution's most outspoken opponents.

The themes of visuality and power clearly influenced Tony Bennett in his *Birth of the Museum*. He argues that the museum can be understood only in terms of a nineteenth-century tendency to see culture as useful for governance:[20]

[T]he conception of the museum as an institution in which the working classes – provided they dressed nicely and curbed any tendency towards unseemly conduct – might be exposed to the improving influence of the middle classes was crucial to its construction as a new kind of social space.[21]

The observation that museums offered an opportunity for top-down 'improvement' of the working classes is compelling, and does seem to apply to the museums in this book. The Hunterian and Oxford museums were probably too exclusive for working-class people to attend, however. Yet many critics of Foucault have pointed out that the prisoners in panopticons, the patients in hospitals, the lunatics in asylums, and the visitors in museums were not empty vessels waiting to be filled with ideology.

Bennett conflates the form of the Familistère at Guise with typical shopping arcades, the department store and custom-built public museums, claiming that

> Relations of space and vision are organized not merely to allow a clear inspection of the objects exhibited but also to allow for the visitors to be the objects of each other's inspection – scenes in which, if not citizenry, then certainly a public displayed itself to itself in an affirmative celebration of its own orderliness in architectural contexts which simultaneously guaranteed and produced that orderliness.[22]

The relations of space and vision are important, but not all acts of looking are equal. The scopic reciprocity to which Bennett refers is not evident in many art museums, including Durand's ideal museum, Schinkel's Altesmuseum in Berlin, and Smirke's British Museum in London. Historians have put quite a lot of pressure on the meaning of 'orderliness' as a sign of social control, but do we as historians honestly think curators ought to have arranged their collections in a disorderly fashion? Or, given that there are different kinds of order, a fashion which they believed to be disorderly? Obviously there were similarities in the spaces of museums, shopping arcades and department stores, but these can be explained by the perceived need for cheap natural lighting. Architects could fit more items under the skylight if they added balconies to a room.[23] Furthermore, the display of objects was not equivalent to the display of human beings. Some museums (the ones with open halls and balconies) may have lent themselves to 'seeing and being seen' on a Sunday afternoon, but most museums would be a last choice for a bourgeois promenade – following the opera, the park, the shopping arcade, and even the street. Many museums were not even open on Sundays.

Cultural theorists have certainly broadened the study of museums, but historian Steven Conn has demonstrated how much more historical detail we need to know before we make such grand claims about museums and power. To use just one example, Conn has argued that the 'crude equation of knowledge equals power' is 'at once critically insightful and profoundly shallow.'[24] The observations of museum theorists help draw attention to sociological issues of power and knowledge, but architectural history is perhaps better served by focussed historical studies, founded on archival research, original texts and drawings, and the buildings themselves.

MUSEUMS OF ART

The art museum has been more thoroughly studied and fully theorized than the natural history museum, and much can be learned from recent scholarship in this field: that museums create or reinforce categories of knowledge; that apparently neutral exhibitions have underlying political meanings; that processional movement through galleries often presents a hierarchy; that public museums paradoxically claim to be elite and democratic at the same time; that objects displayed on pedestals become like relics, the museum like a (false) shrine. There are, of course, many exceptions to these observations. One of the earliest museums, the Alte Pinakothek in Munich, offered the visitor many choices rather than one processional path. The similarities between museums of art and natural history are instructive, as are the differences. Both derive their authority from the authenticity of their objects, in spite of the fact that both types of museums display objects of varying degrees of truth – Roman copies of Greek sculptures, overcleaned paintings, reconstructed skeletons of cast fossils, and dioramas. Authenticity in the museum is a much-valued but elusive concept, as many authors have made clear.

Art museums at least have *some* unique objects. Natural history museums, on the other hand, have banished freaks and mutants from their collections. Only exceptional visitors go to a natural history museum to see a particular famous fossil. (As one of my students in a museum seminar remarked, why would you go to a natural history museum in a foreign country? They all have the same stuff inside, right?) Art museums are the cultural tourists' primary destinations in foreign countries. Visitors to Cairo go to the Egyptian Museum to see the mask of King Tut, and travelers to Rome go to the Vatican to see the Sistine Chapel, but few out-of-town visitors in Cairo or Rome wander into the museums to look at stuffed sparrows. For most people, it is the typicality of specimens that makes one collection much like another. Therefore the exact strategy that nineteenth-century naturalists used to professionalize the museum – to distinguish it from the cabinet of wonder – is the strategy that today lessens the enthusiasm of all but local visitors.

Duncan and Wallach's provocative 1980 article, 'The Universal Survey Art Museum,' recast the museum as a ritual space, in which people saw themselves as part of the grand tradition of western civilization.[25] In natural history museums, one could argue that humans are encouraged to see themselves as part of nature – as part of the food chain here on earth, or as a speck in the solar system. Many nineteenth-century museums, on the other hand, presented humans as above animals, but below God. In theorizing about natural history museums in the Victorian age, we must constantly remind ourselves that for some visitors, museums were displays of Creation. As historians of science like Peter Bowler and John Hedley Brooke have shown, many Victorians reconciled their religious beliefs with evolution, embracing theistic transmutation, 'the belief that nature unfolds according to a recognizable divine plan.'[26]

Adrian Desmond, historian of Victorian science and noted biographer of Darwin and Huxley, offers this clear explanation of the relationship between evolution and religion: 'Evolution cradled within an agnostic framework seems obvious today, precisely because we have inherited the victor's mantle. But it was far from obvious in 1870. Then the English public schools and universities shunned science as useless and dehumanizing. Their world was of character-forming Classics and Theology.'[27] Although ideas about transmutation had been circulating for decades, the *Origin of Species* was published in 1859, and it is likely that afterward more visitors saw natural specimens as emblems of evolution – but these interpreters did not replace the people who visited natural history museums in order to see God's work; religious visitors were not going to recant their creed after one afternoon in the dinosaur gallery. Indeed, there were even more people who believed in both God and evolution – this was just as true then as now. The architecture of museums can only *suggest* a particular view: it cannot determine meaning, and it cannot separate people from their beliefs.

THE PLACE OF KNOWLEDGE

Traditional histories of science have given experiment a privileged place, but it is important to remember that in the nineteenth century, observational science was the cutting edge. Darwin conducted experiments throughout his life, but many of his important discoveries were achieved through close observation. Historian John Pickstone suggests that 'museological/diagnostic' science, medicine and technology was central to Victorian practice until it was pushed out of universities by experimental sciences, beginning in about 1860.[28] Pickstone finds a museological emphasis in many areas of nineteenth-century science – not in just the obvious fields like geology, but also in medicine, geography, chemistry, and analytical engineering, where the prime goal was to classify and diagnose.[29] Historian James A. Secord describes the museum as the 'central institution' of the period:

> Zoologists and botanists classified living beings; astronomers studied the distribution and order of the heavens; chemists analyzed new compounds; geologists mapped strata and their fossils; philologists compared different languages. Not surprisingly, the museum – not the laboratory – was the central institution of Victorian science.[30]

Despite the importance of these institutions, architectural historians have spilled much more ink over Victorian houses and churches than over museums.

Historians Adi Ophir and Steven Shapin have suggested that if scientific knowledge is local rather than universal (a common claim among social constructionists), then we need to study those local places.[31] The authors pose the rhetorical question: 'What if it [knowledge] possesses its shape, meaning, reference, and domain of application by virtue of the physical, social, and cultural circumstances in which it is made?'[32] *Nature's Museums* proceeds from the position that knowledge does indeed derive meaning from its physical situation. The intersection of science and architecture is a fruitful area of investigation, not just for the nineteenth century but in almost any epoch, because it illuminates such important topics as the role of architecture in the social construction of knowledge, and the cultural legitimization of scientific theories through their association with particular architectural sites. Personally, in my university-level teaching at architecture schools and in art history departments, I have found that students readily accept the fragmentation of knowledge; students gleefully concur that certain notions in architecture (proper proportion, universality or style) are social constructions, but when they turn their attention to science, they are faced with pesky truths, and blithe epistemological assumptions look weak. And although many postmodernist critics would argue otherwise, science stubbornly presents its audience with facts: the earth really does move around the sun, not the other way around. But scientific facts and the discourse about them constitute each other: they are mutually reinforcing. Thus the task of the historian is not to dismiss science as social behavior disguised as truth-seeking, but to ask what scientifically constituted facts meant historically (or mean today). And these are cultural questions.

THE HISTORIOGRAPHY OF SCIENCE AND ARCHITECTURE

Scientists and architectural historians both study the material world. And historians of science and architecture share similar methods. Both fields were traditionally marked by the valorization of heroes, an obsession with innovation rather than ordinary practice, a tendency to follow individual careers rather than general movements, and 'presentism,' a tendency to value only those parts of history that foretell current doctrines. In the last three decades, architectural historians have cast aside the view of monuments as timeless, formal expressions, and thus historians have attempted to place architecture in the context of its own time. But 'context' and 'time' are both vexed issues. As *Nature's Museums* will try to suggest, a building does not have a unitary context: institutions have multiple identities, and different audiences approach each work of architecture with their own preconceptions. In each of the following chapters, information on the museums comes from journals (like *Nature*, the *Builder*, and *Building News*), daily newspapers, precisely worded competition guidelines, minutes of committee meetings, architects' statements, letters, drawings, and (of course) the buildings. Science was a social practice, and the architecture of natural history museums presented science, in its many aspects, to a complex public. Furthermore, the concept of nature varied depending upon audiences, places and times. To a certain extent, audiences participated in the construction of architectural meaning, and although the research to prove that such construction occurred is difficult to conduct, architectural historians would benefit from developing methods that truly address context and audience in addition to studying the buildings as objects.[33]

Perhaps the most we can say for certain is that architecture carries meaning, but not the same meaning to everyone and not the same meaning over time. Philosopher Nelson Goodman put forth this position in 'How Buildings Mean' (1985), and compared architecture to science in this light:

> A building, more than most work, alters our environment physically; but moreover, as a work of art it may, through various avenues of meaning, inform and reorganize our entire experience. Like other works of art – and like scientific theories, too – it can give new insight, advance understanding, participate in our continual remaking of a world.[34]

The recognition that buildings mean in many ways, that buildings allow for 'our continual remaking of a world,' is relevant to any discussion of architecture. Sophie Forgan makes the same point when she writes: 'the analysis of space in a strict Foucauldian manner does not take sufficient account of the fact that buildings have multiple meanings at any one time, and that the way they change and evolve is as important as the way they are constructed.'[35] Forgan's statement probably holds true for all architecture, but it is especially important for understanding nineteenth-century architecture. Victorians did not aim for universality; the architects of these museums aimed for distinctive, specific and local communication. Furthermore, I will argue here that this highly evocative architecture contributed to local and temporary meanings of nature. Although I am sure I cannot prove every case equally well, or convince every reader, if this book's premise stimulates further research, then one of its goals will have been achieved.

Natural history museums presented knowledge in the form of specimens; the objects of nature were captured, stuffed, pinned down and categorized, sheltered beneath iron and glass canopies or crowned by Romanesque towers. The museum buildings offer proof of the Victorians' grand belief in the expressiveness of architecture. And today the displays are historical evidence of our relationship to the natural world. With the rise of environmentalism, natural history is in a sense more popular than ever, but audiences can now gain access to nature through greatly improved zoos and film documentaries. The Victorian displays that relied entirely on the viewer looking at the objects are beginning to disappear, and they are being replaced by installations that move and talk. New media challenge the museum, this Victorian invention, a taxonomic collection of still life. This book is an historical argument, not a preservationist call to arms, but I do hope that readers of *Nature's Museums* will see Victorian natural history museums as historically valuable. Definitions of nature change, but these buildings offer a window onto the conflict and ambiguity of Victorian natural knowledge.

Architects and museum curators worked together (with varying success) to make well-lit, logical, meaningful buildings, which, in turn, created architecture for scientific display where none had previously existed. My approach embraces contradictory concepts of nature, from nature as resource to be capitalized to nature as the second book of God. *Nature's Museums* allows the buildings themselves to act as a guide to the Victorians' understanding of the natural world. It is hoped that this book will bring Victorian concepts of nature into clearer focus, so that we can better understand the museums of Darwin's century.

chapter 1

Museum Vision

'Sights Unseen Before'

In the seventeenth century, collectors gathered natural specimens in a quest for the absurd, curious or monstrous. Nineteenth-century naturalists, on the other hand, sought to distinguish themselves from the idiosyncratic, private collectors of the previous centuries. A slow but decisive change, which can be characterized by a shift from displays of curious things to displays of typical objects, occurred from the seventeenth century to the nineteenth. In Britain, the shift can be explained by an enthusiasm for natural theology, which called for natural objects to be displayed as examples of God's work. The kinds of extraordinary objects that were displayed in cabinets of curiosities (two-headed kittens and unicorn horns) were not explicative of God's second book – so they had to be excised from the natural history museum. Furthermore, as science became more of a profession and less of a gentleman's pastime, science museums had to reflect that seriousness in their displays and in their architectural presentation. The careful visual scrutiny required to comprehend myriad objects demanded purpose-built, naturally lit structures. This chapter leads the reader through a brief architectural history of collections and displays, emphasizing that vision – the visitor's need to closely scrutinize selected objects – was a programmatic impetus for the later, Victorian architecture of display.

THE PROBLEM OF CLASSIFICATION: ADAM'S TASK

Taxonomy was central to the study of the natural world, and the classification of the natural world had its spatial corollary in the built world of the museum. The power to name the animals, of course, has biblical resonances: 'whatsoever Adam called every living creature, that was the name thereof. And Adam gave names to all the cattle, and to the fowl of the air, and to every beast in the field' (Genesis, 2: 18–19). Naming did indeed indicate power: dominion over nature, national pride, the pre-eminence of one philosophy over another. Foucault famously refers to his encounter with a passage in which Jorge Luis Borges quotes a 'certain Chinese encyclopedia,' which, Foucault said, 'shattered all the familiar landmarks of my thought.' In the Chinese encyclopedia, animals are divided into categories including: 'belonging to the Emperor,' 'sucking pigs,' 'fabulous,' 'stray dogs,' 'included in the present classification' and 'having just broken the water pitcher.'[1] As the museum theorist Eilean Hooper-Greenhill points out, the classification system of the Chinese encyclopedia puts a certain kind of pressure on western museums: 'if we accepted as "true" the classification that Foucault describes, the work of curators in identifying, controlling, ordering, and displaying their collections would have to begin all over again,' and, furthermore, western taxonomies facilitate some epistemologies, and prevent other ways of knowing the world.[2]

The cabinet of curiosity – a glorious summation of knowledge for the Renaissance or Baroque collector – was disorganized and nearly useless by the standards of the nineteenth century, and Victorian museums appear cluttered to today's scientists. Specialist debates within taxonomy (such as where to place the furry but egg-laying platypus) are beyond the scope of this study, but the larger import of taxonomy must be emphasized. Museum designers had to allow for a seemingly endless set of categories and sub-categories, but these were not as fixed as we might assume. In 1836, arrangements were made to house Cambridge University's natural history collections in the new library, and in 1855 Oxford's natural history museum was clustered with state-of-the-art laboratories, lecture rooms and lecturers' offices. In Victorian Scotland, the nation's most important natural history collection was displayed alongside machinery, model ships and mass-produced decorative art. The original competition for the Natural History Museum in London included a patent museum, and early plans for the Museum of Natural History in Dublin devoted the ground floor to cow sheds, needed for the annual agricultural exhibition.[3]

One of the most disturbing aspects of classification in Victorian museums is that the natural history museums in Amsterdam, Washington DC and New York City, all contained objects made by non-western people. Historian Mario Baglioli writes: 'Science museums . . . have seen their discourses analyzed and often deconstructed – especially the naturalizing representations of racial differences and gender roles embedded in many natural history exhibits, or some science museums' attempts to shape national identities through the celebration of a nation's scientific and techno-logical "monuments" and heroes.'[4] Some natural history museums equated non-western people with nature itself: people were presented as close to nature, or natural. In the early twentieth century, anthropologists would have unabashedly called the people of Africa and Oceania, Native Americans, and sometimes Asians, 'primitive.' Since high art was the sign of civilization, primitive people could not, by such a definition, make art. Therefore the objects made by people of color could not be placed in art museums; instead, they were displayed in the natural history museum. As art historian Mieke Bal has shown, museum strategies that seem invisible to the visitor carry political meanings: the placement of rooms, labels and choice of objects all come from a western colonialist perspective.[5] Ironically, given its rampant imperialist policy, the case in Britain is somewhat different. The strength of natural theology as a philosophy engendered a different taxonomy, and some naturalists saw a line between things made by the hand of God and things made by the hand of man.

THE IDEA OF COLLECTING: NOAH'S TASK

Noah's Ark was, metaphorically, the first natural history museum. The Ark was an architectural vessel designed to house and preserve the animals, although there were no visitors, no public: only Noah and his family. The seventeenth-century German Jesuit priest Athanasius Kircher believed the study of nature would prove that the Bible was an accurate account of historical events, and held a particular passion for the Ark. He pictured it in 1675 as a three-storey, rectilinear box, with animals on the lowest level, food storage on the second level, and birds and humans on top.[6] While Kircher's illustration does nothing to convince us of the Ark's seaworthiness, Noah's management skills astonish (Figure 1.1). Noah has collected pairs of typically unruly snakes, lions, leopards and camels, and he efficiently guides them up the gangway to protect them from the imminent deluge.

The social history of collecting has captured the attention of scholars in many fields: history, art history, anthropology, the history of science, cultural studies. In particular, the cabinet of curiosities, or *Wunderkammer*, of the seventeenth and eighteenth centuries (once considered to be a meaningless jumble of objects) has emerged as a fascinating site of scholarly investigation. While not exactly precursors to the museum, cabinets of curiosities suggest that collecting may be seen as a reflection of social values, especially a desire for dominion over nature. Museum theorist Krzysztof Pomian defines the *Wunderkammer* as a collection with 'encyclopedic ambitions, intended as a miniature version of the universe, containing specimens of every category of things and helping to render visible the totality of the universe, which otherwise would remain hidden from human eyes.'[7] He also theorizes that the *Wunderkammer* existed in a liminal realm between religion and science, where curiosities spoke to elite visitors about the secrets of nature: '[I]t was a universe to which corresponded a type of curiosity no longer controlled by theology and not yet controlled by science, both these domains tending to reject certain questions as either blasphemous or impertinent, thus subjecting curiosity to a discipline and imposing certain limits on it.'[8] Cabinets of curiosities fulfilled many functions: the display of personal power, good taste, the advancement of prestige, the establishment of self-identity.[9] But as Pomian points out, the mysterious objects

Figure 1.1
Athanasius Kircher,
Arca Noë
(Amsterdam:
Waesberg, 1675),
p. 122. Noah loading
pairs of animals onto
the Ark. By
permission of the
British Library,
460.c.9.

held a more important epistemological value, by suggesting a cryptical and power-ful way of knowing. Arguing that strange objects act as 'hieroglyphics,' Pomian suggests that they 'make the universe comprehensible, as long as they are cor-rectly deciphered.'[10] *Wunderkammern* were privately owned and only accessible to those the owner deemed worthy. This type of collecting was a show of power directed at other nobles, or rivals in other states, and was not directed at the general population. Museums of wonder communicated a moral to the visitor: against the creative works of nature and art, the specter of death loomed.[11] Time, 'the destroyer,' was represented by quickly fading flowers, skulls, or *memento mori* paintings.

Before collecting and display emerged as ways to disseminate knowledge, know-ledge had to be exhumed from its usual resting place: the book. Summarizing the sites where knowledge was produced in the seventeenth century, historian Paula Findlen writes: 'Knowledge, formerly embedded in texts, was created by a com-munity of collectors, experimenters, and visitors whose viewing of nature estab-lished its authoritative image.'[12] By the nineteenth century, scholars were already accustomed to displays of knowledge, and museum keepers hoped to establish an authoritative image for their work.

Findlen emphasizes the importance of collecting to the larger issue of the acquisi-tion of knowledge: Collecting provided an important mechanism to facilitate the transition of natural philosophy from a 'largely textual and bookish culture, difficult for all but the most learned to access, to a tactile, theatrical culture that spoke to a multiplicity of different audiences.'[13] (The theatricality of displays stayed with museums: a ghost from Baroque Italy, it trailed the display of natural objects well into the nineteenth-century, when professional museum keepers shunned spectacle and theatrics.) Findlen also emphasizes the drama of early museums: 'When col-lectors brought nature into the museum, . . . they attempted to recapture not only the totality of nature but also the excitement, conflicts and expectations that their initial voyages in the vast "natural" theatre had produced.'[14]

One of the most important collections belonged to Ferrante Imperato, an apothecary who amassed his cabinet in the sixteenth century in Naples. It was not the largest of its kind, but we know it from the frontispiece of a catalogue in which Imperato is shown surrounded by the fruits of a life's labor (Figure 1.2). The image does not show us much about the architecture, and what we can discern must be mediated by conventions of representation; but this much seems clear: it was a room in a house, not a free-standing building; it had one window, deep enough to contain a small desk; the room was about twice the height of a man; its walls were completely covered with bookshelves, cupboards, and hanging specimens; the ceiling was a flattened barrel-type vault. The room is a background for the wondrous objects, but is not itself particularly adapted to the act of observation.

For a moment, we might look at Imperato's museum through Victorian eyes. By nineteenth-century standards, the lighting was all wrong – the single window on one side of the room was insufficient and lopsided. Natural historians needed to handle and measure specimens, so an alligator pinned to the ceiling was not exactly con-ducive to scientific work. Victorian museums were supposed to make it easy for scientists to *look*. Many museums included balconies, so that the largest number of specimens possible could be packed beneath the skylight. After finding the Italian's architecture a disappointment, a Victorian naturalist would find the collection a horrifying spectacle, since the objects were selected for their scarcity, rather than

typicality. A monstrous lizard (split in the middle, with two sets of hind legs and two tails) was proudly displayed on the upper edge of the left vault; this would seem unprofessional (if not scary) to Victorian museum curators. Two dogs scurrying around, both of which resemble very small lions, would have been unwelcome in later museums, where carrying a walking stick or umbrella was a breach of etiquette. Furthermore, Imperato's objects were not well organized: the vault contained a few starfish on the left, and one starfish on the right; fishes and shells were scattered throughout; the crab was nowhere near the lobster; an armadillo was perched near the foot of a tall bird. Similar objects were not classed with other similar objects, thus breaking a central rule of nineteenth-century museum design. The objects seem to have been placed either where they looked good, or where there was space. The Victorians wanted to observe specimens which were instructive about general principles in natural history – not nature's quirks, God's inexplicable moments of bad taste. Ugliness, and sometimes beauty, were too extreme to teach lessons.

Olaus Worm's collection is also well-illustrated in the frontispiece for his catalogue, although it does not show the collector and his guests, as did Imperato's (Figure 1.3). Worm's museum introduces another vexed issue in museum classification, because at a glance the spectator can see that human-made items are included with the natural specimens. One can see stuffed quadrupeds, fish, parts of incomplete animals, bows and arrows, paddles and footwear. The images attempt to capture the awe visitors must have felt upon viewing these rooms filled with natural specimens, human artifice and books. Recent studies on seventeenth-century natural history suggest that curiosity was a value in itself: ' "curiosity" was not originally a psychological attribute, but part of an early modern practice of collecting and display.'[15] The links between objects in these cabinets might have been magical or

alchemical, but once the understanding of those links was gone the cabinets themselves seemed irrational and confused.[16]

A WAY OF SEEING

Art historian Svetlana Alpers has emphasized the fact that these objects were collected not only for political meaning but also for their visual power: 'Much has been said of the ideology of power, political and intellectual, engaged in both the collecting of objects and the taxonomic manner of ordering them. But I want to stress that what was collected was judged to be of visual interest . . .'[17] Alpers proposes that museum vision is a 'way of seeing,' and that once an object rests in a museum, there is no way to view it other than as an object of visual worth. The museum setting actually dictates vision. I agree with this observation, and take it one step further, by suggesting that the particular architectural setting of each museum also shapes the way visitors see and understand objects.

Are cabinets of curiosities really precursors to the natural history museum? Museum expert Eilean Hooper-Greenhill warns against 'the search for "origins" and a "tradition"' because it leads to 'a search for similarities rather than differences, and the specific set of political, cultural, economic, and ideological relations that

characterises different historical manifestations is rendered invisible, and is therefore effectively lost.'[18] Douglas Crimp also rejects the link between cabinets and
museums, saying 'Anyone who has ever read a description of a *Wunderkammer*, or
Cabinet des curiosities, would recognise the folly of locating the origin of the museum
there, the utter incompatibility of the *Wunderkammer*'s selection of objects, its system of classification, with our own.'[19] Crimp goes on to remark in an endnote that the
title of Impey and MacGregor's *The Origins of Museums: The Cabinet of Curiosities in
Sixteenth- and Seventeenth-Century Europe*, is an example of the 'obliviousness of traditional art historians to questions posed to cultural history by Foucault's archeology.'[20] First, Crimp was mainly concerned with the art museum, while Impey and
MacGregor were not. Also, Foucault did not suggest that master narratives remain
fixed, but rather that they change over time. Thus a *Wunderkammer* could have a
different system of classification and still illustrate the origins of museums.

Findlen, on the other hand, presents a compelling case that the cabinets of Baroque Italy were indeed early natural history museums, and that early collectors
(including Athanasius Kircher, Ulisse Aldrovandi and Imperato) 'popularized the
study of nature – "science" in its broadest sense – for the urban elite through their
willingness to make learning a form of display.'[21] In the *Wunderkammer*, displays of
nature were used to facilitate learning. At this fundamental level, the cabinet of
curiosities is the necessary precursor to nineteenth-century museums. While Findlen's study of cabinets of curiosities serves as a window into the lives of aristocratic
patrons and naturalists, nineteenth-century museums extended their reach beyond
the upper-class to middle- and working-class visitors.

TRADESCANT'S ARK AND THE ASHMOLEAN MUSEUM

By the middle of the seventeenth century, Tradescant's Ark, as it was known,
emerged as one of the best collections of natural objects anywhere in the western
world.[22] The elder John Tradescant was a gardener who collected botanical specimens. His museum included an impressive array of items: whale bones, a flying
squirrel, brightly coloured birds from India, an elk's hoof with three claws, the
passion of Christ carved on a plum stone, a piece of the true Cross, all kinds of shells
and the hand of a mermaid.[23] In 1656 his son John published the first catalogue of
any British collection, and the younger Tradescant continued at the Ark's helm until
his death in 1662. There was no architectural component to the collection (no special
rooms or lighting effects); it was originally housed in the Tradescants' home in South
Lambeth, outside London, and later moved to a house in Oxford. A poem on their
family monument in the Lambeth graveyard describes how the gentlemen 'liv'd till
they had travell'd art and nature thro', And by their choice collections may appear,
Of what is rare, in land, in sea, and air.'[24]

Elias Ashmole, another important collector in Oxford, had designs on Tradescant's
Ark. Ashmole built a house next to the Tradescants', and sued Mrs Tradescant (the
younger John's widow) for the collection, which Ashmole eventually seized after her
suicide. Ashmole left the valuable Ark's contents to the University at Oxford in
1677.[25] The Ashmolean Museum then became one of the most important cabinets of
curiosities in England. Opening in 1683, it contained natural specimens as well as
exotic objects from foreign lands. The prize of the collection was and remains 'Pow-
hatan's mantle,' four deerskins decorated with shells – a religious wall hanging
owned by the father of Pocohantas in Virginia.

Scholars have debated the identity of the architect of the Ashmolean Museum, with some attributing the design to Thomas Wood, a master mason, and others preferring to give credit to Christopher Wren (Figure 1.4).[26] The Renaissance-style building, completed in 1683, occupied an important site next to the Sheldonian Theatre. It was a narrow, two-storey building with its long side facing the street; there was an elaborate portal on the short side, which was originally intended as a ceremonial entrance from the neighboring Sheldonian Theatre. The interior was less crowded than Ferrante's or Worm's cabinets: Ionic columns marked the longitudinal axis, traditional windows illuminated the room from one side, and it was just tall enough for a giraffe (Figure 1.5). The displays were on the top floor, a large lecture room on the ground floor, and chemistry laboratories were located in the basement, as was typical for that time. When the Ashmolean Museum opened in 1683, anyone could visit for an entrance fee of sixpence. In 1710 the German antiquarian and traveller Von Uffenbach objected to this open-to-all policy, on the grounds that he could 'see nothing well for the crowds'; it was market day, and the museum was packed with 'all sorts of country-folk.'[27] At this same time, however, the Bodleian was allegedly open to visitors, but it was difficult to obtain permission and therefore was less than welcoming.[28] The original Ashmolean's collections were later divided among the University Museum, the Pitt Rivers Museum and the Bodleian Library, and the current Ashmolean Museum of Art and Archeology contains few items collected by Tradescant and Ashmole.[29]

When the antiquarian John Henry Parker, architectural historian and keeper of the Ashmolean from 1870 to 1884, took over his post, he disparaged the 'curiosities' in

Figure 1.4 Original Ashmolean Museum, Oxford, attributed to Thomas Wood, 1683, exterior. Photograph by the author.

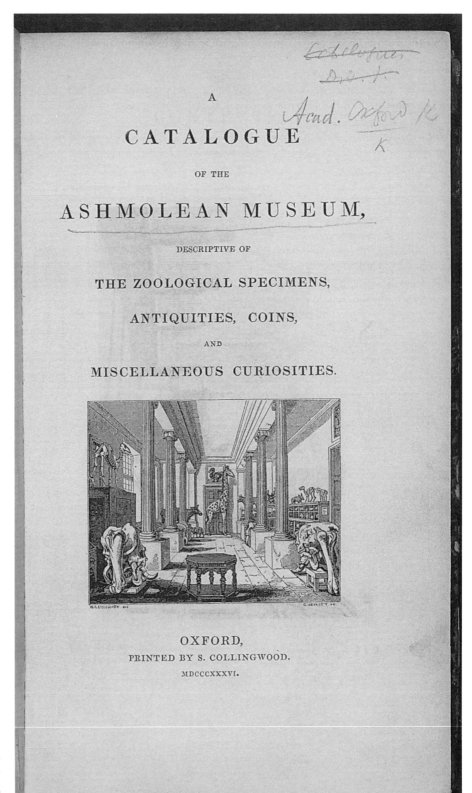

Figure 1.5
Ashmolean Museum,
Oxford. P. B. Duncan,
*Catalogue of the
Ashmolean Museum*
(Oxford, 1836), title
page with drawing of
the interior in 1836.

Ashmole's collection. The sharp edge to his comments offers an opportunity for us to see that the earlier classification systems seemed muddled and unsophisticated by 1870:

> [The Ashmolean] was the earliest collection of its kind formed in England, and chiefly consisted of what are called *curiosities*, without regard to whether they were objects of Natural History – the works of God, or Antiquities, the works of Man, in the olden time. The collection, with the additions of Ashmole, included Birds, Beasts, Fishes, especially the productions of distant countries, all that was comprised under the general name of 'Rarities.' Such was the general character of a Museum down to our own time.[30]

This distinction – between the works of God and the works of Man – dominated nineteenth-century British museums.

As Findlen points out, Baconian philosophy emphasized that science should improve humankind, and to achieve this English gentlemen were urged to open the doors of their collections to a wider audience than on the continent, where museums were the purview of only courtiers and philosophers. By denying the strict boundary between scholar and commonfolk, English museums offended the Italian courtiers, who felt that any knowledge so easily accessible (and on offer for a sixpence) was suspect.[31] Even if post-Enlightenment men of science spurned the *Wunderkammer* for its faulty classification and jumbled presentation, these later men owed to early collectors something more basic: Aldrovandi, Kircher, Worm and Ferrante established specific places for studying nature. They invented rooms with defined boundaries for scholarship and with the distinct purpose of visual scrutiny; these spaces led to the wide range of purpose-built museums in the nineteenth century.

Objects in museums of wonder were included as fragments; no linear development was implied. Historian Barbara Maria Stafford has observed that pre-Enlightenment thought seems more like postmodernism, as it is more open to multivalence. One thinks, for example, of the prized artifacts in *Wunderkammern*, items like the conch shell carved into a drinking vessel, an ostrich egg serving as the body for an ostrich sculpture, or the plum stone carved with the Passion of Christ: these objects were natural and cultural at once, and thus open to multiple meanings. Barbara Maria Stafford has argued that today 'we possess artistic models and visual methods of analysis – many deriving from the eighteenth century – for not receiving pictures passively but entering and reassembling them actively.'[32] Stafford's notion, that the postmodern era encourages us to actively 'reassemble' images, is compelling. She continues:

> The eighteenth century scientific quest for origins, ancestry, and genealogy, however, was permeated by the conviction that such a trove of visual objects possessed a unique capacity to teach, to uncover the relation of known parts to an unknown whole. The creation of galleries, museums, libraries, and natural history cabinets was grounded in a visual encyclopedism persuasively encouraging cross referencing in a disparate public that strolled and paused before minute details and eye-arresting features.[33]

The desire for eye-arresting display lasted further into the nineteenth century than many people think; one weakness with theories that praise the pre-Enlightenment period for being proto-postmodernist is that they unfairly caricature the nineteenth century. Vision in the Victorian museum was every bit as complex and multilayered as previously: visitors were required to assemble information on their own, and what they took away from the museum displays must have varied widely, since it was based on the knowledge they brought with them. Elite scientists often made their opinions clear, but their judgments probably differed from those of non-scientists. Furthermore, historian Anne Secord has studied the lives and interests of working-class naturalists, and found that they valued Linnaeus' systematics long past the time when he was popular among elite scientists. The botanists she writes about would have perceived the museum differently from either their friends (who did not botanize as a hobby) or from upper-class men of science. And all of these groups would find visual 'cross-references' and would 'pause before minute details and arresting features.'

The Enlightenment influenced education in every way: not only was formal education introduced into schools, but informal education changed, too. The emphasis on 'rational amusements' or rational recreation was typical of the entire nineteenth century, and certainly engendered the growth of museums. In the rhetoric of the Enlightenment, order and classification replaced the sense of wonder known to Renaissance and Baroque collectors. In England, the Baconian ideals of the Royal Society influenced collecting. As Findlen explains, 'The cosmological significance of the Renaissance museum had no place in the Enlightenment world view; it was socially and intellectually incommensurable with the new place of natural history in the eighteenth century.'[34] One wasn't supposed to wonder, one was supposed to learn.

HANS SLOANE AND THE FOUNDING OF THE BRITISH MUSEUM

One of the most generous gifts to the eighteenth-century British people was Hans Sloane's donation of his vast collection. It was subsequently housed in Montagu House, the home of the Earl of Halifax, which had been built in imitation of a Parisian hôtel.[35] In spite of the importance of the collection, Parliament did not allocate funds for a purpose-built museum: the objects were fitted into an existing hôtel and opened to the public in 1753 (Figure 1.6). As historian Richard Altick points out, it was ostensibly free and open to the public, but the difficulty of getting tickets, coupled with numerous closed days at exactly the times when working people might be free, made a visit inconvenient, unless one had access to a Trustee and plenty of leisure time. But since the museum was, in theory, open to the public, other collectors after Sloane were inclined to place their objects on view, and the museum helped create a national image for Britain. Visitors to the museum were intended to feel a sense of pride in the vast collections. In a drawing of the interior stair, visitors were awed by the large stuffed animals, especially three giraffes (parents and presumably a daughter – with stereotypically feminine long eyelashes) perched on the landing. The building is clearly domestic, not institutional, architecture – for a moment we might think this image shows the staircase of a rather well-off giraffe family. There is an absence – a lack of specified, purpose-built architecture for display.

The British Museum in Bloomsbury, the building we know today, was designed and built in the 1820s by Robert Smirke. An imposing Greek Revival edifice, it was intended to hold Sloane's collection as well as an increasing number of antiquities,

natural specimens, and the great British Library. The natural history collections were later removed from the Bloomsbury building, and housed in a separate structure in South Kensington – the subject of Chapter 5 of this book.

BULLOCK'S MUSEUM

It was only a short walk from the British Museum to Bullock's Museum on Piccadilly Circus, but it was a world away. Bullock's Museum was originally called the Liverpool Museum, because he relocated it to London from that northern city. It was also known as the Egyptian Hall, after its fashionably styled exterior (Figure 1.7). A privately-run, profit-making popular attraction, it cost a shilling for admission, and played on the confusion between entertainment and education. In 1810 an enthusiastic review in *The Repository of the Arts* claimed a visit was money well spent: 'We have the pleasure of assuring the public that the spirited proprietor of this delightful place of amusement ... meets with that remuneration to which he is so justly entitled.'[36] The museum included many exotic artifacts (exotic to Englishmen and women, anyway), like Maori necklaces made from human bone, canoes of various nations, a mummy, wampum belts, and the shoe of Count Borulaski (a Polish Dwarf). In 1810 Bullock's main room was lit from above by an oval skylight, and the walls remained free for extensive hanging (Figure 1.8). Arms and armour on the far wall, including a knight on horseback, skulk in the shadow of the imposing quadrupeds: an elephant, rhinoceros (in the etching his horn is hidden behind a tall black

Figure 1.7 Bullock's Museum (the Egyptian Hall), 22 Piccadilly, exterior showing Egyptian details and tulip columns at entrance. Aquatint in *Repository of Arts*, 14 (1815) plate 9.

Figure 1.8 Bullock's Museum (the Egyptian Hall), 22 Piccadilly, interior showing display of natural history specimens. Aquatint in *Repository of Arts*, 3 (1810) plate 35.

bird, possibly the vulture mentioned in the catalogue), polar and brown bears, and a zebra. These beasts were corralled within a rough-hewn fence, which contrasted with the finery of a lady dressed in pink who rests against it. The larger (and flashy) animals were displayed in this central area, but the rest of the natural objects were grouped into categories such as quadrupeds, birds, amphibious animals (reptiles, or 'lizards' and 'serpents' were under this category), fishes and insects. Some larger animals were out of order, so that they could be displayed in the artificial forest. The numbered objects corresponded to a catalogue which gave both Latin and British names, details of their origins, and occasional stories. So far, this all sounds as though it would suit any naturalist. But the tone of the catalogue captured Bullock's sensationalism: the rattlesnake is deadly, the lynx ferocious, the rhino untractable and rude, and the polar bear an animal of such tremendous ferocity that it occasionally attempts to board armed sea vessels.[37] The wonder of this museum (as described by *The Repository of the Arts*) was that it offered 'sights unseen before.'[38] Nonetheless, Bullock could also appeal to mainstream Christian values because the rarities in his museum were part of 'the great volume of Creation, the work of an all-wise Providence.'[39]

We can see Bullock's Museum through late Victorian eyes, because Thomas Greenwood, a chronicler of public museums and proponent of museums as serious educational institutions, described the Egyptian Hall in detail:

> [It] was divided into two parts. The large room, with galleries round it, contained the birds, beasts, fishes, amphibia, insects, &c, besides many works of art, particularly various specimens of ancient and modern armour, and curiosities from America, Africa, and Asia . . .

One room of Bullock's contained both cultural and natural objects. Quadrupeds had a special display room, the Pantherion, where animals were posed in reconstructed environments. Greenwood continued:

> The other part contained quadrupeds, and, according to the taste at that time for Greek names, was called the Pantherion. The arrangement of this place was a novel plan, intended to display the whole of the known quadrupeds in such a manner as would convey a more perfect idea of their haunts and mode of life than had hitherto been done, keeping them at the same time in their classical arrangement . . . It occupied a spacious apartment, nearly forty feet high, erected for the purpose. The arrangement of the objects was rather unique. The visitor was introduced through a basaltic cavern, similar in style to the Giant's Causeway or Fingal's Cave, into an Indian hut, situated in a tropical forest, in which were displayed most of the quadrupeds described by naturalists. In addition to these there were correct models from nature, or from the best authorities, of the trees and other vegetable productions of the torrid climes. The whole was assisted by a panoramic effect of distance, which made the illusion produced so strong that the surprised visitor found himself suddenly transported from a crowded metropolis to the depth of an Indian forest.[40]

Visitors entered the Pantherion through a cave, then were surprised by the spectacle of a panorama of the Indian jungle. The stuffed animals were staged in frightening battles; a boa constrictor squeezed the life out of a deer in one famous installation. Bullock's displays exemplified up-to-date taxidermy: the animals were freely posed, their skins fitted over carved forms; Bullock also used arsenic to prepare the taxidermy so that the animals would not decay or become bug-infested. Here at the popular museum, nature was defined as dangerous and dramatic.[41]

We can understand a later Victorian perception of these dramatic groupings because in 1874, a critic objected to the emotional narrative taxidermy groups that were so popular at Bullock's:

> 'Spread-eagle styles' of mounting, artificial rocks and flowers, etc, are entirely out of place in a collection of any scientific pretensions . . . Besides they take up too much room. Artistic grouping of an extensive collection is usually out of the question; and thus when this is unattainable, halfway efforts in that direction should be abandoned in favour of severe simplicity. Birds look best, on the whole, in uniform rows, assorted according to size, as far as a classification allows.[42]

These birds in rows, an orderly uniform system, constructed a kind of museum vision. Once in the museum, specimens were presented as scientific data. The process of science was almost invisible, while the products of science loomed large.[43]

'THE BIRDS AND BEASTS WILL TEACH THEE': PEALE'S PHILADELPHIA MUSEUM

Popular museums, or dime museums as they were called in America, challenged the scientific establishment. In fact, although Bullock's Museum shared much in common with American dime museums, Victorian British critics associated vulgar displays of nature with notoriously profit-driven American culture. The best example of an American museum was the Philadelphia Museum, and its keeper was the multi-talented Charles Willson Peale. The entrance ticket to Peale's Museum read, 'The Birds and Beasts will Teach Thee,' and, indeed, Peale's Museum was meant to both edify and entertain. It contained important scientific specimens like the first complete fossil vertebrate, the mastodon. Peale's primary motivation, however, was to dazzle. He brought taxidermy to a new level of naturalism, and he displayed stuffed and mounted animals in front of paintings made by his talented children to give an illusion of depth (Figure 1.9). The museum included a bloody exhibition of a wolf devouring the head of a mule deer. The deer's skin had arrived in such poor condition that only the head could be used – as a snack for the wolf.[44] The architecture here was merely a pre-existing envelope to house the displays: it was not purpose-built like the Hunterian.

Peale's Museum was first housed in the American Philosophical Society (from 1794 to 1802) and later moved to Independence Hall, where the Declaration of Independence had been signed. The building's original purpose was as the State House for Pennsylvania under British colonial rule. Today it is difficult to imagine a national landmark housing a profit-making attraction, but Peale's Museum was explicitly American, and thus the location in Independence Hall would have enhanced the nationalistic overtones. The mastodon was found in the United States, and it was construed to represent America's greatness at a time when many naturalists proposed that New World beasts were degenerate forms of European animals. Thomas Jefferson had a mastodon bone in the front hall of Monticello to communicate the same meaning. Jefferson presented Peale's Museum with the minerals collected by Lewis and Clark, a gesture that 'symbolically asserted the nation's control over the newly acquired area.'[45]

Even in Peale's time, his enterprise was denounced for being too much a side-

Figure 1.9 Charles Willson Peale, The Long Room, interior of front room in Peale's Museum, 1822. Reproduced by permission of the Detroit Institute of Arts Founders Society Purchase, Director's Discretionary Fund.

show. In 1852, W. S. W. Ruschenberger (later president of the Academy of Sciences in Philadelphia) criticized Peale, saying the 'vulgar and ephemeral curiosity which manifests itself in a desire to see what is not commonly held in nature, or art, expended itself at the Philadelphia Museum.'[46] Worse yet, the word 'museum' itself was diminished by its association with American profit-making institutions. Greenwood, who had also disparaged Bullock's Museum, wrote that 'It has remained for our American cousins to drag the term Museum down to a very low level. On the other side of the Atlantic no good-sized town would be considered complete without its 'Dime Museum,' where every description of monstrosity, natural and otherwise – usually otherwise – can be seen for a modest fivepence.'[47] For Greenwood, who believed museums were meant to be educational, this was an abuse of the good word 'museum.' Peale himself had second thoughts about entertainment without edifying content: after a successful evening performance of an Italian musician named Signor Helene who played the Pandean pipes, viola, Turkish cymbals, tenor drum and Chinese bells – all at the same time – Peale wrote to his son, 'such exhibitions rather degrade a Museum of Natural History.'[48]

The *scala naturae*, usually translated as the Great Chain of Being, was the predominant metaphor for the order of nature in the eighteenth century. The *scala naturae* is indicated in the painting Peale made of his museum in 1822; portraits of famous men hang above the mounted birds, at the top of the hierarchy. Peale represents the ingenuity of mankind (less than modestly) with his own personage, and his dramatic gesture of pulling back the curtain to reveal his collection. At the left foreground of the painting, a dead turkey is draped over a box containing his taxidermy tools: Peale makes a visual equivalent between creating life-like sculptures out of dead animals and painting, because his palette rests on a table nearby.[49] In the theory of the Great Chain of Being, the lowest animals are linked to the highest, Man, in a directional progression of graduated steps. Confidence in the Great Chain of Being did begin to erode in the early nineteenth century, because western naturalists discovered unusual animals, connections between animals, and fossils of extinct (and sometimes grand) animals. With the advent of Darwinism, many elite scientists rejected the simplistic progression, but the idea remained vivid for many personally religious naturalists and for less well-educated enthusiasts.

SCIENCE VS. SHOW

For most of Victoria's reign, men of science tried to keep natural knowledge safe from encroaching theatricality: a stage set would undermine the authenticity of the natural objects, and authenticity was the only reason for museums to exist. If authenticity were not the unspoken *raison d'être* of museums, then naturalists could have studied from illustrated books. Neat rows of skeletons reified natural order, just as surely as a romantic painting (like Edwin Landseer's *The Hunted Stag*, in which hounds drag down a deer caught in the white water of a rushing stream) communicated the violence of nature. In both cases, the skeletons in the museum and the Landseer painting, nature is socially constructed, but its meaning shifts from an appreciation of order in the museum to the Victorian valorization of hunting in the painting. Men of science sought to control the presentation of even the most unusual objects, like the mastodons, so that they would be taken seriously. Curatorship was a ladder for ambitious scientists to climb: these men wanted attention for collecting the best and biggest specimens, and such self-aggrandizement necessarily conflicted with their claim for creating typical displays.

Peale made unsuccessful attempts to start branch museums in Baltimore and New York,[50] but the collection was purchased by P. T. Barnum in 1849–50. This marked the objects' 'descent,' as it were, from science to show. The mastodon was the same physical specimen, but in Barnum's museum, next to Jumbo the Elephant, its meaning as a scientific symbol might have been lost.

DISPLAYS OF NATURAL KNOWLEDGE OUTSIDE THE MUSEUM

Natural specimens could be found outside of museums and popular shows. Many provincial museums contained art and natural artifacts, and literary and philosophical societies often had small displays, as did mechanics' institutes and schools. Often the 'lit and phils' acquired their assorted collections in a haphazard manner, as members left butterflies, fossils or dried botanical specimens to their local group. Commercial galleries (relatively rare at the time) sold natural tidbits to the curious, and many private homes also displayed trophies and decorative taxidermy groups. It is ironic – given that today's natural history museums emphasize wildlife conservation – that so many of the specimens in museums were shot by big-game hunters. Architect Decimus Burton designed a home for the geologist George Bellas Greenough that included two special rooms, one rectangular and the other oval, for his library and cabinet of specimens.[51] Some hunters' private collections became local education facilities, as was the case with William Oswell's trophies; schoolchildren came from nearby Tunbridge Wells to see his animal heads and other African memorabilia. The painter Edwin Landseer owned an impressive collection of heads – zoologists might have reasonably lamented the loss of bodies – including stags, bulls, rams and wild boars. One of the largest private hunters' collections was P. H. G. Powell-Cotton's house in Kent, to which he built additions specifically to house his trophies. Some of the stuffed animals were displayed in dioramas with painted backgrounds.[52] One of the large rooms in Holland House, a Jacobean mansion in Kensington, was lined with black mahogany bookcases filled with printed journals: above the bookcases, boxes of minerals, butterflies and insects completed the decor.[53] And the Harpur and Harpur Crewe families of Calke Abbey collected voraciously; they acquired some things themselves and purchased others from dealers. Thus the saloon at Calke Abbey appears today as a work of Victorian installation art: cases are arranged artistically alongside the furniture, family portraits hang above and below a row of mounted heads and antlers.[54]

VISUAL SCRUTINY: AGASSIZ AND THE FISH

'Trial by fish,' as historian Mary Winsor calls it, was Professor Louis Agassiz's clever (if malodorous) method for teaching his new graduate students that looking was the most important skill for aspiring zoologists. Agassiz, a professor at Harvard and curator of the Museum of Comparative Zoology, initiated each new student by placing a pickled fish in a tin pan, setting the pan on a desk, and leaving the individuals (student and fish) alone together for a week, sometimes longer. He instructed each student not to read about fishes or discuss the project with other students. Students tended to notice peculiarities that distinguished one species from the next, but Agassiz wanted them to see deep similarities – those characteristics which were hidden in plain sight. He said to one pupil: 'You haven't seen one of the most conspicuous features of the animal, which is as plainly before your eyes as the fish itself; look again, look again!'[55] Bilateral symmetry, for example, was a characteristic of the whole vertebrate class, and could be easily identified in the fish. As historian Winsor explains, 'The answer, which Agassiz hoped to impress upon his students by means of their initial lonely exercise, was that even a single individual embodies the layered structure of the hierarchy of taxonomic categories.'[56] Thus one of the most famous stories in the history of Victorian science (if not the history of education) illustrates the value of visual scrutiny as a reliable epistemology in the nineteenth-century context.

Lay consumers of science were also encouraged to learn by looking: vision was a credible way of understanding the world, especially in science museums. James Rennie, a popularizer of natural science and the author of both *Insect Architecture* and *The Architecture of Birds*, clearly explained how the act of examining a specimen brought naturalists the greatest joy:

> The mere collector, who looks only to the shining wings of one [insect], or the green rust of the other, derives little knowledge from his pursuit. But the cabinet of the entomologist becomes rich in the most interesting subjects of contemplation, when he regards it in the genuine spirit of scientific inquiry ... Their differences are so minute, that an unpractised eye would proclaim [them to be identical] and yet, when the species are separated ... [the differences] become visible even to the common observer. It is in examinations such as these that the naturalist finds a delight of the highest order.[57]

Published under the auspices of the Society for the Diffusion of Useful Knowledge, Rennie's books introduced scientific subjects to a mass audience. He argued that by proper organization, even common observers could learn from the objects. This object-based epistemology, as historian Conn calls it, was the founding principle of the Victorian museum.

The 'code' of the earlier cabinet of curiosities was, then, radically different. The cryptic quality was valued by courtiers because it enhanced the curiousness of the collection, and at the same time heightened the sense that the elite visitor was privileged to have such a clue to the meaning of nature. Ferrante Imperato's cabinet and Olaus Worm's *Wunderkammer* offered no special architecture for viewing specimens. Traditional windows were good enough for gentlemen's homes, and good enough for museums before the Victorian era. Perhaps early collectors consciously avoided new imagery, in order to link their pursuits to gentlemanly behaviour. In contrast, British Victorian natural history museums were founded by men who believed in rational recreation for all classes: rationally designed and purpose-built structures were developed for a wide range of audiences.

chapter 2

Displays of Natural Knowledge
in the 1830s and 1840s

A range of co-existing definitions of nature may be seen in three architectural projects from the 1830s and 40s. Patrons at prestigious, private Cambridge University included natural history displays in the plans for a new university-wide library. The Hunterian Museum in London was supported by the Royal College of Surgeons, with occasional governmental grants. Although the society's primary purpose was to promote the education of surgeons, the society supported one of the most important natural history museums in the nineteenth century. Thirdly, the Museum of Practical Geology was a parliament-funded institution that signalled the government's effort to promote science, and symbolized the 'state investment in training the next generation of engineers, metallurgists, and geologists.'[1] These three buildings (one unfinished and the other two ignored by architectural historians) reward our attention not only because they show how difficult it was to establish places for the study of natural history, but also because they offer a much-needed context for understanding the program of the better-known Oxford University Museum.

Historians of science have emphasized that there was no Whiggish progression from gentlemanly hobbyist to secular professional that resulted in our modern-day idea of the scientist.[2] While it is true that in the 1830s there were few opportunities for a young man to support himself by practicing science, and that, by contrast, in 1900 there were positions at universities, government grants, publishing venues, organized societies and paid museum jobs, this fact of history should not suggest that ineffectual dabblers were replaced by 'real' scientists. To believe this teleology would be to assume, based on an incorrect twentieth-century bias, that religious men made poor scientists. We must put aside the twentieth-century division between religion and science in looking at early nineteenth-century museums; the professionalization and secularization of science do not influence this story until after 1860.[3] Men of science, especially lecturers at Oxford and Cambridge, commonly believed that by studying nature they were broadening their knowledge of God. In this view they were influenced by the widely popular writings of William Paley.

Upon its publication in 1802, Paley's *Natural Theology, or Evidences of the Existence and Attributes of the Deity, Collected from the Appearances of Nature*, captured the imagination of British thinkers. The book offered a litany of examples of perfect design from the natural world, each of which proved that only an intelligent Creator could make such delicate contrivances. Paley was enthralled with the sheer diversity of nature: as Psalm 104 says, 'O Lord, how manifold are thy works! . . . the earth is full of thy riches.' Paley began his book with the famous comparison of nature and her Creator to a watch and its watchmaker. If one finds a watch, and cannot understand how it works, the fault lies in the finder. Christians found the natural world to be incomprehensible, but beneath its wondrousness and variety, nature was really as perfectly honed and smooth-functioning as a well-oiled watch. The study of nature would lead to greater understanding of God.[4] Natural theology was more influential in Britain than in Prussia, Bavaria or France. All naturalists in Britain, whether natural theologians or radical evolutionists, would have agreed that the social status of science in France was appropriately high, because the Jardin des Plantes served as a centralized, active, state-funded research institute.

THE JARDIN DES PLANTES AND THE MUSÉUM D'HISTOIRE NATURELLE IN PARIS

Parisian science was the yardstick by which English naturalists measured themselves in the first decades of the nineteenth century. Beginning in the eighteenth century, the Comte du Buffon (1707–1788) enlarged the natural history collections at the Jardin des Plantes and organized a kind of research centre for the natural sciences. The curators at the Muséum d'Histoire Naturelle were also professors, which enhanced its status. The Jardin des Plantes included a menagerie; while there were earlier zoos in Vienna (1765) and Madrid (1775), the live animals at the Jardin des Plantes were more than royal toys, they were intended for scientific study.[5] As architectural historian Paula Young Lee has shown, the Jardin des Plantes was conceived of as a research institution of the highest order, and its misleading name (it was much more than a 'garden') provoked complaints as early as 1790. A topographical map of the Jardin des Plantes in 1853 shows the size of the enterprise: medicinal and botanical gardens, separate galleries to house individual collections, and laboratories (Figure 2.1).[6] No such research institute existed in Britain.

The Parisian garden and its museums offer a glimpse into categories of knowledge and their reification in architecture. Lee also points out that while Étienne-Louis Boullée's well-known design for a museum was without utility, addressed neither collecting nor curating, and was never meant to be built, J. N. L. Durand's project for a museum marked an important change. Durand's museum housed only art, without any natural specimens, thus beginning the institutional separation of art from nature that we take for granted today. In contrast to the Muséum d'Histoire Naturelle, the Louvre (which is routinely taken to be the archetypal art museum) was originally intended as a 'depository of all human knowledge.' (The British Museum did not make such grand claims, but it did contain items that today we would place in separate categories of 'science' and 'art.') The Muséum d'Histoire Naturelle kept the term 'Muséum' in its name (as opposed to the more common 'Musée') as an homage to the *musaeum* of Alexandria. As Lee explains, the term 'Muséum' thus indicated 'the possession of knowledge,' as opposed to the narrower 'possession of things.'[7] This definition of the Alexandrian *musaeum* was also known in England, where in 1836 the Catalogue of the Ashmolean defined the term 'Museum' as 'a place dedicated to the muses . . . , [the term was] applied originally to part of the Royal Palace of Alexandria appropriated for the use of learned men.'[8]

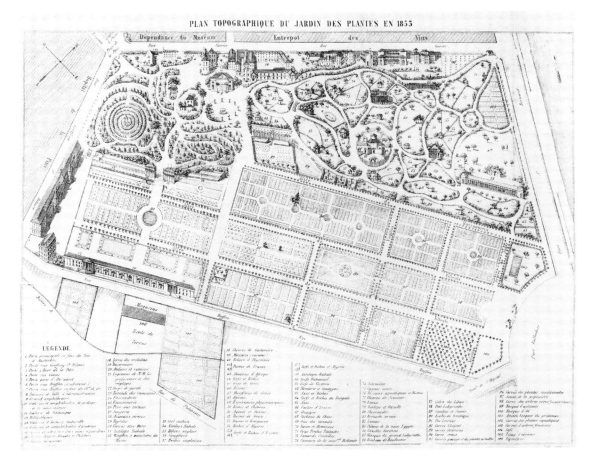

Figure 2.1
Topographical plan
of the Jardin des
Plantes in 1853.
*Guide des Étrangers
dans le Muséum
d'Histoire Naturelle*
(Paris, 1853).

The Jardin des Plantes and its museum buildings were the workplace of Georges Cuvier, the brilliant reconstructive anatomist whose concept of the correlation of forms dictated that animals were holistically perfect, to the extent that they could be rebuilt from any fragment. In 1836 a Select Committee of the House of Commons cited the Muséum d'Histoire Naturelle as an exemplar, and in 1840 the British naturalist William Swainson called it 'the most celebrated in the world.'[9] Although after 1840 the institution stagnated due to budget cuts and public criticism, in the 1830s it was a major influence on British naturalists.[10] For example, in 1831, Cuvier invited Richard Owen, then a young but promising anatomist, to visit him at the Jardin des Plantes. Owen was in awe: in some way, his long career in museum building must date back to that visit. He was especially struck by the arrangement of specimens by taxonomic grouping, which served to illustrate grand principles of natural history.[11] In 1828, the polymath William Whewell, professor of mineralogy, author of one of the Bridgewater Treatises, promoter of natural theology, and later Master of Trinity College, decried the poor facilities for the physical sciences at Cambridge. He was particularly irritated that Cuvier gave osteological casts to Oxford, because Cambridge had no room to keep them.[12] Whewell and Owen were boyhood friends, and Owen's visit to Paris would have only heightened their perception of England's sluggishness in museum construction.

A PLACE FOR NATURAL HISTORY AT CAMBRIDGE: COMPETITIONS FOR THE
UNIVERSITY LIBRARY

In the same year as Owen's visit, 1831, George Peacock, a mathematics professor at Cambridge, expressed his humiliation at the lack of educational displays at his otherwise great university. He did so by noting that he was relieved when the 'most illustrious naturalist in Europe,' probably Cuvier, put off a scheduled trip to England. Peacock said he and the other Cambridge lecturers had 'rejoiced to hear of the postponement of his visit, because it spared them the pain of exposing the nakedness of the land.'[13] Compared to the Jardin des Plantes, the natural history specimens at Cambridge were badly housed: they sought shelter for many years, but never attained a free-standing building. (And they certainly never acquired the grandiose home that their rivals at Oxford later inhabited.) Three competitions over an eight-year period resulted in only a compromised, partially built scheme for natural history displays. At Cambridge, the museum was conceived as part of a large new building that was intended to serve primarily as a library. In the 1820s and 30s natural history was seen as one small part of a vast educational mission at Cambridge, where education was still focussed on teaching the history of ideas from library books rather than teaching the history of the physical world from museum specimens. Theirs was a world in which classical learning thrived.

The natural history collections at Cambridge University had grown out of the private study hoards of several professors. In 1821 a special committee, or Syndicate,[14] first considered the question of how to display the university's geological specimens.[15] By the end of the 1820s, the faculty was planning to extend the University Library to include a large facility for books owned by the university (as opposed to the individual colleges), and they planned to house the natural history specimens and offices in this structure. On 6 May 1829, the faculty appointed another Syndicate (a building committee, in this case) to oversee the construction of the new building.[16] Peacock, a champion of the project, emphasized that the need for science displays at Cambridge was particularly pressing, and that 'the want of such Museums had long been the reproach of the University, and has formed a subject of wonder and astonishment to foreigners visiting the University.'[17] Although professors of geology, anatomy and mineralogy all had useful and valuable collections, they had no place where they could show them to students. Adam Sedgwick, the lecturer in geology, kept specimens in his private apartments, as did Whewell. The anatomy collections were in Queen's College, in rooms which were damp and crowded. Teachers of the physical sciences needed a central location for all their objects, and they looked forward to arranging the items in an orderly fashion.

Having appointed a committee, the faculty decided, in July 1829, to construct a new university building and to adopt the Syndicate's enumeration of its many functions:

> The Syndicate consider it necessary that provision should be made, not merely for a large increase of the accommodation of the Public Library, but likewise for four additional Lecture Rooms, for Museums of Geology, Mineralogy, Botany, and, if practicable, of Zoology; for a new Office of Registrary; for an additional School for the Professor of Physic; and for other purposes connected with the dispatch of the ordinary business of the University.[18]

The program combined in one building what would be several parts of a twentieth-century university: a library, administrative centre, science centre, general classroom building, and museum.

The Syndics invited four promising architects to participate in the competition: C. R. Cockerell, Decimus Burton, William Wilkins and Thomas Rickman and his partner Henry Hutchinson. The site chosen by the Syndicate faced onto King's Parade, just north of King's College Chapel and west of Clare College. It was occupied by the Old Schools, a medieval quadrangle called 'Cobble Court' with one eighteenth-century range which the dons intended to raze, and it embraced the open space to the northwest of King's College Chapel and the old court of King's College.

At this point, the Syndics did not prescribe any particular style of architecture, nor did they propose a budget.[19] The architectural firms were asked to submit their designs by 1 November 1829. Although this was to be a multi-purpose building and not a college, the Syndics wanted the plan of the new building to be that of the traditional collegiate building, the quadrangle. The ground floor of the north range of the quadrangle was set aside for the display of natural specimens, including rooms for zoology, geology, mineralogy and botany. The other schools were also on the ground floor, and the library would cover the whole of the floor above.

Rickman and Hutchinson's submission, along with Cockerell's, are extant, Burton's are now lost,[20] and some of Wilkins's drawings survive but cannot be dated accurately. Rickman and Hutchinson submitted two variants, one Greek and the other Gothic. This was a relatively common practice among nineteenth-century architects, who were not always wedded to one style. (E. M. Barry submitted designs in several styles for the Oxford competition in 1854.) In Rickman and Hutchinson's Greek project, an Ionic hexastyle portico was the focus of the understated composition, an ornamental frieze encircled the building and the pediment included figural sculpture (Figure 2.2). Not surprisingly, Rickman and Hutchinson lavished more attention on their Gothic design, since that style was Rickman's first love and the reason for his considerable fame. His book, *An Attempt to Discriminate the Styles of Architecture in England* taxonomized English medieval architecture; Whewell was a friend and supporter of Rickman's, and he called the guidebook 'his usual travelling

Figure 2.2 Thomas Rickman and Henry Hutchinson, Competition entry, perspective of the University Library in the Greek style, 1829. British Architectural Library, RIBA, London: Rickman & Hutchinson [13] 4.

companion.'[21] Rickman and Hutchinson had won the competition for New Court at St John's in 1825–26 with a Gothic design, so they were known at Cambridge for their recent work. Their second entry for the library competition showed a recessed north range, with a symmetrical east facade and a central portal flanked by crenelated towers (Figure 2.3). The ornament was derived from the style Rickman himself termed 'Decorated' – not as plain as Early English and not as extravagant as Perpendicular.

Cockerell was devoted to one style: his own synthesis of Roman and Greek elements in a modern but always classical idiom. He also submitted two schemes for the prize. In the simpler of the two he used a decastyle Ionic colonnade, surmounted by a balustrade and a largely unadorned attic. The most dramatic element in the design was a pair of curved exterior staircases leading up to the library level (Figure 2.4).[22] The classicist sent a letter with his competition designs, explaining why he chose to submit the two Greek designs for the time-honored purpose of a library:

> It is presumed the Grecian style is most appropriate to a classical institution; is suited to all ages, as containing the essential principles of beauty and magnificence in a superior design. Of the Gothic it may be observed . . . that it is less-suited to an academic building than the Grecian . . . [And] tho' a temporary celebrity has [been] attached [to it] of late years, it never has been esteemed in comparison with the Grecian at periods in which fine art has been cultivated & will again probably sink into disrepute except in the restoration of the ancient monuments of the Country.[23]

In addition to finding the Gothic style faddish and likely to 'sink into disrepute', Cockerell suggested that any neo-Gothic building on this particular site, in the shadow of King's College Chapel, would look foolish: 'the beauty of the *chef d'oeuvre* near it must be greatly to the disadvantage of any attempt to apply it [the style] here.'[24] Of course, one could turn this argument around by concluding that a classical

Figure 2.3 Thomas Rickman and Henry Hutchinson, Competition entry for first competition, perspective of the University Library in the Gothic style, 1829. British Architectural Library, RIBA, London: Rickman & Hutchinson [13] 2.

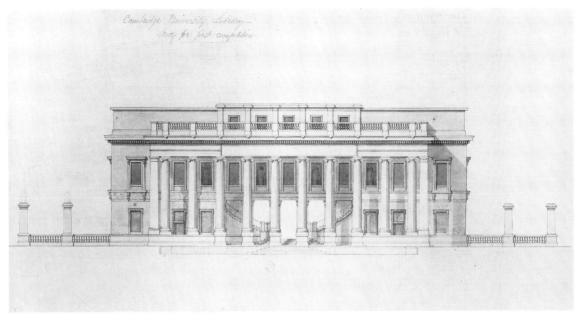

building next to a masterpiece of Perpendicular Gothic would also be at a 'disadvantage', but partisan debates about style are not known for their logic.

Communication between museums and lecture rooms presented a compelling problem in early nineteenth-century university buildings, because while the traditional subjects of mathematics, theology and classics could be taught without demonstrations or props, in science lectures students needed to see the specimens as their teachers spoke. This type of teaching was relatively new to the university setting and required a novel spatial solution. The special problem of the classroom type was spelled out by Whewell's colleague and architectural historian Robert Willis in 1853, when he wrote an analysis of the lecture rooms needed by Cambridge University:

> For the consideration of the accommodation required, the Professors may be divided into two classes: namely, Literary Professors, including all those whose lectures require neither Museums, Laboratories, nor any other appendage to the Lecture-Room; and Scientific Professors, who lecture upon various branches of Natural and Experimental Science, each of which requires Museums, Laboratories, or Apparatus-Rooms.[25]

The Syndicate chose Cockerell as the the winner of the first competition. After consultation with Peacock, Cockerell refined his plans during the winter of 1830. Unfortunately for him, as he laboured, people in Cambridge were changing their minds about the entire project, especially about the cost of the new work and the number of old buildings that would be torn down.[26] In the spring of 1830, the Syndicate decided to re-evaluate the program and budget for the University Library, and they then called for a second competition in which the same architectural firms were asked to prepare designs. Decimus Burton did not send in plans for the second round, claiming he was busy with other projects. By excusing himself, he escaped the aggravation of this second competition, which proved terribly divisive. In

Figure 2.4 C. R. Cockerell, Elevation of the University Library, 1829. The simpler of the two designs that Cockerell submitted to the first competition. By permission of the Syndics of Cambridge University Library, Manuscripts Department, Add. 9272/4/19 (formerly Tab.a.2.).

the ensuing debate, professors and architects joined forces: Peacock supported Cockerell while Whewell defended Thomas Rickman.

The second set of instructions specified: 'The Style of Architecture to be Grecian,' perhaps because Cockerell's earlier arguments regarding style had struck a chord with the Syndicate, or possibly even to discourage Rickman.[27] The second instructions, like the first, asked architects to combine many functions in one building. The plan was to be 'a complete hollow square,' and the architects were again told where to place the museums, schools and library within the building. In order, from west to east, would be the geology museum, mineralogy gallery and botanical gallery. The updated guidelines differed from the first in omitting the zoology room and indicating that only part of the new building would be constructed – the part on the old King's College court, which could be built without tearing down any old structures. Also, the architects now had a budget. The first phase of the building could cost only £25,000. That the Syndics wanted this part (the north range of the quadrangle comprising the museums) built first suggests that the scientists had proven the urgency of their needs.[28]

Cockerell did not rest on his laurels; he produced several new lavish watercolours for the 1830 competition in the hopes of securing a second victory. One watercolour perspective captured the view looking north, past King's College Chapel. The drawing shows the new library set before a grand piazza which is separated from King's College chapel by a low wall punctuated with classical statues (Figure 2.5). For the 1830 competition, Wilkins submitted a scheme that would have saved Steven Wright's Old School building (1753–58); he no doubt hoped this cost-saving measure would appeal to the Syndics, but it did not. Neither Wilkins's preservationist designs nor Cockerell's inventive proposal prevailed in 1830. On December 10 the Syndics hired Rickman and Hutchinson. Peacock wrote a pamphlet in which he supported Cockerell by arguing that only his plans adequately accommodated the natural history displays. He claimed Cockerell's museum galleries 'were arranged *en suite* and formed a continued range of 225 feet, an extent of accommodation [of] which no similar example exists in England, and which if properly furnished, would speedily redeem the character of this University from the just charge of

Figure 2.5 C. R. Cockerell, Entry for second competition, perspective, 1830. By permission of the Syndics of Cambridge University Library, Manuscripts Department, Add. 9272/4/30.

possessing no adequate means of teaching natural knowledge.'[29] But it was not enough to win the votes of practical-minded Syndics, who were already annoyed with Cockerell for disregarding their instructions by adding a basement storey and zoology museum.

In supporting Cockerell, Peacock listed the many faults of Rickman's design: it had too many steps, a narrow court, and poor lighting.[30] Lighting was emerging as a key issue in museum design, and Peacock condemned Rickman and Hutchinson's flat skylight as 'the most miserable of all species of lighting and ventilating,' because it left part of the wall in shade.[31] A flat, overall skylight also created glare on the vertical surface of display cases. (In contrast, the early Hunterian Museum did not have an overall flat skylight, but was glazed only around the edges of the curved ceiling.)

It is difficult for historians to explain Rickman's victory, because the exterior and interior drawings are lost; only plans remain (Figures 2.6 (museum level) and 2.7 (library level)). Whewell emphasized Rickman's functional planning in his pamphlet, which answered Peacock's point for point.[32] Where Peacock supported his favoured architect by claiming he would build a dazzling museum, Whewell argued that Rickman's planning was superior, directly connecting each lecture room to the exhibition spaces. Whewell was probably in a better position than Peacock to judge what the teachers of the physical sciences really needed, since Whewell was reader in mineralogy and Peacock was a mathematician. Rickman connected the lecture room to the museums by placing the theatre at the northwest corner of the building, with the museums on the floor below, linked to the upstairs by three different staircases. Rickman had carefully connected all the lecture rooms to the museums, a problem Cockerell only partially solved.

Although the second Syndicate publicly announced its reversal, the report nominating Rickman was never submitted to the faculty Senate for confirmation. By the end of the nineteenth century, the reasons for the ensuing four-year delay were

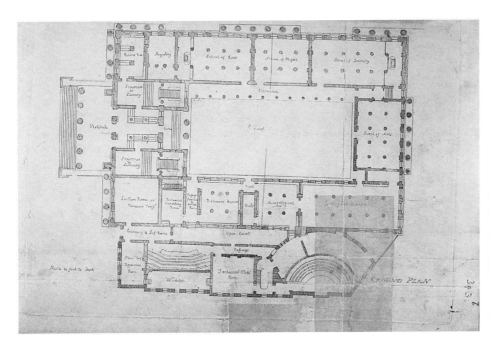

Figure 2.6   Thomas Rickman and Henry Hutchinson, Competition entry for second competition, plan of lower level with museums, 1830. By permission of the Syndics of Cambridge University Library, Manuscripts Department, *History of the Library*, vol. 1: fol. 393b.

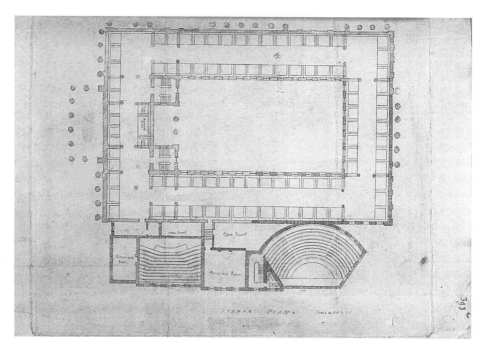

Figure 2.7   Thomas Rickman and Henry Hutchinson, Competition entry for second competition, plan of upper level with library and lecture rooms, 1830. By permission of the Syndics of Cambridge University Library, Manuscripts Department, *History of the Library*, vol. 1: fol. 393c.

already lost to historians.[33] In 1835 a third Syndicate decided that only another competition would settle the matter fairly, so the architects Rickman, Wilkins and Cockerell were asked to submit still more designs.[34]

Cockerell's designs for the third competition finally swayed the judges. The elevation of the main block of the east wing was a compact Greek Ionic design with a nine-columned portico (Figure 2.8), recalling the long colonnade in one of his 1829 competition entries. The short end of the north wing, with arches that broke through their entablatures, contrasted with the rectilinear main block.[35] The west elevation was less formally composed than the east entrance front. Two lecture rooms projected from the facade and were marked by pediments and grand Greek Ionic columns; again the arched windows, like the one on the east end of the north range,

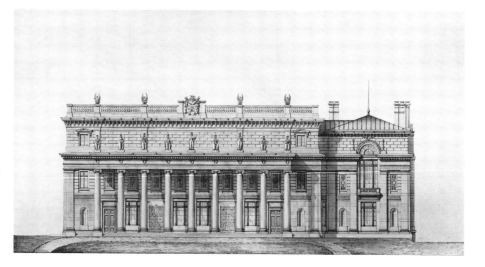

Figure 2.8   C. R. Cockerell, University Library, elevation of east facade, 1837–40. This was the final winner of the three competitions, but only the north wing (on the far right of this image) was constructed. By permission of the Syndics of Cambridge University Library, Manuscripts Department, Add. 9272/2/3 (formerly Tab.a.2).

showed Cockerell's tendency to fuse Roman and Greek precedents in his reinterpretation of the classical past. Again, the library was on the upper floor, so the zoology museum could be lit only partially from above (Figure 2.9, ground plan). In a section drawing sketched along the side of a different plan from the same set, Cockerell showed his solution to the lighting problem in detail. He cut an oval out of the floor of the library, thus making a balcony on that level, and thereby permitted natural light to illuminate both the library and the natural history collections on the first level, where he drew a stuffed deer, elephant, and horse (Figure 2.10, detail of section of ground floor).

When the Senate voted in 1836, Cockerell won by a large margin: 60 votes to Rickman's 9. Wilkins received no votes at all.[36] The temperamental Cockerell had disregarded the instructions by adding a zoology museum in 1830, and in 1836 he again made life difficult for the Senate by refusing to agree to a budget. Only the north range of the quadrangle was ever constructed; the schools for divinity, medicine and law, meant to share the ground floor with the science museums, did not find accommodation in the library building, because after the first £25,000 were spent, funds to complete the remaining three sides of the quadrangle were never raised.[37] An engraving shows the construction of this wing in progress, affording a glimpse of the ground floor, where the collections were displayed (Figure 2.11). Only mineralogy and geology were accommodated in Cockerell's building.[38] The ground-floor galleries were a well-known attraction at Cambridge, but accessible only to scholars. Sedgwick appears in a drawing from 1842, introducing visitors to the mastodon skull and Irish elk skeleton (Figure 2.12). But the library was the real centrepiece of the program at Cambridge, and the showpiece of all of Cockerell's designs; its uninterrupted barrel vault evoked visions of Étienne-Louis Boullée's imaginary library designs of the 1780s.

There are several important lessons that can be learned from the library competition at Cambridge. First, at the time of the second competition, the Syndics stated their preference for the 'Grecian style' but with little explanation. This was primarily a library, and perhaps some of the patrons thought the Greek style (and associations with Alexander) evoked the proper seriousness for the building type. Also, this was a university-wide commission for a shared building (not an individual college), and the patrons may have wanted to distinguish the new library and museum from the residential colleges, which tended to be medieval. As will be argued later in this book in more detail, patrons at the Museum of Practical Geology, Oxford, Edinburgh, and London were less concerned about style and than the practical arrangement of rooms – just as Whewell was at Cambridge.

But the most significant lesson to be learned from Cambridge's truncated museum lies in its failure. The status of natural history at Cambridge (from about 1829 to 1836) coincided with the meagre beginning of physical science teaching in British universities. Science was not yet recognized in the curriculum, and the study of the natural world was considered an accessory to a young man's education, not a necessity. No one at Cambridge dared to suggest that the sciences needed a separate building, and even staunch supporters of natural history hitched the fortunes of the museum to the library. Although pervasive, well-diffused natural light was a basic requirement for museums, no one at Cambridge seems to have requested that the natural history collections be on the top floor of the new building. The library, which of course also required good lighting, unquestionably received the best architectural position. The Syndics's decision reversals, coupled with Cockerell's abbreviated

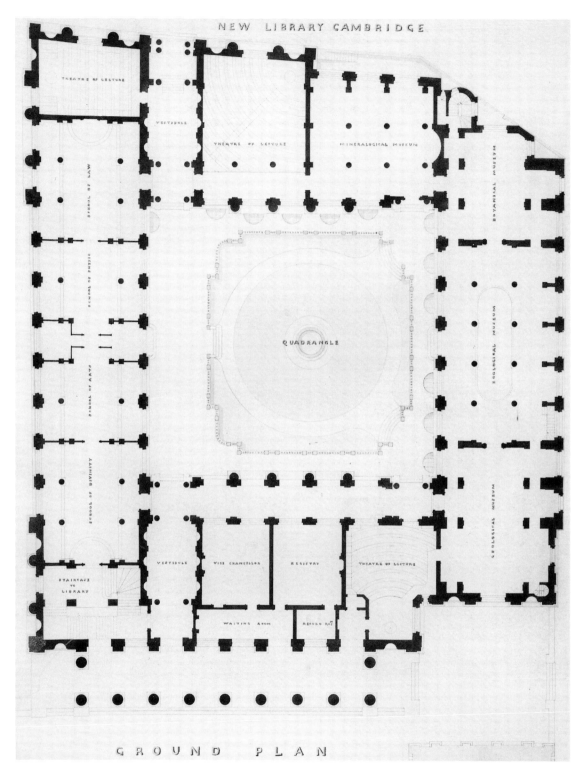

NEW LIBRARY CAMBRIDGE

QUADRANGLE

GROUND PLAN

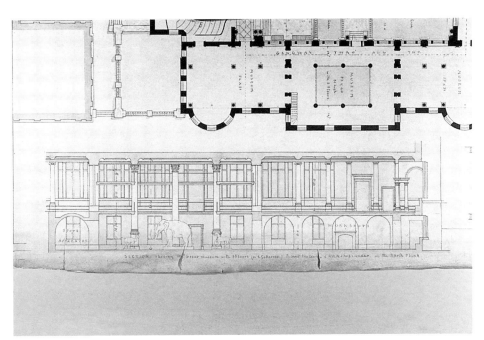

Figure 2.10 C. R. Cockerell, University Library, detail, section of the museum (lower) level, showing elephant and other mammals. By permission of the Syndics of Cambridge University Library, Manuscripts Department, Add. 9272/2/2 (formerly Tab.a.2).

Figure 2.11 C. R. Cockerell, Former Cambridge University Library, 1837–42. Engraving showing building under construction, *Cambridge University Almanack* [sic] 1839. By permission of the Syndics of Cambridge University Library, Map Room, Tab.b.204, fol. 38.

final building, have been described by historians as a disappointment. The history of the Cambridge University Library can also be interpreted as a metaphor for the struggles of early nineteenth-century natural knowledge. It is not surprising, given the place and time, that Cambridge in the 1830s had no grandiose building devoted to the study of the physical world. The books trumped the rocks and bones.

Figure 2.12 C. R. Cockerell, Drawing by George Scharf, Sr, showing Adam Sedgwick in the Cambridge University Library, lower level, natural history collection. By permission of the Syndics of Cambridge University Library, Map Room, Views.X.2, fig. 32.

G. Scharf lithotint

CAMBRIDGE GEOLOGICAL MUSEUM, 1842.

C. Hullmandel's Patent.

HUNTERIAN MUSEUM OF THE ROYAL COLLEGE OF SURGEONS

Whewell and his friend Owen pursued parallel tracks in nineteenth-century science – Whewell in the academy, Owen in the museum. Whewell was a university lecturer, a Fellow at Trinity, a man who made few discoveries and yet held enormous power as an 'adjudicator of science.'[39] In spite of his influence, he did not live to see a monumental, free-standing natural history museum at his beloved Cambridge. Owen stood in a better position to build museums, because he worked in them: he established England's reputation as a museum-making nation. Owen's first success in building a new museum came with the renovations to the Hunterian Museum of the Royal College of Surgeons.

The Royal College of Surgeons was a professional society that had its roots in the ancient guild of barbers, and the college received its natural history specimens when the physician John Hunter (d. 1793) sold his collection, which he originally kept in a building behind his home on Leicester Square, to the British government. When the government gave custody of the collections to the Royal College of Surgeons, the college was instructed to give 24 annual lectures and to open the museum to the public. But because the museum was paid for by the College of Surgeons, with only occasional parliamentary grants, it was primarily a medical museum for use by physicians. Entrance to the Hunterian was granted only to visitors who had a letter of reference from a member of the College of Physicians. Access was easier at the nascent British Museum in Montagu House. The first Hunterian museum opened on Lincoln's Inn Fields in 1813.[40] It was a modest temple-fronted building; in an early architectural design, the inscription on the entablature read 'Quæ Prosunt Omnibus Artes,' or 'These Arts Benefit All' – an obvious rationalization of the use of government money for the surgeons' private study collection (Figure 2.13). Designed by George Dance and James Lewis, the main salon was long and narrow,

QVÆ PROSVNT OMNIBVS ARTES

Figure 2.13 George Dance, Hunterian Museum of the Royal College of Surgeons of England, London. Exterior, Drawing from *c.*1808, negative no. 426/64(16). Photograph courtesy of Conway Library and the Trustees of Sir John Soane's Museum.

lit by three circular lanterns, with a gallery all round (Figure 2.14). The lighting system was reminiscent of the work of John Soane, Dance's friend and former pupil. It most clearly recalls the Dulwich Picture Gallery by Soane. A detailed section plan (signed by both Dance and Lewis, and dated 1805) indicates that the building was divided by a centre spine (Figure 2.15). To the visitor's right, as he or she entered, were the keeper's office, an oval room (of unclear purpose) and then the three main rooms that formed the museum. To the visitor's left, the secretary's office was followed by a courtyard and lecture theatre toward the rear. The keeper's apartment was on the upper floor on the Lincoln's Inn street side. (This was the home of William Clift and his daughter, the future Mrs Richard Owen.) Because the museum was intended for the training and use of physicians, the specimens were organized by physiology.[41] For example, the digestive organs or respiratory organs of various animals were displayed in jars alongside one another.[42]

In 1827 Richard Owen, who was later called the 'British Cuvier', took his post at the Hunterian. He worked there for 29 years. (His next post began in 1856, when he moved to the British Museum which then contained natural specimens in addition to antiquities.) Owen spent 57 years of his life working in these two museums, a fact which makes him the most important museum keeper in Victorian Britian.[43]

In 1833, even though the Dance and Lewis building was only 20 years old, Owen decided that an entirely new structure was needed. Consequently, the Surgeons demolished the galleries – the rooms that had been lit by drum-shaped lanterns.[44] Owen had never liked the building to begin with; he later described it as 'costly, cumbrous, and ill-lit.'[45] Besides, a recent visit to Paris had inspired him. Charles Barry was the winner of a limited competition for the building renovation. He

Figure 2.14 George Dance, Hunterian Museum of the Royal College of Surgeons, Interior showing domed museum rooms lit by lanterns, *c*.1813. Reproduced by kind permission of the President and Council of the Royal College of Surgeons of England.

maintained Dance and Lewis's Greek portico, but extended the building upward by one storey. According to a contemporary guidebook, this extension contained 'artificial stone' – cast concrete covered with stucco.[46] Barry also renovated the interior by constructing a rectangular main room with two balcony levels (instead of one, as in the former building) supported by Doric columns on the ground floor and a flat panelled ceiling with a deep glazed cove (Figure 2.16). An ancillary exhibition room was also added then.

Although the Hunterian was already an important museum, Owen wanted to extend its usefulness beyond medicine – to geology and paleontology. He even dreamed of making it the national museum of natural history, a dream he took with

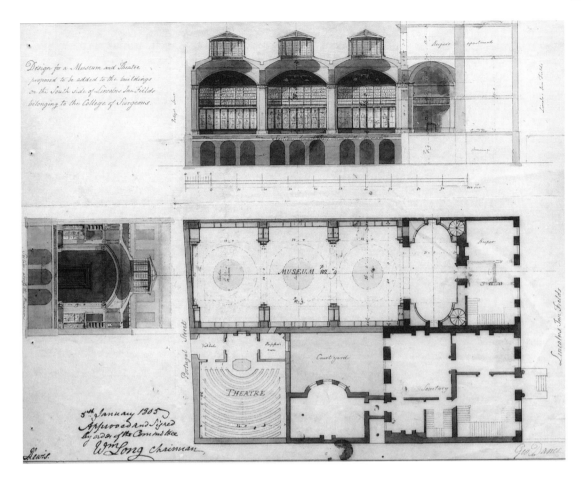

him to Bloomsbury in 1856.[47] He therefore acquired skeletons of both living and extinct animals for display. His placement of the mylodon (an extinct giant sloth) and glyptodon (an extinct giant armadillo) near the entrance was spatially significant: the visitors' first impressions were of two magnificent paleontological finds, presumably unrelated to medical research.[48] As described by historian Adrian Desmond, the Hunterian 'reopened in February [1837] in a typically lavish way with the Duke of Wellington, Sir Robert Peel, and 500 guests. Visitors flocked to the magnificent new museum, with its three-storeyed galleries packed with exhibits and supported on Doric pillars. Everything was on show, from an eight-foot Irish giant to chimpanzee skeletons, platypuses, and fossil armidillos.' (Figure 2.17)[49] Later, in 1845, the *Illustrated London News* celebrated the spectacle: the writer particularly enjoyed seeing the skeleton of the Irish giant (whose early death, he scolded, 'was precipitated by excessive drinking'), the preserved bodies of two men who had been impaled on metal poles, a portion of Napoleon's intestines preserved in spirit, and the conjoined skulls of a two-headed Bengali boy who lived to the age of four, when he (or they) were killed by the bite of a cobra.[50] Owen's desire for a serious research collection was just that – a desire. He had no control over newspaper reporters, who relished the miraculous, gargantuan, and monstrous. Owen's curatorship at the Hunterian included building new spaces, and he maintained this enthusiasm for construction throughout his career. The Hunterian was a landmark in the display of natural

Figure 2.15 George Dance, Hunterian Museum of the Royal College of Surgeons, Plan and section, negative no. 426/42(12). Photograph courtesy of Conway Library and the Trustees of Sir John Soane's Museum.

Figure 2.17 Charles
Barry, Hunterian
Museum of the
Royal College of
Surgeons, Interior of
the main room.
*Illustrated London
News* 7 (4 October
1845) 209.

specimens; the 1813 museum by Dance and its successors by Barry were purpose-built displays with top-lighting and balconies. This *parti* inspired many later museums, including London's Museum of Practical Geology.

THE MUSEUM OF PRACTICAL GEOLOGY: 'IMMENSE MINERAL RICHES'

The Museum of Practical Geology was a government-funded science institute: a museum plus a 'think tank', and it had to be, as the name suggests, Practical. Unlike the Hunterian, its patron was not a professional society, but rather a much more complicated constellation of organizations and individuals. The Museum of Practical Geology contained four distinct agencies: the Geological Survey, the School of Mines, the Mining Record Office, and the Museum of Practical Geology. Geology itself was a multifaceted enterprise, and included among its practitioners wealthy men who travelled widely and romanticized the outdoorsy pleasures of fieldwork, academics like Adam Sedgwick and William Buckland who argued that geology should be studied not for its economic uses but because it broadened the mind, and engineers, metallurgists and miners. All of these careers existed at the same time, and no one particular route should be seen as more serious than any other, even if (at the time) the gentlemen diminished the accomplishments of engineers and surveyors.[51]

According to historian Roy Porter, 'systematic professionalization first came to English geology from 1835 through the bounty of the Geological Survey.'[52] The fashionable geologist Henry De la Beche, son of a Caribbean planter, was originally employed to colour the maps of the Ordnance Survey. Historians of science have emphasized that the practice of science was ordinarily a gentleman's right well into the nineteenth century, and that this right was derived from the notion that a disinterested gentleman had nothing invested in the outcome of scientific observation or experiment, and therefore would have no reason to lie.[53] When he took

Figure 2.16 Charles
Barry, Hunterian
Museum of the
Royal College of
Surgeons, Interior
after Barry's
renovation to
Dance's original
structure, 1837,
drawing by
Sheppard.
Reproduced by kind
permission of the
President and
Council of the Royal
College of Surgeons
of England.

this paying position, the geologist Roderick Murchison labelled De la Beche a 'jobber', thereby implying that his scientific propriety was compromised.[54] De la Beche knew a good deal when he saw one, and his position at the Survey allowed him to remain a powerful figure in the practice of geology. The Geological Survey became a separate institution by act of Parliament in 1845, and by then De la Beche was the director of four chairs: Mining, Geology, Chemistry (held by Lyon Playfair) and Zoology (held by Edward Forbes).[55] Later, in 1854 several branches of the institution (the Museum, the School of Mines and the Geological Survey) were transferred to the newly formed Department of Science and Art: this transfer constituted an alliance of the Museum with Henry Cole's educational institutions in South Kensington.

The Museum of Practical Geology brought together and displayed materials gathered by the Geological Survey, and, as such, defined nature as useful. Royal patronage graced the project when Prince Albert opened the Museum of Practical Geology on May 12, 1851. As the Prince described it:

> it is impossible to estimate too highly the advantages to be derived from an institution like this, intended to direct the researches of science, and to apply their results to the development of the immense mineral riches granted by the bounty of Providence to our isles, and their numerous colonial dependencies.[56]

This was not basic science (as we might call it today), but applied science. And, as Prince Albert explained, the museum would serve as evidence that God was smiling on the British Isles when He deposited all that coal in the midlands. Since the museum displayed many specimens gleaned from colonial sites, it also represented the economic success and the promising future of colonialism.

As was typical of nineteenth-century museums, the collection was formed first and a purpose-built structure erected later. The Geological Survey collected specimens in the course of the geological mapping of Great Britain, and the Museum of Practical Geology became the resting place for its recently gathered rocks and minerals. One part of the collection, a group of building stones, was greatly expanded in 1839 when the stones, which had been gathered together for possible use in the Houses of Parliament, were donated to the Museum.[57] The specimens were used by engineering and mining students at the Royal School of Mines. In the museum's early years, didactic exhibitions were kept in a house at the northern end of Whitehall,[58] but the Museum of Practical Geology quickly outgrew those quarters; and when it required larger and better facilities in the late 1840s, the Office of Works oversaw the completion of a new building to house the geological exhibits, laboratories, a lecture hall, and offices of the Geological Survey and the Mining Record Office. The main goal of the institution was to present science as useful for a vital industrial economy.[59] Such a goal does not necessarily imply that everyone who visited the museum accepted its message as solely economic, nor did all of its employees. John Phillips, later an important science teacher and museum keeper at Oxford University, was a natural theologian, not a utilitarian. Victorian culture combined commerce and God with relative ease.

The Office of Works selected James Pennethorne to design the new Museum of Practical Geology because he was already involved in other projects at the Office, including metropolitan improvements such as the planning of New Oxford Street (1843–47).[60] The Office of Works chose a centrally located site, a narrow plot between Piccadilly and Jermyn Street owned by the Crown. Originally, planners at the Office of Works wanted to include shops on the noisy Piccadilly side and so located the entrance on Jermyn Street (Figure 2.18). In fact, in the nineteenth century it was often called simply the 'Jermyn Street Museum.' Although Adrian Desmond calls the Piccadilly frontage 'prestigious,' it is also possible that government leaders did not want their building adjacent to garish attractions (like Bullock's Egyptian Hall) on Piccadilly – a second reason for placing the entrance to this educational establishment on the 'far more genteel street.'[61] The Piccadilly side had six large arched windows that lit the director's office, secretary's office and the library (Figure 2.19).

De la Beche himself chose the stone for the Renaissance facade. He selected Anston dolomite, the same stone he had recommended for the Houses of Parliament.[62] The Museum of Practical Geology was an in-fill building, with front and rear facades only. The site did not allow for the typical Renaissance palazzo plan – four exterior walls contrasting an arcuated inner court – but Pennethorne adapted the Renaisssance arcuated style to the rear facade, facing Piccadilly. The front of the museum was then like the front of a palazzo, and the rear like one slice of a Renaissance courtyard. The style of the new museum was similar to the new gentlemen's clubs on the Pall Mall, a few blocks away (Figure 2.20). For a practical educational museum to resemble a gentlemen's club might at first seem improbable, but the museum's designers and chief officers were gentlemen, and middle- and upper-class people comprised the primary audience, although it did offer special evening lectures for working men. The club-like appearance lent an air of respectability to this exemplar of rational recreation.

Figure 2.18 James Pennethorne, Museum of Practical Geology, Jermyn Street, London (demolished). Elevation drawing, entrance facade on Jermyn Street, 1846–1851, final design showing rectilinear fenestration.

Figure 2.19 James Pennethorne, Museum of Practical Geology (demolished). Photograph of rear facade on Piccadilly. Reproduced by permission of the Director, British Geological Survey.

The exterior of the museum had a special appeal, something no other museum could boast. The facade itself contained one of the museum's main exhibitions, for its portal was built out of a wide selection of English polished specimen stones.[63] Newspapers reported that 'the very doorway gives a short lesson in the geology of England.'[64] The interior continued this didactic effort, with polished column shafts made of various indigenous stones ringing the entrance hall. This built-in display – the architecture itself – served as a basis for the teaching of geology at the museum. After walking into the grand entrance hall, visitors would climb the stairs to enter the main display area of the museum: a rectangular room covered by a shallow vault with glazed haunches and a central skylight (Figure 2.21). A balcony ringed the main

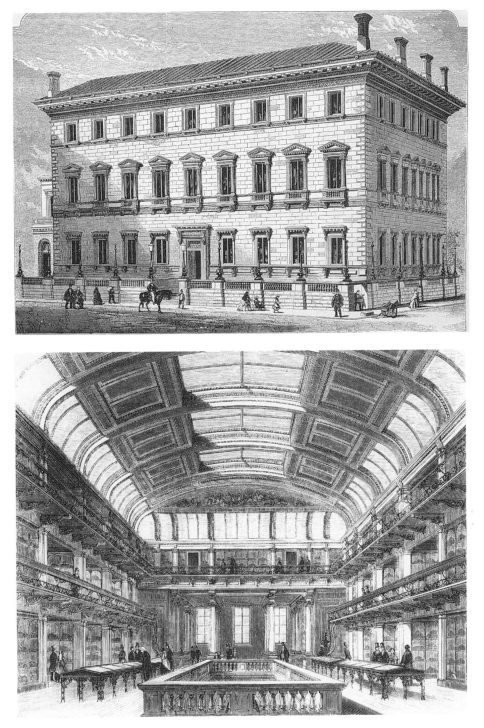

Figure 2.20 Charles Barry, Reform Club, Pall Mall, London. 1837–41. *Building News* 4 (1858) 271.

Figure 2.21 James Pennethorne, Museum of Practical Geology (demolished), interior, 1846–51. *Builder* 6 (28 October 1848) 522.

room and offered extra display space closer to the skylight. This balcony was similar to the one at the Hunterian: balconies were logical in science museums because toplighting was costly, and balconies maximize the number of objects that can be placed beneath a partly glass ceiling.

The lecture room was an important part of the Museum of Practical Geology's plan (Figure 2.22). The lecture hall not only consumed the lion's share of the building's ground floor space, but it gave the institution a public, welcoming image. When visitors arrived at the museum, they could walk directly through the entrance hall (Figure 2.23) into the lecture room. This was used by the School of Mines, but evening lectures for the museum were also held there. In addition to visiting museums, attending public lectures was one of the primary ways for mechanics and artisans to learn about science, and these educational programs received government support throughout the Victorian period. In 1853, the 600 spaces allotted for the

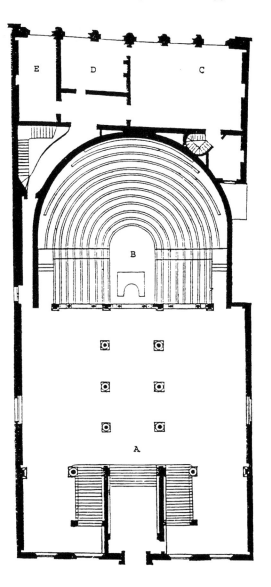

Figure 2.22 James Pennethorne, Museum of Practical Geology, plan, 1846–51. Drawn by Michael Piga.

A.ENTRANCE HALL FOR BRITISH MARBLES   B.THEATER   C.LIBRARY
D.DIRECTOR'S ROOM   E.SECRETARY'S ROOM

GROUND FLOOR PLAN

Figure 2.23 James Pennethorne, Museum of Practical Geology, interior of lower level. *Illustrated London News*, 18 (24 May 1851) 446.

Evening Lectures for Working Men were filled up in just two days.[65] The demonstrations of scientific experiments amazed the crowds, and many Victorian scientists were acclaimed for their lively lecturing style. The *Illustrated London News* depicted Scottish chemist Lyon Playfair lecturing to a packed theatre in the museum in 1852 (Figure 2.24). Playfair, like De la Beche and Huxley, promoted science as practical

MUSEUM OF PRACTICAL GEOLOGY.—DR. LYON PLAYFAIR'S LECTURE.—(SEE NEXT PAGE.)

Figure 2.24 James Pennethorne, Museum of Practical Geology, lecture hall, 1846–51, Lyon Playfair lecturing. *Illustrated London News*, 20 (21 February 1852) 161.

for British society. For Playfair, ' "searchers after truth" were not dreamy idealists. They were "the horses of the chariots of industry".[66] Desmond and Doughty both misread the image of Playfair lecturing by assuming the speaker stood in front of windows on the Piccadilly side, when in fact the curve of the seats in the picture, correlated to the plan, shows that the backdrop behind the speaker consisted of interior windows that screened the auditorium from the Hall of Marbles.[67] Aimed at the working class, the evening lectures at the Museum of Practical Geology were a popular form of entertainment and education, and the planners of the Edinburgh Museum hoped to duplicate such lectures in Scotland.

Pennethorne was opinionated on the subject of museum design. He objected that the rooms in the National Gallery were not lofty enough, and were not bright enough. Pennethorne favoured diffuse light, such as that which could be obtained through thick glass: in short, he said that the galleries 'should be a mass of light, not lighted only by rays of light.'[68] The phrase 'mass of light' indicates his preference for a skylight, rather than side lights (windows) which cast a bright raking light on paintings and the vertical surfaces of glass cases.

Most of the specimens were on the second floor, which was accessed by either a grand stair or stairs in the corners (Figure 2.25). The specimens in the exhibition cases at the Museum of Practical Geology were part of an overall program which taught the viewer how natural resources were transformed into commercial products: the raw materials were exhibited with the tools necessary to effect their transformation. The exhibitions also displayed all the intermediate stages between the natural and manufactured product – between iron ore and steel, clay and porcelain, skins and leather. These exhibitions were highly selective and didactic. In 1874 Howard Becker extolled the clarity of the museum's displays, which allowed visitors to study many properties of a single stone:

Figure 2.25 James Pennethorne, Museum of Practical Geology, interior of lower level. Reproduced by permission of the Director, British Geological Survey.

The specimens are admirably arranged in separate lines of cases placed in such juxtaposition that the progress of any one metalliferous mineral may be traced from the geological stratum whence the ore is extracted through the various processes of manufacturing till the metal ultimately assumes the forms required for use or ornament.[69]

The museum's name had been 'economic geology' before it was changed to the similar 'practical geology': this practical use of nature (as resource for capitalization by the empire) was its *raison d'être*.

The uses of different materials were explained to visitors on the ground floor. Upstairs, the balconies ringing the main room were arranged stratigraphically (Figure 2.26). As Forgan describes, 'So while the ground floor, the horizontal plane, was devoted to the uses of geology, to those processes which took place on the surface of the earth, the vertical plane, the galleries above, displayed the structure of the earth in terms of its geological record.'[70] The lower galleries contained the oldest (or earliest) rocks. Around these galleries were displays of rocks arranged in the order of increasing closeness to the earth's surface. Again, quoting Forgan:

[the collections] formed a sort of stratigraphical column, one that did not rise vertically, which would have been impractical given the number of fossils which had to be exhibited to demonstrate it, but was instead wrapped round the two galleries. The lower gallery started from the earliest – the Lingula flags or Cambrian – at the lower west edge and moved to the Permian at the eastern corner, whereas the upper moved round from the Jurassic to the Eocene to the Oligocene epochs. The lower gallery therefore covered the older Palaeozoic era, and the gallery above contained more recent fossils of the secondary and tertiary eras.[71]

Figure 2.26 James Pennethorne, Museum of Practical Geology, interior of main display area. Reproduced by permission of the Director, British Geological Survey. A man on the upper balcony provides a sense of scale in this photograph of the display cases, which are full of specimens from floor to ceiling.

The arrangement assumed that visitors would follow one particular path around the partly curved balconies. As one circulated through the museum, one examined the objects. This arrangement was obviously not as radical as the ramps of Frank Lloyd Wright's Guggenheim, but the directionality, curved walkways and central skylight achieved some of the same spatial goals that the American architect attempted to attain 100 years later.

The Museum of Practical Geology was intended to be especially useful to Victorian architects, because of its collection of building stones. The *Builder* suggested

> there is no public educational institution which should be of greater interest to the architect. Besides affording means to the student, of acquiring essential knowledge of geology as a science, it contains an important collection of samples of building stones, and an extended series of metalliferous and other mineral products, with examples of their application in art.[72]

The reporter from the *Builder* asked that the museum produce a catalogue of building stones and extend that collection to the out-of-doors, for experimental purposes:

> Excepting the specimens of marbles which are worked into pedestals and vases, few of them can be sufficiently examined. The slates are heaped together, almost out of sight. But, besides specimens to be preserved indoors, the architect desires to see others, worked into mouldings, under the action of the weather and exposed in all different positions relative thereto.

The Museum of Practical Geology also bears comparison to Bentham's panopticon. At first glance, one might think Pennethorne had the prison model in mind. But this metaphor should not be pushed too far, because the strength of Foucault's reading of Bentham lies in his theorization of the internalized gaze. The fact that one could stand at one edge of the light well and survey the Geological Survey is an appealing notion, suggestive of the powerful gaze of the naturalist, but it does not do justice to Bentham or Foucault to simply substitute rocks for humans. We can reasonably measure the similarities in this way: the curved balconies with their bounty of specimens do seem to lay themselves out for inspection, and the subtitle of Bentham's book – 'the inspection house' – resonates with the few surviving illustrations of the Museum of Practical Geology. The museum was primarily intended for use by naturalists and miners: their gaze might give them a sense of dominion over nature, or a sense of the value of human industry over the natural world. Most of the visitors to this museum would have had the conviction that the complete geological wealth of Britain was, as Prince Albert said, left there by God as a blessing for Britons.

Becker, again commenting on the museum in the 1870s, lauded it because 'the natural materials may be studied as to their lithological character, their geological order, or their mineralogical constitution; the artificial productions, exhibiting the results of labour and science, may be investigated in a commercial, scientific, or artistic spirit.'[73] This was the highest achievement for a popular museum: it was not only successfully didactic, but it operated on several levels at once. The link between science and commerce cannot be overstated – it will reappear in the Crystal Palace as well as in the Edinburgh Museum of Science and Art.

The University Library at Cambridge, the Hunterian, and the Museum of Practical Geology all included purpose-built display spaces for natural knowledge. Their designers would have preferred to make ceilings of glass to achieve the best possible lighting (in a country known for grey weather!) and for arranging the greatest number of valuable objects beneath the diffuse light of such a glass ceiling. The sheer number of specimens may seem a jumble to the modern viewer, but in the nineteenth century, before minimalism dampened modern vision, the visual arts (from interior decoration to the decorative arts to painting to set design) were crowded with detail and accretive ornament. So the objects of science, which were organized carefully, might not have seemed unintelligible to Victorian audiences. These three museum projects from the 1830s and 40s already suggest the range of definitions of nature that were presented in the introduction: from nature as capitalistic resource to nature as God's second book.

chapter 3

Nature as Creation

The Oxford University Museum

Let us ever apply ourselves seriously to the task [of scientific inquiry] feeling assured that the more we thus exercise, and by exercising improve, our intellectual faculties, the more worthy we shall be, the better shall we be fitted, to come nearer to our God.[1] (Lord Wrottesley, at the British Association for the Advancement of Science, Oxford, 1860)

At the 30th annual meeting of the British Association, Lord Wrottesley, President of the Association, congratulated his audience on the state of science. He addressed his fellow men of science (those who studied chemistry, physiology, astronomy, and geology, among other fields), imploring them to continue their studies of 'the course of the planet and comet through boundless space . . . the world's history written on her ancient rocks, the sepulchres of stony relics of ages long gone past . . . the secret mysteries of form and being in animal and plant; discovering everywhere connecting links, and startling analogies and proofs of adaptation of means to ends.' And Lord Wrottesley looked forward to future researchers singing an even more complete and 'glorious hymn to the Creator's praise.'[2] This was a grand vision of the sciences as integrated with religion; the study of natural knowledge would allow Oxonians and their guests to better understand God.

Such a connection is well known to historians of science, who have researched the related realms of intellectual discourse in the nineteenth century, especially at Oxford and Cambridge, where natural theology (the belief that the natural world should be studied in order to reveal the greatness of God) dominated scientific thought.[3] The opposition of science and religion, often taken for granted in the twentieth century, is a social and intellectual construction, not a fact of history.[4] Our notion of science warring with theology was consciously developed in the latter half of the nineteenth century, most notably by T. H. Huxley, who was also waging a class-based battle to keep the Anglican elite from controlling the practice of science. But at the time the Oxford University Museum was commissioned, in the 1850s, science and religion were not opposed. This intellectual background is essential if we are to place the museum – a major monument in British Victorian architecture – in its proper context. Study of the museum allows us to examine key issues such as the influence of John Ruskin, the use of iron and glass for a non-utilitarian building, and the alleged triumph of the Gothic style over classicism.[5] Since Ruskin's involvement has been discussed extensively in other art historical literature, the details will not be repeated here. The iron and glass roof will be reinvestigated, not for its structural innovation, but from the point of view of the clients, who were well-informed professors of science and who wanted the same advantages of top-lighting that they recognized in earlier science museums such as the Hunterian Museum of the Royal College of Surgeons and the Museum of Practical Geology. The 'Battle of the Styles' will be addressed here to suggest that some of the patrons at Oxford preferred the classical design; thus the Gothic style was not an inevitable choice, as is sometimes assumed.[6] A few days after the President of the British Association told his audience that science brings men closer to God, another conference session was held in the library of the recently completed Oxford Museum, during which T. H. Huxley and Bishop Wilberforce disputed briefly over the origin of mankind. Natural theology was just beginning to lose ground to secular science, but the museum had already been designed, built, and was ready for occupancy. This important Victorian building may best be understood through a reconsideration of the inter-relationship between science and religion.

A SCIENCE CENTER FOR OXFORD

The decision to build up-to-date science facilities was a reaction to the new demands placed upon higher education in Britain. At the start of the nineteenth century, Oxford and Cambridge prepared their students for the clergy, for teaching in public schools, for professions such as law, or for no job at all, because, as members of the gentry, they might choose not to work. In contrast to German universities, which already functioned as modern research centers, Oxford and Cambridge taught an established body of knowledge. Profound study of mathematics, theology and classics was their curriculum, not the acquisition of novel, broad-based knowledge. In the early Victorian period, new secular universities in northern industrial cities began to challenge the pre-eminence of Oxford and Cambridge. These new universities, like their German counterparts, emphasized science and technology.[7] Oxford and Cambridge maintained their affiliation with the Anglican Church – no dissenters were allowed to enroll, and attendance at college chapel was mandatory. Much later in the nineteenth century, the success of technologically advanced nonsectarian universities in Scotland and even Germany forced Oxford to reconsider its old-fashioned curriculum, but in the 1850s Oxonians plainly rejected utilitarian science. The new building would announce, metaphorically, the university's decision in 1850 to set up an Honours School in Natural Science. Although they still had to pass examinations in classics, theology and mathematics, students in the new program could concentrate on studying the physical world. The new science edifice at Oxford should be regarded not as a secular institution, but as one with quasi-religious goals rooted in natural theology. The museum was meant to be a place where students could contemplate authentic physical wonders of Nature and the greatness of godly design.

THE NECESSITY OF A MUSEUM FOR VISUAL INSTRUCTION ABOUT THE NATURAL WORLD

The University Museum at Oxford was not a museum only. The Oxford Museum was more like the 'science centres' of today's universities than it was like a museum, because it also contained lecture rooms, professors' offices, a library and a laboratory, in addition to a number of display areas, all cobbled together under one roof.[8] The collections of the University Museum were brought together from several different places at Oxford: rocks and gems had been in a small geological display in Clarendon Hall, the anatomical collection had been exhibited in rooms in Christ Church College, and many natural historical specimens had been housed in the Ashmolean Museum.[9] The Ashmolean gave its natural objects to the new science museum, but kept its archeological collections – a range of artifacts from prehistoric flints to Anglo-Saxon jewelry.

John Henry Parker, keeper of the Ashmolean in the later nineteenth century, was eager to bring his collections up-to-date by dividing the collection into human-made and divinely created objects. Together, the collections of the Ashmolean and the new museum (although housed separately) would offer students an opportunity to observe and handle material objects, thus offering Oxonians a world of knowledge beyond theology, classics and mathematics – museums offered students a chance to learn from the visual scrutiny of matter. Parker and the keepers of the new museum rejected displays of 'curiosities' as objects lacking in scientific value. The presentation of curiosities and rarities represented a distant, eighteenth-century world, not to be confused with the serious specimens that would be displayed at Oxford. If naturalists wished to teach students about the orderliness and beauty of God's universe, they would necessarily reject the display of *Wunderkammer* rarities like human horns.

The decision to set up the Honours School was not prompted by waning Anglican influence at Oxford; on the contrary, the study of natural objects was seen as part of teaching about Creation. Oxford in the 1840s was the center of a theological storm. Theologians in the Oxford Movement hoped to revitalize the Anglican Church by reviving pre-Reformation forms of piety – including increased ritual and more elaborate church architecture. While some Anglo-Catholics, like John Keble and Cardinal Newman, opposed the rise of science (as represented by the British Association for the Advancement of Science) others like Reverend E. B. Pusey did not. In fact, Pusey donated funds to enhance the museum's sculpture.[10] There is no reason to assume that all conservative theologians opposed the study of science, or that they necessarily would have perceived the new science building as a threat. Typically, members of the BAAS (notably William Whewell) were liberal Anglicans who promoted the idea that the study of natural knowledge led to Christian humility rather than atheism.[11] It was too early to predict the specter of Darwinism, and even after the publication of *The Origin of Species*, many naturalists reconciled their Anglican religious beliefs with the study of nature.[12]

THE MUSEUM AS AN EPITOME OF NATURE

In May 1853 the Reverend Richard Greswell (1800–1881), a founder of the Ashmolean Society and an energetic proponent of the new science building, wrote a memorial (a public letter) imploring his fellow Oxonians to build an encyclopedic museum, in which each specimen would occupy in the Museum '*precisely the same relative place* that it did in God's own Museum, *the Physical Universe in which it lived and moved and had its being.*'[13] Greswell consulted museum experts in London, who agreed that it would be possible to display the natural history collections at Oxford so that they presented an accurate, though reduced, representation of the natural world. Greswell's opinion was typical of his time: the study of natural science was a kind of religious contemplation, and the scope of the museum's displays was thus enormously important in communicating that religious purpose. He complained that the naturalists were discussing different rooms for the new building based on 'unsound principle[s],' and, to his credit, the principle to which he referred was hardly a principle at all; the building committee had simply asked the keepers how much space they needed for their existing departments. A better starting point, Greswell thought, was to look at the natural world itself, then divide up the total space by relative importance. Greswell believed too little space had been given to general zoology, and he thought that mineralogy could be placed in side rooms, because those specimens needed less light than 'the more delicate and interesting forms of Animal Life.' The notion that the museum should be built to house the collections as they currently existed was, to Greswell's thinking, short-sighted. The professor had a point: if the allocation of space were based on the randomness of the collection existing at Oxford, an exceptional amount of space in the new museum would be taken up by bugs. This was not a mere inconvenience; it was a serious misrepresentation of the harmony of natural design, making it 'impossible to exhibit, *in a natural series*, that uniformity of plan, which every principle of sound reasoning convinces us must belong to the system of creation and the representation of which is *the final end and purpose of every well-arranged museum*.'[14] Greswell did not want the space divided up by the proportional quantity of species; he held a common Victorian belief in a hierarchy of species which progressed toward more complex animals and placed humankind at the apex.

REPORT OF BUILDING COMMITTEE, FEBRUARY 1853: THE EARLY PROGRAM

In 1852 the Convocation (the Faculty Senate) appointed a delegacy (a building committee) to scrutinize the university's precise needs for the Museum's science departments.[15] In addition to several science teachers and college masters, the delegacy members included the prominent physician Henry Acland and Greswell. The delegacy concluded that, indeed, Oxford University should have facilities for the study of the natural world. They also agreed in February 1853 on a site in the University Parks – close to the countryside, but within walking distance of the centre of town. By combining the different physical science departments in one new science building, the Convocation promoted a particular philosophical view of the sciences as interconnected. As the notes from a meeting of Convocation on May 9, 1849, explained:

> That whereas it would be consistent with a Philosophical view of the connexion of the sciences, that all the materials, explanatory of the Structure of the Earth and of the Organic Beings placed on it, should be arranged, in distinct departments, under one roof, together with fit accommodation for preparing, studying, and lecturing on the same, it is much to be desired that a building should be erected, within the University, in which these several objects may be carried out.[16]

'All the materials, explanatory of the Structure of the Earth and of the Organic Beings placed on it' would be housed in the new science edifice. Like Noah, the architects of this building faced a challenge of biblical proportions.

The committee went on to direct that distinct rooms should each hold a different type of natural specimen, and that these rooms be skylit, be laid out in a row (*en suite*), and be tall enough to have a balcony level:

> the museums are to be all on one floor; lighted from the roof; not warmed by open fireplaces; high enough to admit of gallery; not less than 30 feet wide; having each a separate entrance for the Professor; but communicating *en suite* in the following order, viz. Chemistry, Mineralogy, Geology, Zoology, Anatomy, and Medicine.[17]

Significantly, the committee members assumed the museum display area would be 'lighted from the roof,' undoubtedly because skylights offered diffuse, inexpensive, consistent natural light. No architect invented this *parti*: it was the clients' mandate. It is clear from the minutes of the meeting that the delegates wanted the display space to be toplit, and they repeated this desideratum in the later written guidelines for the competition.

THE INFLUENCE OF EARLIER MUSEUMS ON THE OXFORD PATRONS

Greswell consulted two of the most capable architects in the country, G. G. Scott (1811–1878) and Charles Barry (1795–1860) in 1853, to find out how much museum Oxford could get for £30,000. After studying the *Report of the Delegates* of February 1853 Barry concluded that the type of museum the delegates wanted could not be built for less than £50,000; G. G. Scott gave Greswell the same estimate. Despite the expert advice, the delegacy retained the £30,000 budget. Charles Barry, whose son, Edward, later finished second in the competition, was an acknowledged museum specialist. As Greswell explained it : '[Barry] . . . was selected, not as the Architect of the Houses of Parliament, but *as the Architect of the [Hunterian] Museum of the College of Surgeons*, and a pupil, in this capacity, of Professor Owen.'[18] The Hunterian Museum was a model for the delegacy's requirement for the toplighting and the galleries. Professors at Oxford were also influenced by London's Museum of Practical Geology. In addition to its toplighting, the Museum of Practical Geology was known for its built-in selection of polished specimen stones, which predated the stone column shafts at Oxford.

THE COMPETITION

Henry Acland was a well-known teacher at Oxford and the major force behind getting the museum built. Acland believed in natural theology, and saw the museum as a means to exhibit God's second book. He was a tireless supporter of the building project. After the *Report of the Delegates* was completed in February 1853, he and others lobbied for eight months until Convocation voted to approve its recommendations in December 1853. A few weeks later, in January 1854, the delegacy reconvened, ready to build. In April the delegates decided to hold an open competition for a two-storey building, stipulating a plan that (rather awkwardly) demanded three sides of a quadrangle, with an open side allowing for further expansion. It was at this point in the building's history that one of its most striking characteristics was established: the competition guidelines stated that the courtyard was to be covered by a glass and iron roof. The guidelines placed no restrictions on style.[19]

By October 1854, 33 designs were submitted by a range of architects.[20] As required in the instructions, the designs were identified only by mottoes. The three judges, Philip Hardwick, C. R. Cockerell and T. L. Donaldson, were architects (but not devoted Goths) who were well prepared for this job, and they quickly deduced that none of the entries could be built for the specified £30,000. In spite of this warning, the delegacy reaffirmed the £30,000 limit, assuming that competition entries could be scaled down later, and ordered the jurors to proceed. The judges chose four designs that best answered the needs set forth in the guidelines, and then narrowed those to two. These two were coded *Fiat justitia ruat coelum* – meaning 'Let justice be done, though the heavens may fall' and *Nisi Dominus aedificaverit domum*, the first half of the phrase, 'Unless the Lord builds the house, they labor in vain who built it.' These were later identified as from the offices of E. M. Barry, and Deane and Woodward, respectively.

BARRY'S CLASSICAL ENTRY

Edward M. Barry (1830–1880) was the third son of architect Charles Barry. Since Greswell had recently consulted Charles Barry about the Oxford museum project, E. M. Barry probably had inside knowledge about the competition, and the younger architect might have been influenced by his father's Hunterian Museum, but since the competition instructions specified that the natural objects had to be in a covered courtyard, he could not use the exact lighting scheme from the Hunterian. He entered the competition with an apparent intent to please the delegates, no matter what their stylistic preferences, by submitting four designs in three different styles (one Roman, one Gothic, and two Renaissance); in a typically Victorian strategy, Barry based three of the designs on the same floor plan. Like many Victorian architects, Barry did not connect *any* particular style to the display of natural historical objects. The jurors chose one of the Renaissance projects as a finalist in the competition, a Palladian quadrangle with an inviting Corinthian portico (Figure 3.1). Barry's runner-up competition panel is still extant, and goes a long way toward explaining his success – it is a well-rendered watercolour showing the glistening white quadrangle beneath a cloudy sky, with happy Oxonians ambling across a wide green lawn. Barry broke the competition rules by using colour, but he was able to exhibit the high-quality drawings at both the Royal Academy and the Society of British Artists.[21]

Students would have entered Barry's building by climbing a flight of steps and walking through a one-storey entrance hall from which they would emerge into the dramatic two-storey, light-filled space, covered by an iron and glass vault. With more specificity than the guidelines called for, Barry's plan showed the zoology, chemistry, mineralogy and experimental philosophy collections arranged in display cases (Figures 3.2 and 3.3). The fact that Barry spelled out the location of each type of object recalls the level of detail of the 1853 *Report of the Delegates*, but that earlier document asked for different categories to be placed in separate rooms, which the 1854 guidelines had abandoned in favour of all the collections residing in the courtyard.

Barry employed a central glass barrel vault, flanked by smaller vaults, for his glass-covered courtyard, as is clearly visible in his section drawing (Figure 3.4). The exhibition cases were cleverly designed so that the objects were stored within the structure. The spaces between iron piers would have been filled with specimens, so that the piers formed the sides of the cases and the supports for the upper level. The

supports on both levels were like walls that had been made useful by virtue of being hollow and metal – rather than solid and stone. The barrel vaults referred directly to Joseph Paxton's bright, airy Crystal Palace. On the one hand, the Crystal Palace was not an obvious source for a permanent, academic science building, since it housed a temporary and popular showplace for industrial and decorative arts. On the other hand, the Crystal Palace was the best-known ferrovitreous building in the world, and when, in the 1854 guidelines, the delegates asked for an iron and glass roof spanning a large space, at least some of them must have been thinking of the Crystal Palace. Archival evidence from 1856 proves that delegates did discuss the iron and glass structure of the Crystal Palace as a point of comparison for the Oxford Museum's roof: 'Mr Woodward thought that a thicker glass would be very desirable – because, it is necessary to make the roof of the Museum stronger, more completely waterproof, and durable, than the roof of any Railway Station, or the Crystal Palace' and again, 'Questions having been asked as to the probability of the roof leaking – Dr Acland instanced the Crystal Palace as a specimen of leaking, and Mr Phillips the Jermyn St. Museum as a specimen of the contrary.'[22] The *Athenaeum*'s reporter noted that while many designs ignored or concealed the iron roof, Barry's *Fiat Justitia* celebrated it.[23]

At the display of the 33 competition drawings in the Radcliffe Library, Barry's Palladian design attracted the most attention. (The drawings had been displayed for a few weeks so that the faculty senate could vote on them.[24]) On December 9 (a few days before the vote) Acland held an evening reception to allow prominent Oxonians to view the drawings for a final time. Gas lighting had recently been installed in the library and the drawings looked especially fetching. Enthusiasm for the new building infused newspaper accounts. According to one article, Barry's was more favoured by those present:

the objects which attracted the most attention and absorbed the most interest were the designs for the new Museum . . . [These] were ranged on screens in the gallery, and during the whole of the evening there were crowds scrutinising and criticising their respective merits. The two selected by the Delegacy for the approval of Convocation were naturally those most sought for and discussed; but as far as we could judge, the Palladian design appeared to be most popular.[25]

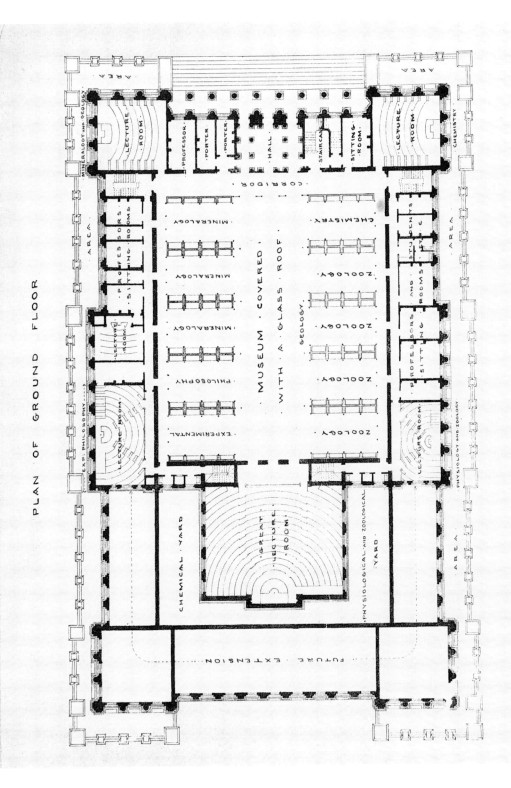

PLAN OF GROUND FLOOR

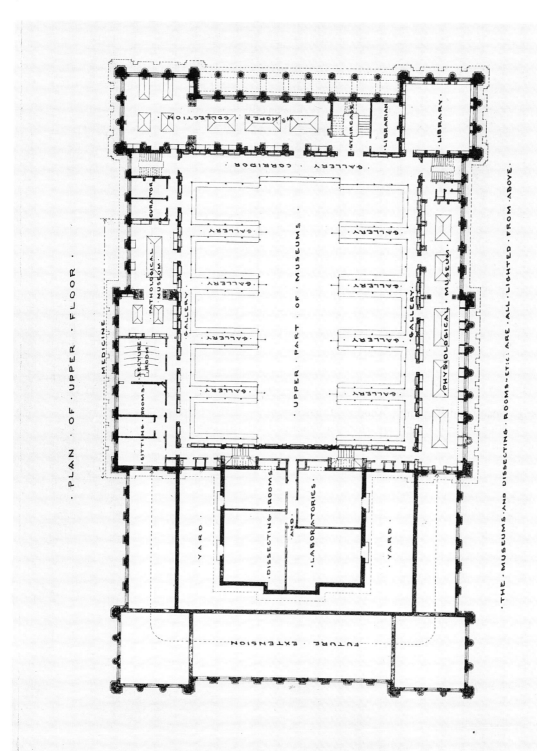

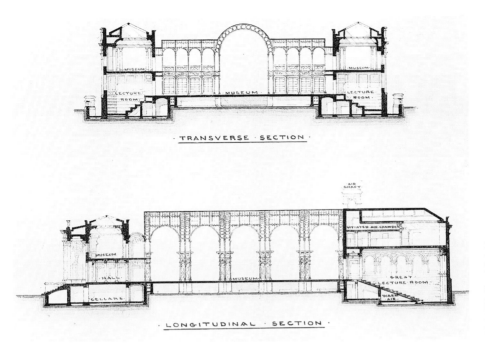

· TRANSVERSE · SECTION ·

· LONGITUDINAL · SECTION ·

Figure 3.4 E. M. Barry, Competition entry for Oxford University Museum, section, 1854. By permission of the British Architectural Library, RIBA, London, C4/21 3.

DEANE AND WOODWARD'S GOTHIC ENTRY

Thomas N. Deane and Benjamin Woodward, partners in an Irish architectural firm that had not yet built in England, submitted a Venetian Gothic design with a silhouette reminiscent of Flemish town halls, but the actual competition drawings are now lost.[26] Woodward was the firm's principal designer, and his most ambitious project before the 1854 competition had been the science building at Trinity College, Dublin, which also included an exhibition space for natural specimens. Woodward's work, at Oxford and elsewhere, was characterized by contained masses, striking surface texture and sculpture, and polychromy. Other than drawings of the side elevations recently discovered and published by Frederick O'Dwyer, the earliest known images of the Oxford facade are the contract drawings from 1855 (Figure 3.5).[27] This image from 1855, which is similar to a perspective published that year in the *Builder*, shows the compact facade and simple outline.[28] On the ground storey, Woodward employed mostly modest two-light windows, while on the upper level he elaborated slightly, using two pointed lights and a quatrefoil. Short buttresses met the ground, dormers dotted the roof line, minor asymmetries in this arrangement (corresponding to different-sized rooms inside) enlivened the exterior, and, in the central tower, the tall portal broke the stringcourse of the second register, with the steeply pitched tower ending in a flat top, crowned by a delicate iron rail.

STREET'S 'URGENT PLEA'

Among the members of the Oxford community who answered the *Report of the Delegates* was the architect George Edmund Street, who published *An Urgent Plea for the Revival of the True Principles of Architecture in the Public Buildings of the University of Oxford* some time after February 1853 – far in advance of the competition, but still

Figure 3.3 E. M. Barry, Competition entry for Oxford University Museum, upper floor plan, 1854. By permission of the British Architectural Library, RIBA, London, C4/21 2.

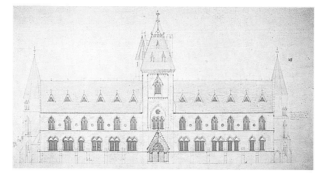

Figure 3.5 Thomas
Deane and Benjamin
Woodward, Oxford
University Museum,
contract drawing,
elevation drawing of
the west front, dated
21 February 1855.
Oxford University
Archives/Bodleian
Library, UM/P/3/5.

important in the museum's history. Street worked for the firm of G. G. Scott, established his own office in 1849, and wrote thoughtful, broad-minded articles for the *Ecclesiologist* magazine, starting in 1848. From 1850 to 1853, he outlined his position that the Puginian phase of the Gothic revival was confined by excessively strict historical and geographical bounds. Augustus Welby Northmore Pugin, the polemical Catholic writer and architect, was of course England's most outspoken antagonist of classical architecture; while Pugin's writings laid the foundation for Street's criticism, Pugin promulgated English Gothic only. Street valued early and late Gothic, Spanish and Italian styles, religious and secular medieval buildings. He had high hopes for the success of the Gothic revival in the town that nurtured the theologically conservative Oxford Movement.

Street surmised that the university was likely to build in one of two styles, classical or fifteenth-century Gothic (called Third Pointed or Perpendicular), and he set out to dissuade the university from both. He was especially appalled by what he considered the wasteful expense and false grandiosity of the recently erected Taylor Institute, designed by C. R. Cockerell, the architect for the library at Cambridge, Oxford's ancient rival. In the Institute, windows that had been built for the sake of symmetry were later blocked up, and a portico was built but never used. Also, Street complained that it was impossible to tell the purpose of the Taylor Institute from its exterior.[29] He argued that the pointed arch was the greatest mechanical advancement in architectural history, and thus its absence from classical buildings made them technologically backward. The classical style was, to him, 'foreign, contrary in its construction to natural principles, and unsuited in its effects to English habits, and in its design to our English climate.'[30] He served as architect for the diocese of Oxford from 1850 to 1881, and therefore Bishop Samuel Wilberforce was his patron. Oxford was Street's town: he had a personal stake in the quality of its architecture.

Street hoped that Oxford would adopt medieval, or what he called Christian, architecture 'in any of its future works,' but he especially hoped it would be used for the new science edifice (Figure 3.6). His logic was compelling:

> there seems to be a peculiar propriety in selecting the style which, above all others that have ever existed, took nature and natural forms for her guide and ornaments, in a Museum intended mainly for the reception of a collection illustrative of Natural History. Surely, where nature is to be enshrined, there especially ought every carved stone and every ornamental device to bear her marks and to set forth her loveliness [sic].[31]

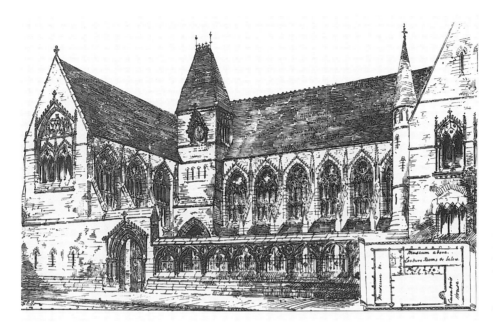

Figure 3.6 George Edmund Street, Proposed Oxford University Museum, perspective, 1853. G. E. Street, *An Urgent Plea for the Revival of the True Principles of Architecture in the Public Buildings at the University of Oxford.* (Oxford and London: John Henry Parker, 1853).

As appealing as it is, this quotation from Street was probably not a determining factor in Deane and Woodward's success, because, among other reasons, the competition was not decided until one and half years after the publication of Street's essay.[32] According to the *Builder*, there were more competition entries – twelve – in the Gothic style than in any other single style; however, there were 21 other entries in a range of styles from Elizabethan to Greek.[33] In previous debates about nineteenth-century natural history museums, a link between natural history and naturalistic design was not stressed. Even in other pro-Gothic arguments for the Oxford Museum, no other theorist voiced the opinion that the naturalistic ornament of Gothic was peculiarly proper for a museum of natural objects. Most theorists, including Street himself, made a much more general claim for the Gothic style – that it was universal and therefore suitable for many new building types. Writers found it a more useful strategy to promote Gothic architecture as practical and adaptable; indeed, Gothicists would have hindered their own cause if they had associated their style too strictly with an uncommon building type such as a natural history museum.

RUSKIN'S OPINION

Acland's friendship with Ruskin had begun in their college days, and it remains a contingency of history that generated remarkable events in Victorian architecture. Ruskin's opinion about the competition has been analyzed by many scholars, most recently O'Dwyer, and it is clear that the critic influenced his friend greatly. Ruskin wrote to Acland two days after the reception, while the competition entries were still on display in the Radcliffe Library, complaining bitterly about Barry's design. In this private letter, he seems to have offered strategies to Acland for defending their shared preference for Deane and Woodward's Gothic entry. Ruskin was particularly aggrieved at what he reckoned was the underestimation of the classical building's cost – Ruskin had asked Philip Hardwick, a juror, if he had taken the sculpture into consideration when estimating that *Fiat Justitia* (Barry) would cost the same as *Nisi Dominus* (Deane and Woodward), and Hardwick said he had not considered the sculpture. Ruskin then described how, as he spoke to Hardwick, G. G. Scott (who was not a judge in the competition, but who had consulted with Greswell about the museum) joined the conversation. Scott said 'the *stone dressings* (external carved work) of FJ, would cost *at least double* that of ND.'[34] It should come as no surprise that Ruskin hated the classical design; even when he compared it to other Venetian Renaissance works, it drew sharp reproach:

> [T]hough I do not like Italian designs in general, I have had more opportun-
> ities of studying them at Venice by the greatest masters – San Michele –
> Sansovino – & Palladio, than many architects have had, and that FJ is one of
> the most commonplace & contemptible imitations of those masters I have
> ever seen.[35]

Ruskin wrote this condemnation of Barry's project on the same day that Acland published his own persuasive pamphlet in support of Deane and Woodward. Later, after the winners were announced, Ruskin remarked that Woodward's design was 'by no means a first rate design, yet quite as good as is likely to be got in these days, and on the whole good.'[36] Despite his guarded opinion, Ruskin was pleased that the Gothic style was chosen by the university Convocation. Historians have tended to celebrate Ruskin's role in the museum, and the building is often used as an illustration of his theories. Because Ruskin was not himself an architect, his theories can be demonstrated only through the works of others. In retrospect, this connection seems obvious. But what did the professors of science at Oxford – well-educated, internationally known scientists who already knew what sort of building they wanted – what did they really think of Ruskin and his theories? Clients voted on the competition entries just six months after architectural history's hero, Britain's best-known art critic and Oxford's native son suffered a humiliating personal defeat when his wife's plea for annulment was granted on the grounds of his impotence. Ruskin's ideas clearly influenced a few of the clients, especially Acland, but his name must have caused shudders at the delegacy meetings.[37]

ACLAND'S PAMPHLET PROMOTING DEANE AND WOODWARD'S DESIGN

Appearing on December 11, 1854, Acland's pamphlet, like Ruskin's letter, argued that the architect of the Palladian *Fiat Justitia* did not follow the instructions – his building had three floors instead of two. The architect had placed rooms in the basement, which Acland deemed unnecessary in a building to be set on four acres of land. Acland also disliked the fact that E. M. Barry's plan was a symmetrical block – a plan that would make it difficult to build an attractive extension when it was needed. Acland's defense of *Nisi Dominus* was based largely on its practicality: the central museum space was ample; the corridors behind the arcades allowed for further display of objects; there was plenty of room for the Hope entomological collections; and the laboratory building was set apart from the main building. In this well-written affirmation of Gothic, Acland pleaded that science not be severed from the traditional medieval collegiate associations:

> Whether these arrangements ought, or ought not, to be placed in an edifice harmonizing with the Collegiate associations of Oxford, is a point which there are many more competent to discuss than myself; but it may be fairly asked whether it is desirable to detach these new Sciences from those old associations? and whether they cannot be combined with our old Architecture, as in 'Nisi Dominus' they are?[38]

Acland believed that the study of the natural world should be integrated with the other academic pursuits at Oxford – and similarly housed. Science in the nineteenth century did not have futuristic undertones (like modern-day physics), for while the methods for studying the physical world were new, the subject of this new scientific inquiry – God's grand plan as presented in nature – was ageless. In Acland's mind, the choice of a medieval style for the new science building would make science appear to be a legitimate part of Oxford's physical and intellectual landscape; it would make science part of Oxford's history. Acland believed it was desirable to combine new sciences with old (meaning medieval) architecture, but Victorian Gothic architecture was, in a sense, modern as well. Thus *Nisi Dominus* provided both a link to Oxford's past *and* a statement of Oxford's modernity.[39]

THE CLIENTS DEBATE THE MERITS OF THE FINALISTS: DECEMBER 12, 1854

It has been generally reported that the views of the clients were polarized into Gothic and classical camps.[40] A more accurate survey of the extant pamphlets, however, suggests a less orderly story. Earlier, in 1853, two pamphlets appeared which discussed style, one by Street (previously discussed) proposing fourteenth-century Gothic, and the other by an anonymous author (possibly Parker) proposing thirteenth-century Gothic.[41] While the competition drawings were on display in December 1854, the Acland pamphlet openly promoted the design by Deane and Woodward. The archives of Oxford University do not preserve any pamphlets promoting the classical style, although some may have been published, and most of the other surviving pamphlets concern finances rather than style. Most importantly, the minutes from the major meeting of the building committee (December 12, 1854) do not suggest strict polarization of opinions on style.

Although two different contractors agreed to build either *Nisi Dominus* (Deane and Woodward) or *Fiat Justitia* (Barry) for £30,000, the speakers at the December 12 delegacy meeting predicted financial doom, and thus spent the meeting trying to guess which architect was more likely to overrun the budget. About a dozen men were present, at least five spoke, and their conversation provides excellent evidence as to how the Battle of the Styles (which is so familiar in the Victorian architectural press) was understood by educated people who were not experts on architecture. John W. Burgon, fellow of Oriel College and the first delegate to speak, claimed that while he usually preferred Gothic, he hoped this time the Italian design would be chosen. He disliked the turret and towers of Deane and Woodward's design, saying it was 'absurd' to make the porter 'sleep up in the clouds because you wanted elevation to give effect to the building.'[42] Burgon also 'found fault with the ecclesiastical character' of *Nisi Dominus*, and he recognized that pointed windows, necessary for the Gothic style, would never let in as much light as square-headed windows. Furthermore, he said that while other people had objected to the unfinished appearance of Barry's design (indeed, the large lecture hall would have jutted out the back of the building), Burgon said Woodward's was worse, having a 'strange, bizarre, and utterly detestable' appearance on its east end, which was the unfinished side of the quadrangle. He hoped the University would eventually come up with enough money to complete Barry's classical quadrangle. Barry's design could have been extended on the back; however, the extension would not have allowed for a larger museum, since the display area was hemmed in by the lecture theatre.

M. J. Johnson (1805–1859), the university's astronomer and the head of the Radcliffe Observatory (hence his official title of 'Radcliffe Observer'[43]) spoke in opposition to Burgon. Johnson thought the building should aim to hold the eccentric collections which Oxford already owned, and he believed that 'the multifarious character of the collections rendered all attempt to arrange them in a symmetrical form useless,' and therefore classical architecture, rooted in symmetrical planning, was an illogical choice for the science buildings. Importantly, Johnson recognized that Deane and Woodward's design, which had an awkward wall at the rear, allowed for extension of the display space. The university should choose a style, Johnson argued, which 'did not recognise symmetry as one of its essential conditions[; it] . . . was one of the chief characteristics of Gothic that it admitted of irregular development and might be made applicable to any purpose.' Earlier, Greswell had hoped the new museum would be an epitome of nature, but Johnson seems to have given up on that idea. Pugin's notion of 'picturesque utility' is evoked in Johnson's view that a Gothic science center could be comprised of a cluster of buildings – the composition could be additive. Johnson himself went to work every day in a bilaterally symmetrical classical observatory building which had been completed in 1784; perhaps he was weary of the rigidity of such a plan. On the issue of the porter's apartments, Johnson suggested the towers would provide him with purer air than the cellar. On the question of ecclesiastical overtones, Johnson asked 'why should you not imitate so good a thing as the ecclesiastical architecture of the 13th century, which was based on sound principles of construction and utility.' He also pointed out that Deane and Woodward's design was 'no more ecclesiastical than many Hôtels de Ville on the continent.'

Professor John Phillips (1800–1874) was almost as important a client as Acland.[44] He was a geologist who had worked in museums for his entire career. From 1840 to 1844, Phillips had worked for the Geological Survey, housed in the Museum of Practical Geology, and he also worked at Trinity College, Dublin, from 1844 to 1853, in buildings designed by Deane and Woodward. Phillips was designated to become keeper of the Oxford museum when it opened, and he was the person set to occupy the curator's cottage. Even though he was an extremely well-informed client, he expressed no strong opinion, saying that he saw 'much merit in both' finalists. He believed that, with minor alterations, either design could be adopted. He came to Oxford as reader of geology in 1853, and his views were similar to Acland's: that nature proved the existence of an intelligent Creator.[45] Acland closed the meeting, but his comments were not well recorded in the minutes. Of course, we know his opinions from the pamphlet he produced. The notes mention only that he made a 'statement about the practical advantages of a Gothic Building over a Classical for the purposes of a Museum.'[46]

Acland, Johnson, Burgon and Phillips were knowledgeable, thoughtful clients who discussed many issues – style, where the porter sleeps, how much light gets through a pointed window, how the odd collections would fit in a symmetrical building, and how much it would all cost. In sum, one outspoken patron (who usually preferred Gothic) in this case preferred classical, two patrons favoured Gothic, and one thought they were equally suitable. On the subject of presenting an ecclesiastical image, one objected but did not give clear reasons, the other three who spoke at the meeting saw no contradiction between medievalism and the practice of modern science. Unfortunately, at this otherwise informative meeting the delegates did not discuss the merits of the Crystal Palace-like vault in Barry's design contrasted with the specifically Gothic ferrovitreous roof in Woodward's. It is ironic that the exact part of the design that modern historians admire – the Gothicized roof – might *not* have been a factor in the success of Deane and Woodward. In any case, the delegates did not discuss it directly.

THREE VOTES TAKEN

Barry's section drawings were so clear and evocative, they might well have helped his cause – not enough for him to win, however. There were three votes taken at Oxford, and the first vote indicates that both *Nisi Dominus* and *Fiat Justitia* were far from ideal. First, the convocation voted on whether *either* of the designs should be accepted; this motion was carried by a rather narrow margin of 70 to 64. If three professors had changed their votes, then there would have been no clear victor, Gothic or Palladian, in the competition. In effect, both sides would have lost. But the convocation did decide to go ahead and build a science centre, so they took a second vote to choose between the finalists. This time they voted 81 to 38 in favour of Deane and Woodward.[47] The third vote was to elect a new delegacy to oversee the completion of the project.[48]

THE GENERAL PLAN

University bureaucracy slowed the construction of the museum.[49] The cornerstone was laid on June 20, 1855, and the structure was completed in 1860.[50] Since the competition guidelines specified the general layout of the building, and Deane and Woodward had followed the instructions, the University Museum consisted of three sides of a quadrangle with a covered courtyard (Figure 3.7). One of the contract drawings shows a section through the corridor running round the central hall, but does nothing to indicate the iron structure.[51] The 1855 contract drawings show the chemistry laboratory housed in a separate building, creating an even more obviously asymmetrical plan. Although the plan of the quadrangle has been compared to Charles Barry's Reform Club (which also had a glass-covered central hall), the traditional colleges of Oxford, almost all of which were three- or four-sided quadrangular buildings which included dormitories, common rooms, chapels and libraries, supply more local sources. The members of the building committee at Cambridge, like the delegates at Oxford, had requested a quadrangle for their new Library and Natural History Museum in the 1830s.

THE EXTERIOR

Woodward altered his original exterior, but he did so only because of restricted funds, not because of any creative change of heart (Figures 3.8 and 3.9). Woodward heightened the chemistry laboratory and reduced its lantern, omitted buttresses from the facade, and made the corner stair turrets symmetrical.[52] One of Woodward's

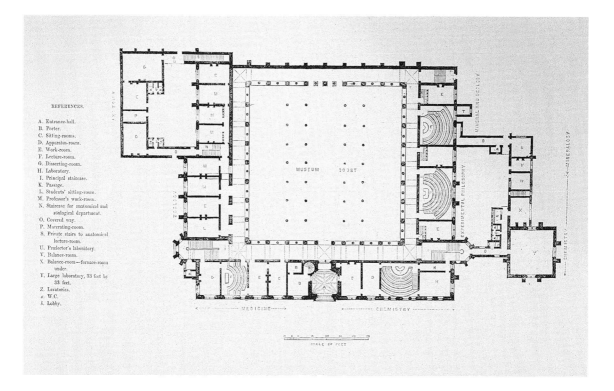

decisions after the competition was to remove the buttresses from the facade; critics said the removal worsened the effect of the building, which lacked a plinth and rested uncomfortably on its site. A reporter for the *Building News* remarked with displeasure that it 'looks for all the world as if the two uppermost stories of a three-storied building had been cut off, and then laid upon the ground; or as if the whole fabric had sunk up to the waist in soil.'[53] Woodward also changed the roof of the tower, settling on a complete, pointed form rather than the truncated pyramid seen in the contract drawings. Some scientists later objected to this change, because it deprived them of a flat perch on top of the tower for weather experiments.[54] At the time, critics complained that the University Museum looked 'bald,' but the crisp, economical exterior quality might have presented science in a more modest light than a bombastic facade – besides, as G. G. Scott and Charles Barry and the later jurors pointed out, the museum's budget was too small.

THE INTERIOR: AN IRON AND GLASS ROOF SURMOUNTING A CLOISTER

Students entered the building through an imposing wooden door beneath a carved portal. The building's light-filled central space surrounded by a two-storey arcade, is one of the most charming in Victorian architecture (Figures 3.10 and 3.11). The courtyard resembled a cloister, and Thomas Greenwood, author of *Museums and Art Galleries* (1888) described it using that term:

> The central court is covered in with [sic] a roof of wood and glass resting on iron pillars. This method of roof lighting gives the best effects, and for this the chief court is admirably suited. In this large hall are placed principal collec-

Figure 3.8 Thomas Deane and Benjamin Woodward, Oxford University Museum, 1855–60. Photograph by the author.

Figure 3.9 Thomas Deane and Benjamin Woodward, Oxford University Museum, 1859. *Building News* 5 (1859).

tions, ranged partly on the ground floor in the centre and partly in the corridors which surround the building. These are arranged on the principle of a double cloister, one part being over the other. These cloisters afford space for additions to the specimens and give access to the various professors' lecture rooms ... The shafts of the cloister as well as those of the windows are of different varieties of stone, illustrating the principle geological formations of the British Islands.[55]

Figure 3.10 Thomas Deane and Benjamin Woodward, Oxford University Museum, 1855–60. By permission of Oxfordshire Photographic Archive, Oxfordshire County Council, no. 2938, interior *c.*1870, showing court as cloister.

The fact that this interior resembles a cloister shows a link between science and religion – the professors' offices around the edges are like cells, and the interior of the court (where a garden would grow in a monastery) is filled with natural specimens. The ambulatories are not actually outside, but given the transparency of the roof, the spaces are light and airy. (Of course, the image of a monastery as a model for scientific contemplation was, much later, exploited to great effect by Louis Kahn at the Salk Institute.)[56] Through the pointed arches of the cloister's arcade, students could reach offices and classrooms. Structural polychromy gave the arcade a vigorous play of warm colours and a rich texture. Against the courtyard side of each pier were placed life-size statues of famous men of science. The liveliness in the arcade was complemented by the iron and glass roof, supported by painted iron piers.

The middle aisle of the court was marked by a row of sharply pointed arches; the two side aisles were slightly narrower but of the same construction. Woodward made no attempt at true vaults; instead, the iron column for each bay supported a pitched roof, and curved elements, resembling pointed arches, are suspended from the pitched members. In this way, Woodward and the contractors were imitating Gothic form without actually using Gothic principles of construction. The clustered piers, for example, are hollow in the center (an efficient use of cast iron but impossible in stone), and the court design shows some innovative thinking about the peculiar technology of iron.[57]

'THE ONE IN THE MANIFOLD': DIVERSITY IN THE ORNAMENT

The iron capitals, accented in the design, were elaborately decorated with leaves, fruits and flowers (Figures 3.12 and 3.13). Woodward took great care that these floral shapes would not be conventional motifs, but rather communicative of the variety

Figure 3.11 Thomas Deane and Benjamin Woodward, Oxford University Museum, 1855–60. By permission of Oxfordshire Photographic Archive, Oxfordshire County Council, no. 9636, interior *c*.1870, showing osteological collection.

and complexity found in nature. His sources ranged from lime, chestnut and syca-more, to water-lily, passion-flower and holly,[58] and this close observation of the natural world obviously recalls G. E. Street's romantic description of the medieval architect's method.

The O'Shea brothers, the craftsmen who traveled from Dublin to Oxford to carve these naturalistic decorations in stone, created an ornamental program of surprising variety, displaying a knowledge of medieval precedent as well as unusual skill. Deane and Woodward were well-informed followers of Ruskin before they actually met him, and at the Oxford Museum they carried out one of Ruskin's most import-ant tenets – that workmen should be given freedom in the design of ornament. One

Figure 3.12   Deane
and Woodward,
Oxford University
Museum, 1855–60,
interior, visitors
among the iron
columns. *Building
News* 6 (1860) 271.

early chronicler of the museum portrays the O'Sheas as simple men who copied nature with devout realism: 'Every morning came the handsome red-bearded Irish brothers Shea, bearing plants from the Botanic Garden, to reappear under their chisels in the rough-hewn capitals of the pillars.'[59] In other words, authentic natural specimens rather than artistic conventions were models for the ornament. As many theorists have noted, the acanthus leaves on classical columns are stylized and identical, but the capitals at the Oxford Museum are all different. The great variety of the decoration is a reflection of natural theology, which held that if scientists studied the diversity of nature, they would eventually find a unity. Or, as Owen wrote in a Christmas card to Acland, 'The One in the Manifold,' meaning God may be found in the multiplicity of nature. Trained to look closely at nature in the manner of observational science, Ruskin, too, saw the infinite variety of the natural world expressed in specific plants, rocks and mountains. O'Dwyer has convincingly argued that Ruskin counseled Woodward about the building and especially the ornament; Ruskin even complained about the architect's pestering: 'I've told Woodward fifty times that I'm busy at present and yet they [sic] keep after me.'[60] Although he fought against the clients' preference for iron and called the overall design 'not first rate,' Ruskin appreciated the ornament, which evidenced a careful study of nature.

Figure 3.13 Deane and Woodward, Oxford University Museum, 1855–60, interior, ornamental detail on iron columns. *Builder* 18 (23 June 1860) 399.

The column shafts, all from British and Irish stones, formed a polished statement of national pride (Figure 3.14). Phillips supervised this project; when he had trouble locating blocks of stone large enough for the shafts, Woodward had proposed that foreign marble be used; but his suggestion 'was by no means warmly welcomed, and no one advocating it, it was rejected.'[61] The columns were also didactic. Phillips devised their arrangement, and had each stone clearly labeled at the base so that students could learn to distinguish various types of marble and granite. Deane and Woodward had used similar columns of Irish stone at the museum at Trinity College, Dublin, but, again, the better-known example was Pennethorne's Museum of Practical Geology, which had an architectural display of geological specimens built into the fabric of the museum.[62] In all of these museums, similar building parts made of different types of stone exhibited taxonomic difference, indicating again that Victorians took for granted that one could learn by looking. The architectural display of geological materials in these three museums communicated geological variation. At Oxford, the University Museum became part of the edifying display; while the carved stone capitals *represented* natural specimens, the stone column shafts actually *were* natural specimens – or, seen through the lens

Figure 3.14 Deane and Woodward, Oxford University Museum, interior, 1855–60, marble columns surrounding the courtyard on the second level. Photograph by the author.

of natural theology, they were authentic examples from Creation that had a function (supporting an arch), an educational value (geological information) and intrinsic beauty. Phillips, a natural theologian like Acland, would have assumed that this impressive display of God's intricate geological creations would reinforce Christian wonder.

ENGINEERING AS DISTINCT FROM OXFORD SCIENCE

As a general rule, Ruskin and some of his followers disliked modern materials, such as iron, in which duplicate forms could be produced without the hand of an artist, thus tending toward utilitarianism.[63] He even told Acland he would have nothing to do with the museum if were to be made of glass. His contempt for the Crystal Palace was well known. But, despite Ruskin's theories, the museum delegacy from the start demanded an iron roof, and they proceeded to build one, although the professors may have actually understood little about the constructional principles of such a design. The delegates had asked for an iron and glass roof to cover the courtyard because they sought perfect natural light, but received an expensive interior that has captured the imagination of later historians because it joined the Gothic style to a new technology. The roof was expensive because the engineers, Skidmore and Company, miscalculated the compressive strength of wrought iron, and the piers began to bow. It was rebuilt using cast iron for the piers. One delegate sounded a prophetic warning, when, in the spring of 1856, he suggested that they not ask for funds until they knew more about erecting the glass roof, considering 'the want of experience in such matters, owing to its being a new invention.'[64] At this same meeting, Acland complained that the roof might leak; Woodward suggested they use extra thick glass to make the roof stronger than those of railway stations and the Crystal Palace; and Phillips recommended they look at the Museum of Practical Geology (his former employer) where 'the glass would bear a man's weight, & where he has never known any leak.'[65]

Today still more confusion arises from the twentieth-century association of science with engineering.[66] We are accustomed to the idea that science and engineering are related disciplines, and they are often grouped together at modern universities. This connection, however, did not hold true at Oxford and Cambridge, where Buckland and Sedgwick 'promoted geology, then the newest of the natural sciences, under an explicitly non- or even anti-utilitarian banner, and not for any economic purpose.'[67] But this link between science and engineering is an outgrowth of the professionalization of science, promoted especially by Huxley, which occurred later in the nineteenth century, after the Oxford Museum was built. Huxley, called the 'Devil's Disciple' by religious critics, tried to wrestle science away from the Anglican thinkers (like Acland and Owen) who held important professorships and curatorial posts, and who dominated the scientific societies. Huxley, who did not have ties to the Anglican elite, began his career as a physician and struggled for years to gain acceptance into scientific circles. It is Huxley's world of secular science that we in the twentieth century have inherited. But since the clients for the Oxford Museum were natural theologians, they most certainly did not identify themselves with utilitarian engineers, and thus it is anachronistic to claim that the 'iron of the Crystal Palace' represents 'science.'[68] Perhaps the timber, iron and glass roof should be seen in the context of other toplit display spaces, rather than as a symbol of clashing worlds of religion and science.

SPIRITUAL AND MATERIAL AT ONCE: THE PORTAL RELIEF SCULPTURE

Another twentieth-century dichotomy – this time between evolutionism and creationism – tempts historians to see the architecture of the Oxford Museum as either conservative and religious, or progressive and scientific, but this is a blurry lens which has distorted the history of the building.[69] Science and metaphysics may be contradictory today, but they were not so in nineteenth-century Britain – in fact, the ideas did not even exist in the same way they do now. The book *The Oxford Museum*, Acland's personal narrative of the museum's history and significance, appeared in four editions, all of which were used as fund-raising tools for the museum. Acland began grandly by defining nature as 'every known and observed form of matter by which our world and its inhabitants were either made or are maintained, and whatever laws of their construction or for their maintenance have by reason been inferred.'[70] Acland presented the new building as one of broad pedagogical importance; in its walls students would study matter and the laws governing matter. He stressed that the laws of nature would not be studied for their own sake, but because they revealed the harmony of nature. Acland compared nature to the Bible or word of God, calling nature an unwritten, or wordless, expression of God's plan. The museum was not an attempt to reconcile opposites – science and religion – because such a reconciliation was not necessary in an atmosphere fused with natural theology.

As historians of science have shown, most scientists accepted Darwin's theory and at the same time maintained essentially religious beliefs, and there were a range of theories that reconciled evolution and religion.[71] For example, some scientists accepted the principle of natural selection, and assumed that it was a law put into effect by the Creator. It was also argued that God set up the grand strategy of evolution, and that the small changes in each species proved His continued involvement in the natural world. Some liberal theologians believed they were completing Darwin's work by using Scripture to illuminate the spiritual evolution of humankind. Still other religious thinkers believed that evolution proved that man was innately selfish, a theory that aroused evocations of original sin. Most scientists rejected the biblical timeline, but maintained a teleological belief that natural history was developmental and progressive. The patrons of the museum were Christians – Darwinism had not interfered with their faith – and they considered themselves to be up-to-date scientists who deserved an appropriately modern building which would mark the arrival of science at Oxford.

Henry Acland believed that the museum portal sculpture was a physical manifestation of the combined powers of religion and science. In 1859, when the structure of the museum was largely complete but the decorative scheme unfinished, the convocation rejected Woodward's costly entrance porch. John Hungerford Pollen, an associate of Deane and Woodward and a member of the pre-Raphaelite circle, stepped in with a less expensive design. Acland described Pollen's portal program in detail (Figures 3.15 and 3.16):

> It takes the received origin of Man as the basis of thought. On the left-hand side is the first man, Adam, in a state of innocence, holding back the bloodhound, emblem of suffering and death. At the base on the right, Eve is attentively listening to the voice of the tempter, still undecided. From these two ascend flowers and thorns and fruit. These reach to the top of the arch, on which rests the Angel of Life, bearing in one hand an open book, the emblem of intellectual and spiritual life, in the other the dividing nucleated cell, the type of all material function, growth, and decay.[72]

Pollen's angel at the pinnacle of the arch represented the spiritual and physical cycle that includes both growth and decay: the material cell was a starting point for life, and the open book was the origin of spirituality. It is not entirely clear whether this 'book of life' represents the Bible, God's first book, or nature, God's second book, but in either case it is distinctly spiritual. As explained further by Acland: 'The idea contained in the bas-relief is that of evolution, spiritual and material.'[73] Acland here states that the symbolism combines, rather than distinguishes, spirituality and materiality.

Acland's use of the word 'evolution' was not a reference to Darwin's particular theory of evolution, given that different theories of transmutation circulated among Victorian scientists, and the word was in common usage before Darwin.[74] Darwin's revolutionary contribution to science was to propose a mechanism for evolution (natural selection), not evolution itself. Darwin's own teacher, Robert Grant, had been teaching theories of transmutation (based on French science) at the University of London for decades before Darwin came to be associated with the concept. Acland and some of his colleagues might have seen the portal sculpture as a candid representation of the theological and scientific role of the museum. To some viewers, Adam and Eve were represented on the museum because they *belonged* on a building dedicated to nature, and these viewers would not have necessarily cared about, or been offended by, the contemporaneous publication of Darwin's *Origin of Species* (1859).[75]

Figure 3.15 John Hungerford Pollen, Portal sculpture at the Oxford University Museum, 1855–60. The angel is at the apex of the pointed arch. Photograph by the author.

Figure 3.16 John Hungerford Pollen, Portal sculpture. Angel bearing in one hand an open book and in the other a biological cell. Drawn by Lisa Marie Yanni.

THE MEETING OF T. H. HUXLEY AND BISHOP WILBERFORCE

The Oxford Museum was host to an event often assumed to be a violent intellectual clash between science and religion; more recent studies in the history of science, however, have undermined this simple conclusion, suggesting that while secular scientists did attract attention to Darwinism, they by no means vanquished religion from scientific practice. The much-discussed event was a brief dialogue about Darwinian evolution that took place between T. H. Huxley and the Bishop of Oxford, Samuel Wilberforce, at the 1860 meeting of the British Association for the Advancement of Science (BAAS).[76] Although it is usually called a 'debate,' it was actually an impromptu exchange.[77] Darwin did not attend the meeting due to one of his frequent illnesses; but an American scientist, John William Drape, gave a paper on *The Origin of Species*, and the exchange took place during the question-and-answer period after the talk. The Bishop possessed a gentleman's interest in science, especially ornithology, and was a supporter of the new science building.[78] Many historians believe he discussed the weaknesses of *The Origin of Species* with Richard Owen before the meeting – not to prepare a written statement, but to collect his thoughts in case he was called upon to speak. Wilberforce stated that he opposed the *Origin* because Darwin's facts did not support his claims, and that

> The line between man and the lower animals was distinct; there was no tendency on the part of lower animals to become the self-conscious intelligent being, man; or in man to degenerate and lose the high characteristics of his mind and intelligence ... Mr. Darwin's conclusions were an hypothesis, raised most unphilosophically to the dignity of a causal theory.[79]

Actually, many people criticized Darwin for not having enough proof of natural selection, so the Bishop's objections were partly reasonable.

Huxley, who defended Darwin at the meeting, had more on his mind than how species develop in nature. His animosity toward men like Owen, whom he considered to be a member of an elitist cohort of scientists, and Wilberforce, whom he saw as a religious dabbler, was widely known at the time, and the audience expected him to trounce the Bishop. Darwin had hardly mentioned the ancestry of humans in *The Origin of Species*, but readers and the popular press seized on the idea that if his theory was correct, humans were related to apes – not to mention tadpoles and mushrooms.[80] The topic gained widespread popular interest, and it was this exact issue that sparked the verbal eruption between Wilberforce and Huxley. One account has it that Wilberforce asked Huxley if he descended from apes on his grandfather's or grandmother's side, and Huxley responded that he would sooner be descended from an ape than from a 'divine who employ[ed] authority to stifle the truth.'[81] Huxley's own version of the story holds that if the question were put to him 'would I rather have a miserable ape for a grandfather or a man highly endowed by nature and possessed of great means and influence and yet who employs those faculties for the mere purpose of introducing ridicule into a grave scientific discussion, I unhesitatingly affirm my preference for the ape.'[82] Until a decade ago, historians reported this confrontation in such a way as to suggest that Huxley conquered the religious old guard: that the truth of secular science won a battle that day in the Oxford Museum. But the case is not so clear. Ironically, *both* Huxley and Wilberforce considered themselves victors; the debate generated interest in Darwinism, but did not cause an overnight rejection of natural theology. Younger men of science were in the minority at the conference, and although the famous event took place in the new museum, the patrons of the museum were conservative religious scientists. It was, metaphorically speaking, a home that was created for Wilberforce's science, not Huxley's. Victorian men of science were slow to accept Darwinian evolution, and remained convinced of their religious mission for decades after the so-called debate.

Participants at the 1860 BAAS meeting had to pass beneath the Adam and Eve on the portal before attending the discussion on evolution, which was held in the west room (later the library). Acland considered this profoundly important theme – the very origin of humankind – in a letter to Owen after the clash. 'Whatever views Mr Huxley, or you, or Mr Darwin, or the Bishop of Oxford may have as to the essential Nature of Man, you all agree that however he so became, he is in some manner made in the image of God, by the ordinance of God . . .'.[83] Acland's statement reflects the view held by many Victorian men of science: whatever mechanisms governed the natural world, the very beginnings of life were a transcendental mystery. Again, this spiritual explanation for the beginning of nature is represented by the portal angel, who holds both the book (the origin of spiritual life) and the cell (the origin of material life), thereby unifying the two realms. Acland endearingly, if naïvely, assumed that Huxley, the man who coined the term 'agnostic,' would accept that man was made by the ordinance of God. But Acland's letter to Owen – his confidence in a Christian world – reveals that the secularization of science had not yet begun at Oxford.

Owen once had been Acland's teacher and the two remained friends. The opinionated Owen had confronted Acland with his disappointment over the outcome of the competition back in 1855, five years before he coached Wilberforce for the BAAS meeting. Owen cared deeply about the Oxford Museum because it was an important symbol of the ascent of science, and as a museum director himself, who had supervised two renovations of the Hunterian by the elder Barry, architectural issues often occupied his thoughts. Owen read about the competition in the *Athenaeum* and complained to Acland about the defeat suffered by the younger Barry's classical design. Owen reasoned that the Gothic was inappropriate for a science building, since scientific inquiry was invented in the ancient world, not in northern Europe:

> I have read with interest the notices of the several plans for your Natural Science edifice in the 'Atheneum'[sic], the 'Builder,' and other periodicals . . . and have last heard, not without a tremor, that a Gothic style had been selected. The Sciences were not born nor nursed where that style originated.[84]

Owen's voice was a clear call for the classical style, although his career and fame were founded on the belief that nature was God's second book. Like Street, he tried to connect the meaning of one style to the exact purpose of the building; however, Owen chose the opposing style. It is for this reason that we cannot simply link the Gothic style, with its ecclesiastical imagery, to natural theology, a religious view of science. While it must be stressed that there are formal characteristics of the Oxford Museum (the cloister, the variation in the ornament, and the portal sculpture) that communicate ideas about science as natural theology, this highly specific communication does not necessarily preclude other interpretations. The meaning of particular forms (and entire styles) in the nineteenth century was complex and ever-changing, as this reading of the Oxford Museum has tried to show. Perhaps the most we can conclude is that there was no one architectural response that would satisfy everyone or even carry the same meaning to every visitor.

CONCLUSION

The Oxford Museum is an important building in architectural history for at least three good reasons: it raised questions about appropriateness of styles, it was a relatively new building type, and it employed recent technology to cover the courtyard. Thus its history evokes issues of style, building type, and technology – the three great architectural challenges of the nineteenth century. There is an historical litany for this building which repeats dichotomies (classical versus Gothic, science versus religion, art versus technology, creation versus evolution) that are, in fact, not present in Victorian intellectual culture in the same way that we understand them today. Indeed, such clear-cut dualities are perhaps not in keeping with Victorian thought. As Ruskin himself wrote, 'truths may be and often are *opposite* though they cannot be contradictory.'[85]

chapter 4

Nature as Natural Resource

The Edinburgh Museum of Science and Art

A national museum *must not be limited* to Natural History; let it be co-extensive with Art and Science – let it be a nucleus to which the spirited sons of Scotia may give and bequeath pictures, statues, specimens, books and manuscripts. Let it be a place to which your hardworking Sailors, Soldiers, Merchants, and Medical men in active foreign service, may delight to send specimens of Natural History or curiosities connected with rude and less civilised nations . . . Let it contain models of the Geological structure of your country, which in itself is almost an epitome of the world. (Adam White, Scottish naturalist, 1850)

Completed within a year of the Oxford Museum, the Edinburgh Museum of Science and Art presented a different face of natural history.[1] Rather than the second book of God, this 'nature' was more practical and economically valuable than it was a reflection of the diversity of Creation. Since many of the categories of knowledge found in museums today (art versus science, for example) were invented in the nineteenth century, the Edinburgh Museum (today the Royal Museum of Scotland) warrants special attention as evidence of the construction of those categories; it is a monument to this process of negotiation. Dating from the time, shortly after the Great Exhibition, when taxonomies of knowledge were relatively flexible, the program and architecture of the Edinburgh Museum of Science and Art were founded on a now-forgotten organizational schema, in which science, industry and art were presented together, almost as fluid categories.[2]

SCOTTISH NATIONALISM AND SCOTTISH EDUCATION

Victorian Scotland was one of the many political divisions of the British Empire subject to the rule of Queen Victoria and the laws of Parliament; but it retained a distinctive culture, sense of territory, and concept of nationhood. Scotland had been merged with England in the 1707 Act of Union, a political agreement by which Scots accepted the authority of the British monarchy and Parliament. Under the Union settlement, Scotland retained certain distinctive characteristics of her cultural institutions, including the Scottish legal system and universities.[3] This dichotomy resulted in cultural tensions in eighteenth- and nineteenth-century Scotland, because the landed ruling class sought to preserve Scottish national identity while maintaining close ties to the government in London. By the beginning of the nineteenth century, Edinburgh had styled itself as 'the Athens of the North,' and the architectural expression of this revival of nationalism was a succession of sophisticated Greek Revival buildings, including Thomas Hamilton's High School (1825–29), William Playfair's Scottish Academy (1822–26) and National Gallery (1850–57), and the monuments on Calton Hill. The program for the Edinburgh Museum of Science and Art was developed in the context of these demonstrations of Scottish national culture.

The character of Scottish education also influenced the architecture of the Edinburgh Museum of Science and Art. Scottish universities were dedicated to bolstering industry. Instruction at the University of Edinburgh was inexpensive because the classes were large and the terms short. Even men from the country, who worked summer, spring and fall, could attend university in the winter; therefore, many considered university-level education to be a reasonable ambition.[4] In 1867, Matthew Arnold, the English poet, social theorist and education critic, who also served as an inspector of schools, noted that in Scotland intellectual pursuits were linked to industry:

> so far as intellectual culture has an industrial value, makes a man's business better and helps him get on in the world, the Scotch middle class has thoroughly appreciated it and sedulously employed it, both for itself and for the class whose labour it uses; and here is their superiority to the English and the reason of the success of Scotch skilled labourers and Scotch men of business everywhere.[5]

Arnold believed he had identified a Scottish trait – the pursuit of education for the practical ends of industry. Arnold's observations were made a few years after the Edinburgh Museum of Science and Art opened to the public, but his comments still elucidate the general character of Scottish higher education. In contrast to Oxford and Cambridge, where business-oriented education was scorned by gentlemanly instructors and students, universities in Scotland purposely prepared middle-class – as opposed to aristocratic – students for careers in commerce and manufacturing.

The value system of Scottish education explains an important circumstance in the history of the Edinburgh Museum of Science and Art. In 1855 the town council of Edinburgh, which was authorized to act as the board of trustees of the University of Edinburgh, transferred the university's natural history collection to the Board of Trade, a branch of the central British government in London that was charged with fostering economic development in Britain and the colonies. The university gave away its collections, but gained a building when Parliament agreed to pay for a site and a purpose-built structure to display the natural objects to their greatest advantage. Not surprisingly, relations between the university professors and museum staff were unfriendly for years afterward.[6] The city council's decision to donate the specimens to the Board of Trade allowed the university's natural history collections to be free and easily accessible to the public.

THE INFLUENCE OF THE MUSEUM OF PRACTICAL GEOLOGY

The Edinburgh Museum of Science and Art was a direct descendent of the Museum of Practical Geology in London. Dublin already had a relative of the Museum of Practical Geology, its Museum of Irish Industry. *The Daily Scotsman* reported in 1858 that the origin of the Edinburgh Museum could be found in these two other model institutions:

> the various learned bodies, public societies, and representatives of the manu-
> facturing, agricultural and other industrial interests of North Britain, resolved
> to institute in Edinburgh a museum similar to those of Economic Geology in
> London and Dublin.[7]

Aimed at the working class, the evening lectures were a popular form of entertainment and education, and the planners of the Edinburgh Museum hoped to duplicate such lectures in Scotland. The exhibitions at the Museum of Practical Geology were part of an overall program which taught the viewer how natural resources were transformed into commercial products. The Edinburgh Museum adopted this kind of display, exemplifying the Victorian enthusiasm for the dissemination of knowledge, which, as Tony Bennett points out, meant that knowledge ought 'to be put to useful effect in the productive exploitation of nature.'[8]

THE CRYSTAL PALACE: 'THAT PROLIFIC MOTHER'

In the same year that Pennethorne's Museum of Practical Geology opened to the public in London, a more famous industrial display seized tourists' imaginations – the Great Exhibition of the Industry of All Nations, held in the Crystal Palace in 1851. As it had affected the Museum of Practical Geology, the Great Exhibition was a model for the Scottish leaders planning their museum. In 1866 the *Edinburgh Evening Courant* noted the influence of the Crystal Palace on the Edinburgh Museum of Science and Art:

> [I]t may be said to owe its origin to that prolific mother, the Great Exhibition
> of 1851, whose offspring have already spread themselves over the globe. The
> Hyde Park Palace, the creature of a summer, was happily destined to repro-
> duce itself not in the evanescent form of exhibitions, but in the permanent
> shape of museums of art, science, and industry . . . It is, however, more of a
> school than a show. It is meant not merely to please, but to instruct; not less to
> charm the eye than to enrich the mind.[9]

This newspaper reporter voiced a widely held opinion in Victorian Britain: that the success of the Crystal Palace should be perpetuated in permanent museums that would charm the eye, instruct visitors on the state of industry, and inspire manufacturers and workers to invest money and labour in the economy.[10]

94 *Nature's Museums*

THE PROBLEM OF SPECTACLE

Some curators argued that each museum should display every single object in its collection. Until the 1860s, curators aimed to compile complete collections of natural objects, which would enhance the curator's own prestige – as he would then preside over a microcosm of the universe. The desire for encyclopedic display created overwhelming visual spectacles. It is possible that secular scientists did not want their museums to be spectacular, because they wanted to edify rather than entertain. T. H. Huxley, in particular, opposed the display of every object – perhaps for exactly the reason that he did not want a spectacle. Art historian Jonathan Crary remarks that Foucault's famous phrase, 'our society is not one of spectacle but of surveillance' is misleading, because the effect of these two regimes of power coincide. Crary argues for placing the beginning of the society of the spectacle in the late 1920s.[11] But another scholar, Thomas Richards, places it further back, to the year 1851. This precise periodization would seem peculiar, were it not for the singularity of the event: The Great Exhibition, of course. Architectural historians are sometimes so happy swooning over its tectonic purity that they forget the Crystal Palace was full of purchasable, consumable bourgeois stuff, and that the purpose of the iron and glass building was to maximize natural light. The actual items did not carry price tags and could not be purchased on the site, but the glass building allowed visitors to view the free market's best products (porcelain cups, silk pillowcases, the envelope-making machine) under natural light. Richards contends that capitalism produced and sustained a culture of its own in Victorian Britain, and that 'the commodity' became the centerpiece of everyday life:

> The Crystal Palace was a monument to consumption, the first of its kind, a place where the combined mythologies of consumerism appeared in concentrated form [and that it was] descended from the spectacular masques and allegorical processions that celebrated political and economic triumph in the eighteenth century, [thus] the spectacle of the Exhibition elevated the commodity above the mundane act of exchange and created a coherent representational universe for commodities.[12]

The Great Exhibition was probably too large and complex to appear to anyone as 'a coherent representational universe,' but Richards's conclusions about the elevation of the commodity in Victorian culture seem sound. The average middle-class family in England was wary of consumerism, and, according to Richards, the Exhibition served to convince them that spending money was morally uplifting.

Increased trade was the goal of the exhibition. Cole solicited the support of Prince Albert for the grand display of industrial art by convincing him that a peacetime exhibition would promote international harmony. The story of the Crystal Palace's architectural genesis has been told many times, but, briefly, its innovative structure was designed by the gardener Joseph Paxton, who had previous experience as a greenhouse builder. Paxton's Crystal Palace was a spectacular structure filled with exhibitions intended to astonish (Figures 4.1 and 4.2). The west half of the building was filled with British industrial products and commodities, including carriages, a root-washing machine, telescopes and musical instruments. The British Manufactures Division was comprised of fabrics, clothing, shoes, glass, porcelain, and like goods. The only natural objects in the Crystal Palace were raw materials for

Figure 4.1 Joseph Paxton, Crystal Palace, exterior, Hyde Park, London, 1851. V&A Picture Library, 81612.

industry – for example, wool and cotton in the Manufactures Division, and coal and iron in the Machinery Division. A display of slices cut across tree trunks was labeled 'The Vegetable Production of Scotland.' Industrial objects outnumbered the natural ones.

This posed a problem for industrial museums: permanent museums were a recent invention. We have already seen the shift from high-status cabinets of curiosities (located in gentlemen's houses) to public museums of more natural specimens organized according to taxonomic principles. But nineteenth-century museums had

Figure 4.2 Joseph
Paxton, Crystal
Palace, London,
interior, 1851.
Lithograph by
Joseph Nash. V&A
Picture Library.

different audiences: elite men of science wanted to separate themselves from the
show of commodities. However, some professional, secular scientists were comfort-
able displaying natural resources alongside capitalistic products. Dublin, Edinburgh
and other towns were setting up permanent museums to house the same objects as
those from the Crystal Palace; this trickle-down effect from the popular and trade-
related Crystal Palace challenged the nature of museums as purveyors of serious
knowledge. There was one shift, from the curious to the serious; and another, from
the serious to the marketable.

   In 1852 the exhibition closed and the Crystal Palace in Hyde Park was dis-
mantled, but the structure was reconstructed in Sydenham, a London suburb, where
it remained a popular tourist attraction throughout the nineteenth century (see Figure 5.28). Although most scholarly attention has focussed on the first Crystal Palace,
the Sydenham Crystal Palace was in a sense the more important building. It loomed
over all other displays until 1937, when it burned to the ground in a death as spectacular as its life. Paxton personally hoped that the materials from the first Crystal
Palace could be used to re-erect a greenhouse full of exotic plants, a living museum of
botany. Paxton did get the chance to rebuild his Crystal Palace, but not just for
botany. The building had 50 percent more floor space, three transepts (instead of
one) and vaults along the short and long axes (instead of just the short axis). There
was a slope to the new site, necessitating a basement and allowing for a grandiose
staircase. At either end of the building, the engineer I. K. Brunel designed tall water
towers which gave the composition a varied, yet symmetrical, silhouette. While both
Crystal Palaces promoted international industry, the Sydenham palace actually had
price tags on some items.[13]

   At Sydenham, history was emphasized. It was a cluttered spectacle of historical
detail, with courts displaying the architecture of Egypt, Assyria and Moorish Spain,
among others. The Sydenham building also included a concert hall, exhibitions of
stuffed natural specimens, a show of live monkeys and (in the grounds) full-scale
reconstructions of dinosaurs and extinct mammals. Important naturalists took part in
the dinosaur swamp and reconstructions, so it can be assumed that other men of
science (like those in Scotland) would be watching the progress of the Sydenham

landmark. When naturalists and architects planned a Scottish national museum, the 1851 Crystal Palace was fresh in their memories, and the Sydenham Crystal Palace had become a lasting physical presence in England's capital. Enthusiasm for a Scottish national museum emerged from the success and popularity of the crystal palaces.

THE EARLY PLANNING OF THE EDINBURGH MUSEUM

When Henry Cole promoted and organized the Great Exhibition of 1851, he was assisted by the Scot Lyon Playfair (1818–1898). The Department of Science and Art, formed in 1853 as a subdivision of the Board of Trade, was charged with promoting practical science and artistic manufacturing; Playfair, who was Secretary of the Science division of the Department of Science and Art, held an ideal platform from which he could extend educational opportunities to the provinces. A teaching museum in his former home, Edinburgh, was just one of these 'out-reach' projects. There was, however, already a groundswell of enthusiasm back in Scotland for such an institution. In the 1850s several local organizations and individuals joined to develop a plan for a national science museum. The Highland and Agricultural Society was one of the groups that hoped to build a Scottish museum. Its collection of rocks, minerals and agricultural models was already open to the public, but they pledged to donate their objects to begin a national collection.[14] Another early supporter, Adam White (1817–1879), was a Scottish ornithologist and entomologist who worked as an assistant in the zoology department of the British Museum in London. In 1850 White wrote a pamphlet proposing that the Scottish museum should be more than a natural history museum; he imagined it as a place to exhibit a wide range of objects, both natural and human-made. He hoped the museum would communicate the ascent of Scotland in the world arena, as he declared in the passage that was quoted at the start of this chapter.[15]

White's museum was meant to symbolize Scotland's place as a leader among nations and gather objects that Scottish travellers were collecting from across the globe.[16] These objectives were taking shape at the same time Playfair was involved in organizing the Great Exhibition in 1851, and although there was support in Scotland for a museum of natural history, science and industry, the funds for the project came from London through the force of Playfair's work at the Department of Science and Art.

In 1854 Playfair, in the name of the Department of Science and Art, took a major step by asking the British Parliament for funds to purchase land for an Industrial Museum of Scotland. He was granted £7000. The Department chose a site east of Argyle Square, a residential neighborhood near the main quadrangle of the University of Edinburgh. Now Scottish museum enthusiasts had a site, but they needed to raise money and establish a collection of industrial objects. (The university's natural history collections were assembled, but the industrial collections had yet to be gathered.) The process began when Playfair's friend George Wilson, whom he had met when both were medical students at the University of Edinburgh, popularized the museum cause.[17] Wilson was Playfair's most important ally in starting the museum, with Playfair working within the government in London and Wilson lobbying in Edinburgh. Wilson had studied chemistry and technology in addition to medicine, and he compiled an impressive collection of machines for teaching. John Pickstone has suggested that while these activities seem disparate, they were connected by being equally 'museological'; he explains that 'Wilson moved through a world of parallel museums.'[18]

Wilson was appointed director of the Industrial Museum in 1855, when the small industrial collection was kept in temporary quarters and the natural history collections were on display in the university's main quadrangle.[19] In his lectures from the 1850s, Wilson evaluated the state of the industrial arts in Scotland. In a surprising example of self-stereotyping, he avowed that Scots were naturally inferior designers whose cultural strengths (intellectualism, common sense and the avoidance of sensuality) undermined their achievements in the decorative arts:

> We need not be ashamed to confess that other nations have outstripped us of the North in the cultivation of the ornamental arts. Our very virtues as a race have in some respects hindered our aesthetic development. Our dread of the sensuous element acquiring the ascendancy in public religious worship: Our tendency as thinkers, toward intellectual rather than poetical abstractions; and as workers, to keep clear of theories, and idolise common sense: Our love of independence, and our jealousy lest the infusion of foreign elements should undermine our nationality, have made us in some respects hard realists. Above all, as regards the present object, that contentment with simple lodgings, plain clothing, and hard fare . . . [has] stood in the way of our largely encouraging or appreciating the graceful arts.[20]

Although the abstemious character of the Scottish people might have dampened their enthusiasm for an industrial museum in Scotland, Wilson argued that it made the project all the more important. The national museum would introduce Scots to the important concept that utility and beauty were allied, so that they would learn not to fear beauty as a senseless luxury. His artful lectures were fund-raising events in which he justified the expense of a national museum (still in the planning stages) to an audience that was raised in a tradition of restraint and moderation.

Wilson envisioned a Scottish institution that would imitate the Museum of Practical Geology, but would also include exhibits on 'economic zoology' and 'economic botany' as well as 'economic geology.' These three Victorian terms were used to describe natural knowledge as it pertained to manufacturing; thus, displays of economic zoology, botany or geology would include commodities made from natural objects, as well as natural objects with commercial applications. Wilson contended that the commerce of the world dealt 'very largely with mineral, vegetable, and animal substances.'[21] The economy of nineteenth-century Scotland was not a service economy, but one based on manufacturing. Study of the physical world, it was believed, would greatly benefit commercial ventures. As Wilson wrote: 'What are the ends of commercial enterprise? I will name but two: – 1. The making of money. 2. The civilizing of the world.'[22] The ideology at the core of Scotland's national museum, an institution which combined natural history and industry, reflects one Victorian view of natural knowledge: nature served Scottish industry, and industry, in turn, would bring the world together in one civilized market. By combining natural history and industry, the museum would present these subjects to the public as united, not opposing, branches of knowledge.

FRANCIS FOWKE: ENGINEER AND EXHIBITION ARCHITECT

The complex program for the Edinburgh Museum of Science and Art had been developed in the early 1850s, and the site had been purchased in 1854. During this time, the new industrial collection was slowly assembled, objects were stored in temporary quarters, and fund-raising continued. In 1857 the Department of Science and Art asked the architect Francis Fowke, who was employed by the Department, to draw up a preliminary proposal for the new museum.[23]

Fowke had been born in Belfast in 1823. As a young man he had joined the Royal Engineers, the engineering corps of the British Army; his first building, the Raglan Barracks at Devonport (1853), was acclaimed for its innovative sanitation and structure.[24] From that time on, Fowke specialized in the design of inexpensive, easy-to-construct buildings. Fowke's first appointment with the Department of Science and Art was as inspector for the British Machinery Division at the 1855 Paris world's fair. When Fowke completed his three-year tenure in Paris, he was hired by Henry Cole for the Department of Science and Art. As Secretary of the Art division, Cole hired the Department's in-house architects and he promoted Fowke to 'Architect and Engineer' in 1856.[25] Cole apparently decided that the new Scottish museum did not warrant a public competition, and so he gave the assignment to Fowke.[26]

Fowke was well prepared for the commission. He had designed several exhibition spaces, including work at the famous 'Brompton Boilers,' the iron sheds at the South Kensington Museum. In 1856, Fowke had been asked by Cole to build the Sheep-shanks Gallery for paintings on the northern side of the South Kensington Museum. Since lighting was an important consideration in an art gallery, Fowke wanted to insure that light from above would not cause glare (or 'glitter,' in Victorian parlance) on the surface of paintings; thus the proportions of the rooms were adjusted so that light from the skylights would hit above the top of a painting if a viewer of average height were standing about ten feet back from the wall.[27] Similarly, in the museum's other galleries, he sought to limit the surface reflections on the decorative art and natural history displays, many of which were preserved behind vertical or nearly-vertical panes of glass.

Fowke recognized that the purpose of an exhibition or museum was to let the visitors *see* the objects, and that lighting was therefore a key technical consideration. He may have known that critics disliked the lighting at Pennethorne's Museum of Practical Geology (or 'Jermyn Street Museum'), about which one writer complained that visitors could see the rocks, but not the fossil imprints on them:

> If any one will go to the Jermyn-street Museum, so admirably planned in some respects, he may discover that the reflection makes it impossible to see even the very forms of fossils, as those of the lower *strata*, which rather than the mere stones, were the objects of exhibition; and the same disadvantage would be experienced were the contents of the table-cases insects or shells.[28]

This was a serious indictment, and a similar error in a building like the Edinburgh Museum would have discouraged both scientists and casual visitors and dismayed Fowke's employers at the Department of Science and Art. Lighting was the most important design element in Victorian museums, and it was Fowke's expertise.

In April 1857, after Cole asked Fowke to prepare a preliminary report, the members authorized him to produce ground plans and section drawings for the new building.[29] Delays were common in the building of any Parliament-funded institution, and Edinburgh seems to have suffered frequent disappointments at the hands of bureaucrats. Strategists at the Department of Science and Art planned to build the museum in stages, because they did not have enough privately raised funds to build an entire structure at once, and they hoped to coax more funds out of Parliament by requesting money several times, over many years. But museum-planners got off to a poor start, when, in 1857 – in spite of the fact that the Department of Science and Art had a site, an architect, and preliminary plans – the House of Commons failed to vote to increase funds for the Scottish museum. The project lay fallow until the following year, as the specimens piled up in the crowded temporary quarters.[30] In 1858 Parliament did grant funds for the first phase of construction, and a burst of productivity occurred when, in the winter of 1859, Fowke made a new set of drawings for the Edinburgh Museum. In a plan and elevation, Fowke proposed a trapezoidal building (Figure 4.3). The east wall of this 1859 plan corresponded exactly to the line of West College Street, the road between the museum and University of Edinburgh, over which Fowke placed a modest footbridge. Fowke was expecting to cover only the east half of the final site, and since the elevation looked like a complete building unto itself, he was apparently not expecting to extend the building to the west.

Visitors would have entered on one of the short sides of the building and ascended the stairs to the entrance hall, from which the museum's longitudinal grand hall, covered by iron and glass, would have appeared as a nave. At two points along each side of this gallery, Fowke introduced spiral staircases, presumably leading to balconies for additional displays. Visitors could also have walked past these spiral

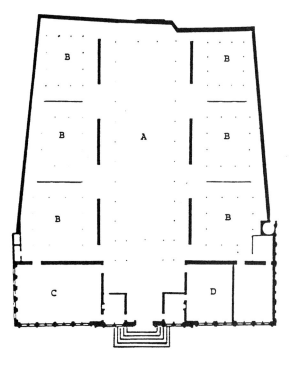

Figure 4.3 Francis Fowke, Proposal for Edinburgh Museum of Science and Art, plan, 1859. The Edinburgh Museum of Science and Art is now the Royal Museum of Scotland. Scottish Record Office, RHP 6524/49. Drawn by Michael Piga.

A.GREAT HALL   B.MUSEUM COURTS   C.PUBLIC LECTURE ROOM
D.ACADEMIC LECTURE ROOMS
GROUND FLOOR PLAN

staircases into 'museum courts' – three on each side of the main hall. These were not actual courtyards, but rather small display areas. Fowke's terminology is significant, because the Crystal Palace had been subdivided into 'courts' as well. Fowke placed lecture rooms and offices at the front of the building, in an arrangement like a 'head house' in front of an iron and glass train shed.

The elevation was a Renaissance design with a slightly advanced central block (Figure 4.4).[31] Fowke divided the facade into three storeys – the first with tall square-headed paired windows, and the upper two with pairs of arched windows and pilasters. One intriguing aspect of the design was Fowke's simple polychromy: the columns between the paired windows were red, the pilasters blue, and, on either side of the middle register of the main block, Fowke planned to set large panels of pink stone. These coloured details were probably not terracotta, but marble or granite, offering the viewer a lesson in geology like that of the Museum of Practical Geology.

The 1859 design was abandoned in 1860 when Parliament passed a bill granting funds to extend the site to its ultimate dimensions by purchasing the remaining houses on Argyle Square and the land of the square itself.[32] This allowed the museum to almost triple its size. In the same appropriation, Parliament offered £25,000 for the first phase of building, to be constructed on the portion of the site which was already cleared. In 1860, when the site was enlarged, Fowke had to revise the design so that the first part of the building could be used as a functional museum until the other two-thirds of the structure were finished.

A plan published in 1867 gives an approximate indication of the shape of the

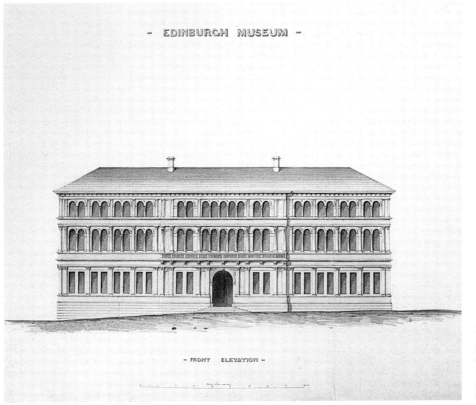

Figure 4.4　Francis Fowke, Proposal for Edinburgh Museum of Science and Art, 1859, elevation. Scottish Record Office, RHP 6542/36.

first phase and its relationship to the site, but does not correspond exactly to two drawings by Fowke from around 1860. In these undated exterior and interior perspectives, Fowke attempted to convey a visitor's view of the first phase of the museum construction. In the exterior rendering, in sepia tones, he depicted the quiet character of the facade; although still Renaissance in inspiration, the central block was now recessed and the wings projected – the reverse of his 1859 composition (Figure 4.5). He divided the main block of the facade into two stories, rather than three as before, but kept the paired arched windows. The projecting east wing, visible at the left edge of the drawing, had the same articulation as the 1859 scheme, with rectangular windows on the ground floor and arched windows above. The central block's cornice was crowned by a balustrade, whose piers bore urns. Behind the balustrade viewers could glimpse the structure of the glass roof. This rendering from about 1860 depicts Fowke's final design for the exterior; thus the museum, which was not constructed completely until 1889, was designed in its entirety by Fowke.

In the interior rendering, Fowke drew the portion of the Great Hall that was planned for the first phase (Figure 4.6). The room had two-tiered balconies on three sides, with delicate iron balustrades at the edge of the balconies. Slender iron columns supported the pitched roof of the Great Hall; the pitched roof beams were supported by half-round arches. Two sets of stairs in the foreground of the drawing may have been an early scheme for a temporary entrance, as described in the *Daily Scotsman*.[33] The accurate plan published in 1867 shows no such stairs (Figure 4.7), and so Fowke must have changed the interior slightly before construction began in 1861.

This first phase was supervised by a project architect in Edinburgh, Robert Matheson, and was completed by 1865. It included the Natural History Hall and a lecture room; a small gallery and the Great Hall (only about one-third of which was built at the time) contained the industrial art collection (comprised of architectural models, glass, porcelain, textiles and scientific instruments), and an ethnology display was installed in the gallery above the lecture room. The building was set awkwardly into the city in the early years, with one-third of the obviously incomplete museum nestled against the university buildings.

Fowke's facade showed the influence of both historic and modern architecture. The Lombard Renaissance was one source for the design, but Fowke also borrowed

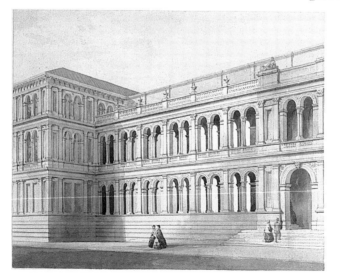

Figure 4.5 Francis Fowke, Edinburgh Museum of Science and Art, exterior perspective, north elevation, signed by Fowke, *c.*1860. © The Trustees of the National Museums of Scotland 1999.

Figure 4.6 Francis Fowke, Edinburgh Museum of Science and Art, interior perspective, signed by Fowke, *c.*1860. © The Trustees of the National Museums of Scotland 1999.

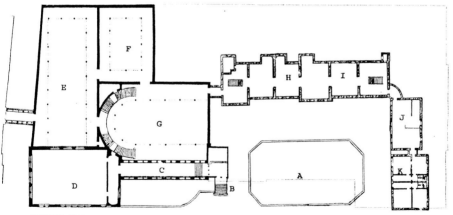

GROUND FLOOR PLAN

A.ARGYLE SQUARE **B.**ENTRANCE **C.**CORRIDOR **D.**LECTURE ROOM
E.NATURAL HISTORY HALL **F.**SMALL HALL **G.**GREAT HALL
H.EDUCATIONAL COLLECTION **I.**AGRICULTURAL COLLECTION
J.AGRICULTURAL COLLECTION **K.**OFFICE

Figure 4.7 Francis Fowke, Edinburgh Museum of Science and Art, plan, 1867. Drawn by Michael Piga.

from contemporary Germany, where the *Rundbogenstil*, a round-arched basis of design, was then being used in the educational centers of Munich and Berlin. The authority of German architectural style had trickled down to Fowke through Prince Albert, who was German himself, and who encouraged Cole to study the cultural centers of German cities as models for South Kensington. Fowke's designs for the Edinburgh Museum were an earlier attempt to adopt the flexible, utilitarian, contemporary German style to a Scottish purpose. Since the museum was a cultural institution, as were many of the *Rundbogenstil* buildings in Munich and Berlin, Fowke's use of the style was reasonable and well informed.[34]

The design for the full facade of the Edinburgh Museum, released to the press at the time of the laying of the cornerstone in 1861, was intended to illustrate the geology of Scotland, thus imitating the Museum of Practical Geology, the Trinity College Museum in Dublin, and the University Museum at Oxford. The *London Journal* compared the design for the Edinburgh Museum to the much more elaborate University Museum at Oxford:

> We understand that the capitals . . . are to embody representative illustrations of the natural history, industry, and geology of Scotland, in a similar manner to that which was so successfully carried out by Messrs. Deane and Woodward, architects, at the new museum, Oxford, which we have already illustrated in our pages. In the carrying out of this somewhat remarkable building, it is further proposed by its promoters to illustrate the granites and porphyries of Scotland by inserting from time to time specimens of these special materials in wide spaces provided for them between the coupled columns of the principal fronts of the elevations.[35]

The reporter for the *London Journal* described inlaid panels of granite and porphyry, and the *Daily Scotsman* also acclaimed the geological display planned for the museum's facade, saying it would 'be ornamented with stone of distinctive colour, selected from various quarries in Scotland. Practically, this feature will in itself form a geological museum.'[36] This proposed characteristic – built-in, didactic, polychromy – is one of the few traits that Fowke's museum might have held in common with Deane and Woodward's. The Oxford rhetoric about nature as natural theology is absent from discourse about the Edinburgh Museum. And the Edinburgh Museum was funded by taxpayers, so the builders were forced to make cutbacks. Unfortunately, the porphyries and marbles were eliminated from the Edinburgh Museum as built, probably to save money.

THE MUSEUM AS BUILT

After the first phase was completed in 1865, the museum, in its truncated form, served visitors until the main block opened in 1875; Matheson was again the project architect. The final phase of construction, under the guidance of another local architect, W. W. Robertson, took place from 1885 until 1889; only then did the structure reach Fowke's expectations – an imposing block-long museum. As visitors approached the completed structure, they saw the two-storey central block set back between three-storey projecting wings (Figures 4.8 and 4.9), and reached the main entrance by climbing broad steps from the street. The channelled foundation accommodated the steep slope of Chambers Street. Columns of red sandstone in the

Figure 4.8 Francis Fowke, Edinburgh Museum of Science and Art, exterior view, 1861–89. © The Trustees of the National Museums of Scotland 1999.

Figure 4.9 Francis Fowke, Edinburgh Museum of Science and Art, exterior, 1861–89. Photograph by the author.

arcades of the second storey, which contrasted with the gray stone of the rest of the building, were the only coloured stones in the facade, a vestige of the more elaborate constructional polychromy mentioned in the papers in 1861; they still serve as both architectural elements and geological specimens. Ornamentation was otherwise sparse, limited to the inscriptions 'Natura,' 'Ars et Scientia,' and 'Industria' beneath personifications of Nature, Art and Science, and Industry, grouped in a triangular composition. Six medallions above the doors, added during the second or third phase of building, contained portrait busts of Michelangelo, James Watt, Queen Victoria, Prince Albert, Isaac Newton and Charles Darwin. The Queen and Prince were represented as patrons, and the others were inspirational exemplars. The image of Watt, the eighteenth-century inventor of the improved steam engine and the only Scot represented, looked across the road at the Heriot-Watt College (now University), a school named in Watt's honor in 1851, for teaching practical science to tradesmen. Michelangelo, the only artist, was the odd-man-out, but his presence on the facade indicates the flexibility of Victorian definitions of art: Michelangelo represented the 'art' in 'industrial art.' In spite of the fact that there was a fine art museum across town, Fowke unselfconsciously included Michelangelo to bolster the image of industrial art.

Fowke's plan was almost symmetrical. The Great Hall, which ran parallel to the facade, was the focus of the plan; other galleries were clustered around it on the rear

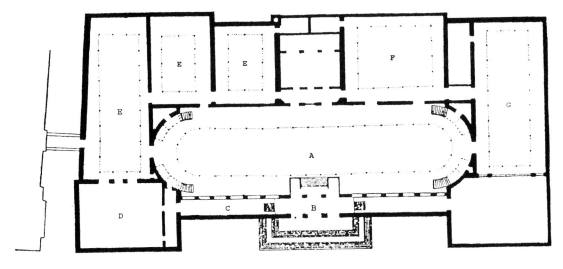

A.GREAT HALL   B.ENTRANCE   C.CORRIDOR D. LECTURE ROOM
E.NATURAL HISTORY EXHIBITIONS   F.MINING AND METALLURGY
G.MACHINERY
GROUND FLOOR PLAN

Figure 4.10 Francis
Fowke, Edinburgh
Museum of Science
and Art, plan, 1861–
89. Douglas A. Allan,
*The Royal Scottish
Museum 1854–1954*
(Edinburgh, Oliver
& Boyd, 1954).
Drawn by Michael
Piga.

and sides (Figure 4.10). The Great Hall enclosed a large, light, airy space, with its pitched roof on delicate timber arches (Figures 4.11 and 4.12). An arcade marked the upper balcony. Originally the tile pavement of the hall was a mosaic of strong colours. The natural history collections were in a long, thin side room with a balcony, also with a distinctly exhibition-style appearance (Figure 4.13).

The mostly iron and glass interior was a physical acknowledgment of the Edinburgh Museum's ideological precedent, the Crystal Palace. Fowke's decision to model its interior on the Crystal Palace was as appropriate as it was obvious. Ferro-vitreous construction was evidence of engineering achievement. The structure itself became part of the museum display as well as part of the entertaining spectacle. Furthermore, this architectural setting for natural objects – a popular show-place like the Crystal Palace rather than a somber museum – suited the commercial emphasis of the Edinburgh Museum's founders and accurately represented the goal of the Board of Trade, the promotion of industry. It did so at precisely the same time the Oxford Museum was proclaiming a different definition of nature, that of nature as God's second book. At Edinburgh, nature was defined as raw material for capitalization by Scotland.

Fowke's later design for the Natural History Museum in London will be discussed in the following chapter, but it is important to note here that, a few years later, critics denounced Fowke for designing a natural history museum that looked too much like the Crystal Palace – too much like a 'bazaar.'[37] But at Edinburgh, the museum founders deemed the exhibition-style building in Scotland well suited to a museum that championed commerce and industry. The Edinburgh Museum of Science and Art did not devalue natural history, but rather presented nature in the company of other, less lofty, objects of knowledge.

Museum theorist Tony Bennett notes that in department stores (like the Bon Marché in Paris) and many museums, the same architectural principle recurs. He argues that centralized buildings with balconies allowed 'the visitors to be the

Figure 4.11 Francis Fowke, Edinburgh Museum of Science and Art, interior, 1861–89. Photograph by the author.

objects of each other's inspection,' and also that 'a public displayed itself to itself in an affirmative celebration of its own orderliness in architectural contexts which simultaneously guaranteed and produced that orderliness.'[38] The main hall of the Edinburgh Museum resembles both the Bon Marche and the Bethnal Green Museum (the children's museum that was originally an offshoot of the South Kensington Museum, later the Victoria and Albert), but this similarity can be explained in many ways. First, many architects at the time believed that these types of buildings required diffused toplighting; a balcony allows more objects beneath the skylight. Second, as Bennett points out, it was difficult to keep track of visitors in old, maze-like buildings such as the Tower of London, but several people mingling in a large unified room are likely to keep watch on each another. Apparently the architectural form that best preserved the objects of national heritage also best prevented shoplifting. These architectural overlaps pose a theoretical problem only when one institution wishes to distinguish itself from another. Department stores benefitted from the association with art museums, for it gave them prestige and a civic presence. The Edinburgh Museum demonstrated to visitors how saleable objects were made by

Figure 4.12 Francis Fowke, Edinburgh Museum of Science and Art, 1861–89, interior *c.* 1890. During this period the main hall was filled with casts of architectural sculpture and the second-floor exhibition featured decorative arts. © The Trustees of the National Museums of Scotland 1999.

Figure 4.13 Francis Fowke, Edinburgh Museum of Science and Art, 1861–89, interior showing side room where natural history collections were installed; Fowke later bragged that his design allowed for the hanging of this large whale skeleton, seen here from the tail end. © The Trustees of the National Museums of Scotland 1999.

Scottish industry, and department stores, in turn, sold some of the same kinds of objects. Both were part of the same process.[39] Thus the architecture of the Edinburgh Museum emphasized the link to stores, shopping arcades, and World's Fairs, to make its support of trade clear.

The supporters of the national museum shared a conception of education based on the assumption that a museum could teach by the mechanism of display. Unlike today's science museums, which draw visitors in with interactive displays (buttons to press, dials to turn, and touch-sensitive computer screens), Victorian museums were founded on the belief that visitors would learn by simply looking at a selection of exemplary objects. At the Edinburgh Museum of Science and Art, industrial and decorative arts, including many objects similar to those that had been on view at the Crystal Palace (such as metalwork, porcelain and patented engines) were crowd-pleasing attractions. Next to these commodities, natural substances from which products could be made – especially rocks and ores – were exhibited with additional geological specimens, including fossils. Since fossils provided information on the age of the earth and its extinct and living inhabitants, geology was linked to zoology. Skeletons, stuffed animals, and animals preserved in spirits, completed the zoology department. The boundaries between natural science, art and industry were made flexible: as Adam White had written in 1850, in the earliest proposal for a Scottish national museum, natural history was made 'co-extensive with art and science.'[40] Thus the categories of 'art,' 'science' and 'industry' were fluid Victorian intellectual constructions that emerged within an educational system that promoted Britain's national industrial agenda.

CONCLUSION

Prince Albert died in 1861, two months after he had laid the cornerstone for the Edinburgh Museum of Science and Art. It was his last public act, and an especially regrettable turn of events for an institution closely allied to the Prince's widely known passions for education and industry. At the cornerstone ceremony, Albert had captured the spirit of the new museum, announcing that it was a practical teaching institution for university students that would at the same time stir the excitement of casual visitors:

> It is particularly gratifying to me to think that in the institution of which I am to-day to lay the first stone the education object will be kept specially in view – that your Museum will not be a mere receptacle of curiosities to excite the wonder to stir the interest of casual visitors, but that by its immediate connection with the University, it will afford the means of supplying the student with practical illustrations of what he has been taught in his class-room.[41]

Albert's reference to practicality showed his approval of German universities, and suggested that Edinburgh was ahead of Oxford and Cambridge. Francis Fowke had responded well to the program of the Edinburgh Museum of Science and Art, recognizing the industrial bent of Scottish education, the ideals of the museum's founders, and the needs of the public. Historians usually give Benjamin Woodward credit for beautifully expressing the function of the Oxford Museum in its form; an assumption that historians know *what nature was* lies beneath any claim of Woodward's success. But the case of the Edinburgh Museum proves that we cannot be sure we know what nature meant to the Victorians, because definitions of nature were local. Francis Fowke also expressed the function of his museum, as the architecture of display. But he proceeded from a different definition of nature – that of nature as resource for trade. Fowke's exhibition-style Museum of Science and Art combined natural history, industrial arts and decorative arts both for the promotion of commerce and for the edification of the middle class.

chapter 5

Nature in Conflict

The Natural History Museum in London

> A vast Bazaar, like the Crystal Palace, or the International Exhibition Build-
> ing, however suitable for other purposes, is not adapted for those of a Natural
> History Collection; – specimens lose scale and importance, the casual visitor
> is bewildered, the student is interrupted, and the display sinks from the
> character of science to that of show. (Robert Kerr, Architect, 1864)

The architectural history of the Natural History Museum in London culminates
many of the themes of this book: scientists and architects debated the scope of the
displays, the suitability of exhibition-style architecture, and the appropriateness of
ecclesiastical imagery for a museum. Historians of science Steven Shapin and Simon
Schaffer encourage the study of scientific controversies, because such moments in
science offer historians a valuable way to distance themselves from history, a way of
maintaining a 'stranger's' perspective on intellectual frameworks that are today
taken for granted: 'Historical instances of controversy over natural phenomena or
intellectual practices . . . often involve disagreements over the realities of entities or
propriety of practices whose existence or value is subsequently taken to be
unproblematic or settled.'[1] In the case of late Victorian natural history, evolution is
the theory that came to be settled, or came to seem 'real.' Beginning in the 1850s,
Richard Owen and T. H. Huxley, a middle-class secular evolutionist of the younger
generation, debated the breadth of the museum's displays, with Owen proposing an
encyclopedic museum of the entire imperial collection, while Huxley preferred a
small didactic museum for the public and a private research centre for naturalists.
Just after the competition in 1864, the architect Robert Kerr and the engineer
Francis Fowke disagreed about the extent to which exhibition-style architecture
should encroach upon museum designs, revealing a tension between the ideas of
the museum as showplace and the museum as scientific research centre. Finally, the
reception of the museum's architecture in newspapers and journals will reveal the
depth of the conflict surrounding the museum (especially its ornament and nave-like
central hall) around the time of its opening day in 1881.[2]

THE PROGRAM AND PRELIMINARY PLANS

When in 1856 Richard Owen became Superintendent of Natural History at the British Museum, he was already an impeccable authority on both natural history and museum design, having supervised the museum at the Royal College of Surgeons in London.[3] Owen believed that the purpose of a natural history museum was to show the greatness of God in the variety of nature. Owen's first task at the British Museum, which at the time subsumed today's Natural History Museum, was to secure government funds for the national natural history collections, and to persuade Parliament to allow the division of the collection into two parts: antiquities and natural history. Anything made by human hands would remain in Bloomsbury, thus enforcing a boundary between God-made and man-made objects, to use Victorian terms. The kind of objects usually displayed in many of today's anthropology museums – carved masks, textiles, canoes, and the like – did not promote natural theology and would have been out of place in Owen's proposed museum.

In 1858 more than a hundred naturalists (probably encouraged by Owen) signed a letter to the Chancellor of the Exchequer, Benjamin Disraeli, complaining of inadequate space for natural history at the British Museum. Too many specimens were out of sight in damp storage areas, and even the objects that were on display, like ornithology, pictured in the *Illustrated London News* on Easter Monday 1845, were overcrowded (Figure 5.1). Men of science concurred that natural history needed to be removed from the British Museum, but this removal led to conflicts over the possible division of the museum into popular and working collections, and the site of these two parts.

Owen was eager to improve conditions, raise money, and organize a new museum, but first he had to contend with skeptics in the scientific community, particularly Huxley.[4] Unlike many Victorian naturalists, Huxley lacked personal wealth, and at

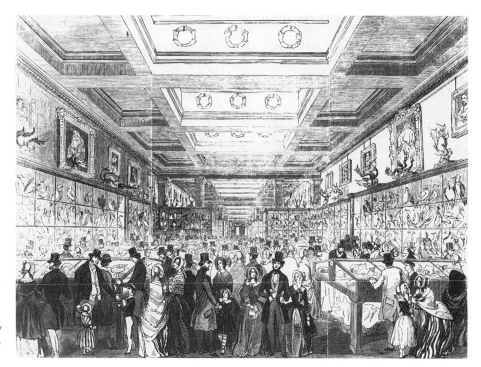

Figure 5.1 Robert Smirke, British Museum, interior, Great Zoology Gallery. *Illustrated London News* 6 (29 March 1845) 201.

first found it difficult to earn a living, although by the end of his career he held several important appointments including Naturalist to the Survey and various lectureships at the Royal School of Mines, where he devoted himself to educating working people. His lectures emphasized the value of objective science and freedom of thought for the daily lives of ordinary citizens. Huxley detested Owen, even though Owen himself had not inherited his wealth. Huxley told his wife Nettie: 'If I hate a man, I despise him,' and he detested no one more than Owen.[5] Throughout the second half of the nineteenth century, Huxley promoted a secular and progressive view of science, which made him a leader among the young men who pursued science as a paid profession rather than a gentlemanly vocation.[6]

In a petition from November 1858, Huxley and eight like-minded men of science, including Charles Darwin, urged that the zoological collections in the British Museum be divided into two major parts: a study series for men of science near the zoo and a popular series in South Kensington, the suburb Prince Albert had promoted as a cultural centre for London since 1851, the year of the successful Great Exhibition.[7] As Huxley wrote to Joseph Dalton Hooker, director of the botanical gardens at Kew:

> The best thing, I firmly believe, would be for the Economic Zoology and a set of well selected types to go to Kensington ... [T]o have a grand scientific zoological and paleontological collection for working purposes close to the Gardens [the Zoological Gardens in Regent's Park] where the living beasts are, would be a grand thing.[8]

Huxley envisioned the extensive scientific collections, bones and folded skins, stored in the drawers and cabinets of a facility where naturalists could conveniently compare specimens to living animals. In accord with Huxley, Darwin saw stuffing skins and rebuilding skeletons as crowd-pleasing techniques and proof of 'a sort of vanity in the curators.'[9] This remark was pointed at Richard Owen, who wanted to reconstruct beasts for a unified, large, encyclopedic museum that would serve as an ideal model of Creation.

The naturalists' discussion over the site reveals anxiety concerning administrative power. Huxley wanted men of science, not bureaucrats, to control the natural history collection, and he believed only the popular collection should be moved to South Kensington, the domain of the government-run Department of Science and Art. As he complained to Hooker: 'I should be sorry to see the scientific collection placed under any auspices as those which govern the "Bilers," ' as he called the Brompton Boilers, in a Cockney accent.[10] The Brompton Boilers housed the South Kensington Museum of decorative and industrial arts managed by the Department of Science and Art, later the Victoria and Albert Museum. Hooker recommended to Huxley that they keep the collections near the zoo not only because of the animals, but also 'to keep out of the K[ensington] Gore people's clutches.'[11] Owen did not originally favour the move to South Kensington either, but the grand size of his intended museum precluded the purchase of land in costly central London.[12] Men of science opposed the move to South Kensington, considered a site for educational museums and spectacular exhibitions like the Crystal Palace, because it signalled their loss of administrative control. In the next few years, Huxley would lose a major battle to Owen: a single unified museum, where the public and naturalists would have equal access to the entire collection, would be planned for a South Kensington site. To some observers, a then-distant suburban site in South Kensington was an illogical choice for the natural history collections, which attracted a working-class audience that in fact lived closer to Bloomsbury.[13]

Site selection continued until January 1860, when the British Museum trustees met to discuss Owen's request for increased space. By a margin of one they voted to move the natural history collections to a site in South Kensington then owned by the 1851 Exhibition Commissioners. Since Parliament funded these national collections, a Parliamentary committee was formed to discuss the political implications. In August 1860 the committee issued a report criticizing Owen's expansive museum, fearing it would overwhelm the public. Although William Gladstone, Chancellor of the Exchequer and a British Museum trustee, sided with Owen and drafted a supporting bill to move the collections, the legislation was rejected by the House of Commons in 1861.

Owen responded with *On the Extent and Aims of a National Museum of Natural History*, a booklet published in 1862, that argued for removal of all natural artifacts from the British Museum. He implored Parliament to grant funds for a modest new building, arguing that it was foolish to spend money to collect specimens when there was no place to display them: 'It is surely unworthy of a great country to profess to have its Museum of Zoology, and to publicly vote, year by year, the sums required for the purchase of specimens; and yet to postpone, year after year, the cost of the simple buildings requisite to render them available.'[14] Owen's primary interest was in planning, both in the arrangement of different-sized rooms and in the placement of the collections, and he never mentioned an exterior architectural design in the *Extent and Aims*. In 1862 his ambition was to get funding for his museum, and if he and Parliament could agree on anything, it was on economy as a virtue.

Owen claimed that visiting men of science would expect a nearly complete display of genera and species, but the sheer number of objects on view would also be a revelation for the public and could carry political meaning. Addressing the British Association for the Advancement of Science at Leeds in 1858, Owen underscored the link between British natural history and British imperialism:

> Our colonies include parts of the earth where the forms of plants and animals are the most strange. No empire in the world had ever so wide a range for the collection of the various forms of animal life as Great Britain . . . Naturalists consequently visit England anticipating to find in her capital and in her National Museum the richest and most varied materials for their comparison and deductions. And they ought to be in a state pre-eminently conducive to the advancement of a philosophical zoology, and on a scale commensurate with the greatness of the nation . . .[15]

Since the British empire's national museum was the only institution in the world that could amass and present such a collection, it followed that it was the empire's duty to do so. Thus the museum's imperial mandate was to assemble the exotic remnants of the colonial periphery. These collections, in Owen's mind, should not be hidden away in drawers and boxes as Huxley and Darwin preferred. Instead, the museum was meant to be an architectural setting that celebrated the act of looking and the ambition of a visible imperial archive. The impact of thousands of objects on view would communicate to foreigners and Britons alike the wealth of the empire in the powerful form of natural knowledge, whose claim to irreducible truth was thus associated with British rule. Furthermore, in his *Extent and Aims*, Owen had invoked the organic truth of nature when he compared his natural history museum to the huge industrial arts displays at world's fairs, claiming that it should

> not be forgotten that truth is something more important, more valuable, more enduring. Above all, the truth as it is in organic Nature; which, as it is slowly and surely evolved, seems, amongst other great ends, destined by Providence to be the instrument for the removal of those errors and misconceptions, which the blindness, pride, ignorance, and other infirmities of man have systematised and would sanctify, to the obscuration and distortion of the rays of divine and eternal truth which have been transmitted from Above for our guidance and support.[16]

Owen's belief in transcendent 'truth as it is in organic nature' echoes natural theology. He did not believe in the biblical account of Creation, or that the species were created all at once. Instead, he believed that Natural Law was an expression of God's will, and that new species could emerge consecutively. This 'continuous Creation,' as he called it, allowed for science to maintain its connection to 'the loftiest of moral speculations.'[17] Thus his life's work in science was to show the divine unity which lay beneath the diversity of animal structures, thus proving godly design.[18] For Owen, a natural history museum was morally superior to an industrial arts display because its ends were at once religious, scientific and imperial.

These arguments convinced neither Parliament nor the press. Newspapers mocked his request for room enough to hang seventy whale skeletons, and portrayed the rest of Owen's proposal as equally outlandish. The most extreme response came from William Gregory, the Member of Parliament for Galway, who regretted that 'a man whose name stood so high should connect himself with so foolish, crazy and extravagant a scheme, and should persevere in it after the folly had been pointed out by most unexceptionable witnesses.'[19] The remarkable irony of the museum's history is that in spite of criticism from politicians and opposition from naturalists, Richard Owen's personal determination and institutional power within the British Museum allowed him to emerge as the ideological leader of its planning.

How did Owen envision the home of natural history? The earliest surviving image is a plan he sketched in 1859 for the museum trustees that assumed 'a plot of ground including ten acres' (Figure 5.2).[20] Visitors would first enter a round room full of British natural objects and 'typical' collections, beyond which was a round theatre. The centrality of the British collection gave architectural expression to the nationalism of Owen's *Extent and Aims*. The typical collection, later termed the Index Museum, was an introductory guide to each branch of natural knowledge. To the left and right off the round room was ethnology, by which Owen meant the physical anthropology of human skeletons. Continuing to the left or right, the collections were laid out in galleries perpendicular to the facade, with mammals closest to the centre, and less complex organisms toward the edges.

THE COMPETITION

Owen's 1859 sketch would have a powerful influence on the final design of the museum. But before any architect could design a building, an existing structure had to be cleared out of the way. Gladstone, now Prime Minister, wanted to purchase the

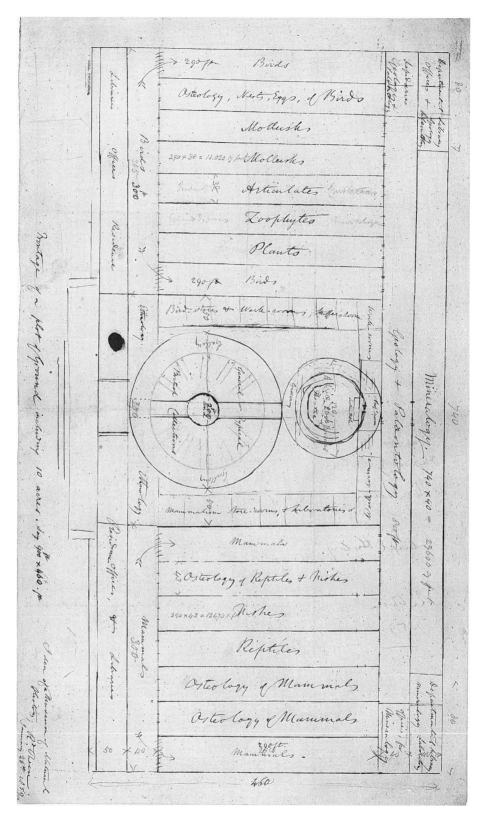

1862 Exhibition Building on Cromwell Road to house the natural history museum, along with a geological museum, a national portrait gallery, a patent museum and the Royal Academy. Not to be confused with the Crystal Palace or the Victoria and Albert Museum, the 1862 Exhibition Building, designed by the army engineer Fowke and since destroyed, was the exhibition hall for the second world's fair in London. Critics disliked Fowke's attempt to supersede the beloved Crystal Palace; reviewers compared its green glass domes to gooseberries, the *Building News* called it 'one of the ugliest public buildings that was ever raised in this country,' and the *Art Journal* remarked dryly that 'it is true that the whole building is large . . . but [its] magnitude serves only to bring out [its] prevailing mental littleness with more start-ling effect.'[21] Members of Parliament disliked Fowke's structure so much that they approved funds for the purchase of the land, but not the building, which was promptly demolished. The Office of Works subsequently approved an open archi-tectural competition for a patent museum and a natural history museum, announced in January 1864, and chose five judges – David Roberts, Lord Elcho, and architects William Tite, James Pennethorne and James Fergusson.[22]

Entrants were expected to prepare a scheme that could be built in several phases, and they were encouraged to consider the architectural context of South Kensing-ton.[23] An elaborate plan, prepared by Owen and his friend Henry Arthur Hunt, consultant surveyor to the Office of Works, was included with the competition instructions, but at the same time the guidelines encouraged the contestants to innovate: 'This plan is referred to for the purpose of showing the requirements of the Natural History Museum according to the view of Professor Owen, but without any intention of restricting the designs to a similar disposition of the required area, or to the forms and dimensions of the several galleries.'[24] Owen and Hunt recommended a three-storey building covering four acres. The lower two floors would be used for display, and the third floor for libraries and offices. Recognizing the importance of lighting, they suggested that the first floor be lit by windows facing narrow light-wells; these windows were to be ten feet off the ground with cases beneath them, against the walls.[25] On the second floor, light could have entered the galleries through similar windows or through a conventional skylight – Owen and Hunt did not specify which. Although the competition included both museums, the plan was for the natural history museum only (Figure 5.3). The Office of Works included a letter from Hunt to William F. Cowper, first commissioner of works, in the competi-tion announcement: 'The materials to be employed would be chiefly bricks, iron, and glass. The exterior . . . would be finished either with coloured bricks or Portland cement, with a proper and suitable amount of architectural decoration.'[26]

The Hunt and Owen plan provided for entrants was centered on a circular room for public lectures, rather than a grand hall as in Owen's earlier sketch. The visitor would have approached the lecture hall through a square vestibule containing twin staircases to the second floor. Most of the galleries, labelled with the collections they would house, were perpendicular to the facade. British natural history was located at the central part of the building (just behind the main hall), indicating its symbolic importance and the practical advantage of keeping this popular collection near the entrance. The labelling offered architects a wealth of information for designing the museum's interior, and indicated by its detail that Owen considered the arrange-ment of specimens to be a serious scientific consideration.[27]

Both the *Builder* and the *Building News* reported on the blind competition, which attracted 33 entrants. The *Builder* complained that many of the projects looked like

Figure 5.2 Richard Owen, Natural History Museum, plan, 1859. The Natural History Museum, London.

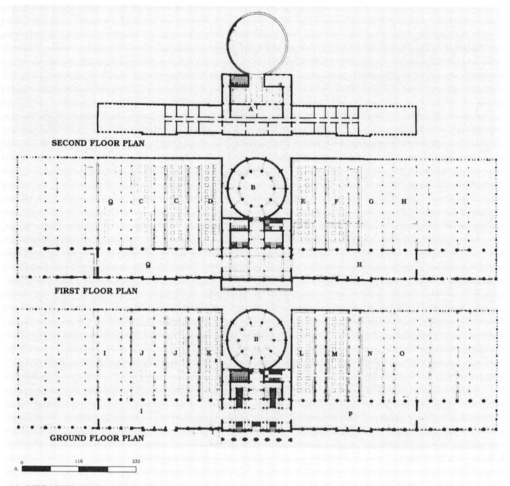

SECOND FLOOR PLAN

FIRST FLOOR PLAN

GROUND FLOOR PLAN

A. LIBRARIES **B**. THEATER **C**. MOLLUSCA **D**. EGGS AND NESTS OF BIRDS AND INSECTS
E. ARTICULATA **F**. RADIATA **G**. BOTANY **H**. MINERALOGY **I**. MAMMALIA **J**. MAMMALIAN
OSTEOLOGY **K**. ETHNOLOGY **L**. REPTILIA AND OSTEOLOGY OF REPTILES **M**. PISCES AND
OSTEOLOGY OF SAME **N**. PISCES **O**. GEOLOGY **P**. PALEONTOLOGY **Q**. AVES

Figure 5.3 Richard Owen and Henry Hunt, Natural History Museum, plan devised for the competition, 1862. Drawn by Naama Ferstenfeld.

the 1862 Exhibition Building, and feared its disastrous replication on its former site.[28] The *Building News* provided short stylistic descriptions of all 33 entries, giving special notice to the one labelled 'Well to build is well to buy,' which the reporter called 'an Italian style building remarkable for the purity of its detail' (Figure 5.4). This entry, by Robert Kerr, was notable for its repetitive round arches across the facade and its mansard roofs. The main block had a high central dome; two smaller pavilions were set in front of the main building. The competition also attracted two Romanesque designs, a 'Greco-Romanesque' entry, and a third design called 'a sort of early Romanesque, and yet there is a Byzantine element about it which will enlist another order of admiration from connoisseurs.'[29] But it could not be said that Romanesque, the style of the building that was ultimately built, dominated the competition. Only one pure Greek design, by Alexander 'Greek' Thomson, was submitted. The entry 'Ad ogni uccello . . . ' ('To every bird . . . ') which was 'illus-

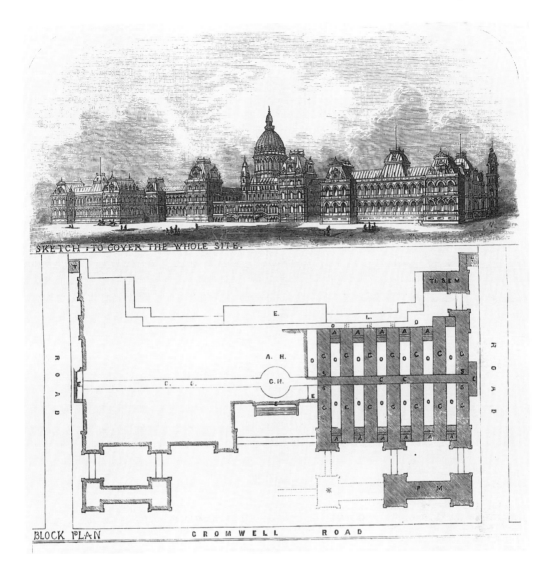

SKETCH TO COVER THE WHOLE SITE.

BLOCK PLAN CROMWELL ROAD

trated by a very taking perspective view, which no doubt will help to place it in the foremost ranks of the premiated,' was also reviewed with admiration.[30] Indeed, the *Building News* proved correct, and the entry with the most elaborate perspective drawing was not only 'premiated' (won some money) but actually won first place for the engineer Francis Fowke (Figure 5.5). The architectural journals indicate that a full stylistic range was represented, but sources do not reveal much more about the complexities of planning.

Figure 5.4 Robert Kerr, Competition entry for the Natural History Museum, exterior perspective and plan, 1864. *Builder* 22 (25 June 1864) 474–75. This design by Kerr was good enough for a second-place finish, but not a first prize.

FRANCIS FOWKE'S WINNING COMPETITION ENTRY

Since three of the competition judges – Tite, Pennethorne and Fergusson – had been outspoken critics of Fowke's 1862 Exhibition Building, it is especially ironic that he won the competition to replace his own maligned edifice.[31] Almost ten years later, Fergusson remembered the puzzlement he and the other jurors felt upon

learning that they had awarded first prize to Fowke, who 'was only known from some terrible things he had done at South Kensington':

> he was brought up as a military engineer, and set to work to design and carry out civil buildings before he had mastered the most elementary principles of the art. He failed of course; but ten years' experience – at the country's expense – had enabled him to remedy the defects of his early education, and his natural aptitude for the art at last enabled him to realise this very beautiful design. It was neither Grecian nor Gothic, but thoroughly nineteenth century; and had he lived and been allowed to carry it out with such ameliorations as further study would have enabled him to introduce, his building would have marked an epoch in the history of architecture in this country.[32]

Indeed, Fowke's plans for the Natural History Museum were monumental, displaying a confidence perhaps derived from his years of work in South Kensington, a neighborhood he helped build with the firm guidance of Henry Cole.

One of the best contemporary descriptions of Fowke's winning design was provided by his successor, Alfred Waterhouse (1830–1908), in a letter to the Office of Works:

> the Competition design prepared by the late Capt. Fowke consisted of a main rectangular block . . . having side-lighted galleries of two stories along the South, East, and West fronts within which were arranged 14 top-lighted Galleries with a Lecture Theatre in the Centre. Behind this block were the present buildings belonging to the Commissioners of 1851 looking into the Royal Horticultural Society's Gardens. In front of this Main building was arranged another block containing the Main Entrance and Staircase surmounted by a Dome 275 ft. high, with rectangular top-lighted courts on either side. East and West of this Central Entrance were two distinct buildings, the one intended for a Museum of Patents and Inventions, the other for a reserve museum.[33]

Operating on strict principles of symmetry, Fowke balanced the Patent Museum with an identical structure labelled 'reserve museum'; picturesque utility was no concern of his. A letter to the *Builder* protested that the entrants were supposed to

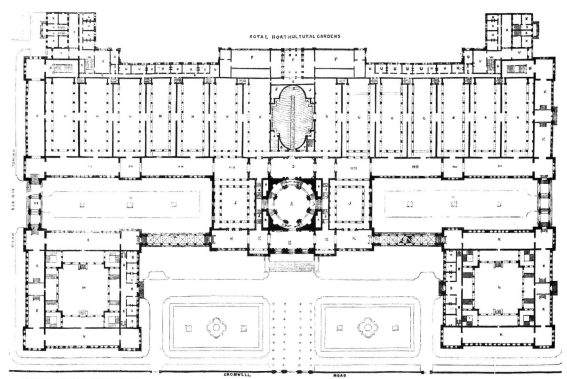

PROPOSED MUSEUMS, SOUTH KENSINGTON.—PLAN OF PRINCIPAL FLOOR, INCLUDING PROPOSED AFTER-APPROPRIATION OF THE WHOLE OF THE AVAILABLE LAND.

design only the first phase of building (estimated to be 600 feet long), but Fowke projected the image of a completed ensemble of buildings stretching 1,100 feet.[34] Fowke's drawing and its accompanying plan suggested a grand spatial sequence (Figure 5.6), perhaps influenced by historical plans known to him from Jacques Androuet du Cerceau's *Les Trois Livres D'Architecture* (Paris, 1559).[35] Climbing the front steps of the Natural History Museum, visitors would have walked through a domed entrance hall, possibly intended to be the Index Museum. From there they could either proceed on axis to the lecture room, or turn right (or left) into a range of seven galleries perpendicular to the Cromwell Road. Each would have been divided into three parts, a nave and two side aisles, with a balcony supported by an iron arcade. Each of these rooms duplicated on a smaller scale the main hall of Fowke's Edinburgh Museum of Science and Art with one gallery level instead of two (see Figure 4.13 in Chapter 4). A section drawing cut through the centre of the cupola depicted the double-height rooms with iron balconies on either side, and revealed (to Fowke's detriment, probably) an expensive, space-wasting entrance hall (Figure 5.7).

Fowke emphasized his lighting system and the clever addition of student rooms above the adjacent 'side aisles' of neighboring first-floor galleries:

> Each room is treated as a wide and lofty nave, with narrow side aisles separated from it by piers and arches, and lighted from above through ground glass in the haunches of a vault roof . . . Over each pair of adjacent aisles a smaller top-lighted room is obtained, communicating with a gallery which crosses the ends of the entire range of rooms on the first floor level.[36]

Figure 5.6 Francis Fowke, Competition entry for the Natural History Museum, plan, 1864. *Builder* 22 (18 May 1864) 394.

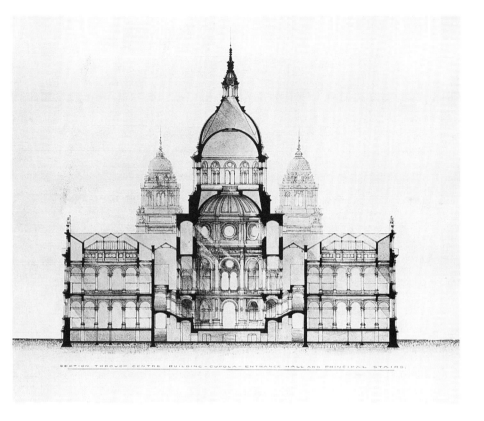

Figure 5.7   Francis
Fowke, Competition
entry for the Natural
History Museum,
section, 1864. This
transverse section
drawing is cut across
the rooms marked 'J',
'A' and 'J' (again) on
the plan. It therefore
shows only a small
portion of the
building: the
entrance hall, cupola,
and two exhibit
rooms. V&A Picture
Library, GF5656.

Special student galleries had not been included in the instructions, but were exactly the kind of rooms Darwin, Huxley and Hooker hoped for – rooms where men of science could scrutinize specimens without interference from meandering members of the public.[37] With the exception of Pennethorne, who had built the Museum of Practical Geology, none of the jurors were natural historians or museum experts, so it is difficult to know whether they picked Fowke's entry because they approved of its functional planning (which Fowke stressed in his description), or because they liked the exterior, or both. In any event, their choice did not please the museum trustees, who complained to the Office of Works that they preferred Robert Kerr's second-placed design.[38]

FOWKE VERSUS KERR: THE MEANING OF AN IRON AND GLASS 'BAZAAR'

Kerr's defense of his design reads today as an exceptional commentary on Victorian museum theory, in which he condemns exhibition-style buildings as inappropriate for science. Although the Crystal Palace, for example, was well loved by the public, such cheap buildings made of modern materials were at the same time disdained by architectural critics, notably John Ruskin. In a memorandum to the Office of Works, also published in the *Builder*,[39] Kerr impugned exhibition-style buildings as impermanent, inartistic and showy structures unsuitable for public institutions.

Branding Fowke's design for the Natural History Museum competition a 'bazaar,'

Kerr claimed that its scale would overwhelm ordinary citizens and hinder serious science students:

> [My own project] presents the *Gallery* principle, as opposed to the *Bazaar* principle so much favoured of later years. A vast Bazaar, like the Crystal Palace, or the International Exhibition Building, however suitable for other purposes, is not adapted for those of a Natural History Collection; – specimens lose scale and importance, the casual visitor is bewildered, the student is interrupted, and the display sinks from the character of science to that of show.[40]

In the *Builder*, Kerr further described a bazaar as 'a place of great height and width, surrounded by balconies and so on, lighted from the roof' – a description which fit not only the Crystal Palace and the 1862 building (Figures 5.8 and 5.9), but also the Edinburgh Museum of Science and Art.[41] Kerr may have known that Fowke had recently constructed this 'bazaar' in Scotland for the display of not only industrial art but also natural history. While Kerr judged that visitors would find the openness of a 'bazaar' bewildering, Fowke probably assumed that visitors to his proposed Natural History Museum in London, like the visitors to the museum in Edinburgh, would enjoy the expansive, spectacular spaces.

Kerr might also have been referring to R. and C. Osler's Gallery (Figure 5.10) (a shop for glass goods) on Oxford Street, or to the Crystal Palace Bazaar, both designed by the architect and colour theorist Owen Jones (Figure 5.11). The Crystal Palace Bazaar was a T-shaped shopping galleria with entrances on Oxford Street and John Street (now Great Portland Street). Its ceiling was made of stained glass held in place by fibrous plaster frames, suspended beneath an iron and glass roof.[42] This architectural special effect must have made shopping at the Crystal Palace Bazaar a dramatic experience. Given its commercial connotations, the word 'bazaar' implied that scientific artifacts would be commodified, compromising the moral and universal goals of Victorian natural history. Kerr assumed that a substantial architectural

Figure 5.8; Francis Fowke, Exhibition Building of 1862, exterior, London, 1862. V&A Picture Library, GX4069.

Figure 5.9 Francis
Fowke, Exhibition
Building of 1862,
interior before
installation of
exhibits. V&A
Picture Library,
Y.577.

structure – galleries with masonry walls, lower ceilings, and traditional lighting
through windows and skylights – would lend legitimacy to science, whereas a lightly
framed exhibition building would reduce the natural history displays to the level of
showmanship. The natural artifacts would remain the same whether placed in a
bazaar or a traditional museum, but to Kerr their meaning as *scientific* objects might
be lost in an exhibition building. This is perhaps the best proof of the claim made by
many sociologists of science: that knowledge gains legitimacy by its local associations. Kerr feared that the setting itself would alter the way the audience would
(literally) see the specimens, and that in a building that resembled a world's fair,
the objects would be degraded to the level of 'show' that was typical of those
exhibitions and private museums like Bullock's.

Fowke, a rather more simplistic thinker than Kerr, published his rebuttal in
December 1865, defending his own design and denouncing the light-wells of Kerr's
plan as 'damp mildew-generating wells,' like 'dank little streets, always open to rain
and rarely to sun, and containing masses of stagnant air.'[43] He did not address the key
issue (science versus showmanship) in his remarks – perhaps he didn't think it *was*
the key issue. For him, this was a planning issue. He concluded: 'the best method
of dealing with large areas devoted to Museums, is to entirely cover the area proposed to be dealt with; as opposed to the method of cutting it up with narrow courts
open to the air.'[44] In attacking Kerr for 'so much space thrown away' in the light-
wells, Fowke pointed out that he had just hung a whale skeleton, 80 feet long, in the
Edinburgh Museum (see Figure 4.14), and that there would be no room in Kerr's
proposed building for a similar specimen.[45] Indeed, Fowke was the more experi-
enced museum designer. But Kerr was the better theoretician. Where Fowke

Figure 5.10 Owen Jones, Osler's Glass Shop, interior, London 1859. Watercolour by Jones. V&A Picture Library.

concentrated on technical details, Kerr cleverly manipulated the discussion to reveal the cultural meaning of the bazaar as a place of bewildering commodification.

Both Kerr and Fowke claimed they had followed the competition plan, with Fowke noting on his drawings: 'This section shews the arrangement of the Model Plan prepared from Professor Owen's suggestions, and is as nearly as possible identical with it both in the disposition and dimensions of the rooms.'[46] Kerr, on the other hand, identified the key idea behind the competition plan as the 'gallery' system (objects arranged in a series of small rooms) as opposed to the 'bazaar' arrangement. To be fair, Kerr overstated the openness of Fowke's plan; although Fowke did cover the ground with one building, he had also broken up the space into smaller rooms, which would not have dwarfed the visitor like the huge, undivided interiors of the Crystal Palace and the 1862 Exhibition Building.

Even though the museum curators preferred Kerr's internal arrangements, the Office of Works kept Fowke and told him to rework the plan. Before Fowke could do so, however, he died at the age of 46. For reasons that remain unclear, the Office of Works gave the commission neither to Kerr nor to Fowke's assistant Liddell, but to Alfred Waterhouse, a young Quaker architect from the north of England with no prior connection to the project, but well known for his planning at the Manchester Assize Courts. Cowper had asked Waterhouse to write specifications for the Law

Figure 5.11 Owen Jones, Crystal Palace Bazaar, London, 1858. *Illustrated London News* (6 November 1858) 442.

Courts competition in December 1865, and he began the project but resigned three weeks later in order to fairly enter the competition himself.[47] Unlike Fowke, Waterhouse was an architect, not an engineer, and he was a devoted medievalist.

ALFRED WATERHOUSE: EARLY DESIGNS AND DRAWINGS

Waterhouse was hired in February 1866 to execute the designs of Captain Fowke, who had not begun the working drawings nor even written an estimate. By the end of that month, Waterhouse had accepted the commission, writing to Cowper: 'my best endeavors shall be used to carry out successfully this great National work.'[48] Even after his death, Fowke continued to influence Waterhouse, who travelled to Edinburgh in 1867 on Cowper's advice 'to examine the Museums there,' presumably Fowke's Museum of Science and Art.[49] Waterhouse later submitted a summary of expenses to the Office of Works, in which he listed 'visiting Dublin Gallery at the First Commissioner's suggestion' under costs incurred in 1866.[50] In Dublin he could have seen Fowke's National Gallery of Ireland as well as Frederick Clarendon's Natural History Museum, a long, thin, rectangular, skylit museum in the manner of Fowke's Natural History Museum proposal (see Figure 6.3).[51]

In February 1867 Treasury officials eliminated the Patent and Reserve Museums from Fowke's original project, leaving Waterhouse with only the Natural History Museum.[52] He retained Fowke's 14 parallel galleries, but changed their widths, alternating narrow rooms with wide. Where Fowke's Natural History Museum housed the round hall in a central projecting block, Waterhouse's new plan placed the round room within the main body of the building. Museum trustees approved this version of the plan in April 1868, but it was never carried out.[53] Throughout 1867 and 1868, hectic times in Waterhouse's office, he met with the keepers of each natural history department to learn about the building's function and refine the plans. He sent 10 drawings to the Office of Works in May 1868, along with a letter explaining the new plans. The curators had complained that the galleries were too lofty and too long, so he reduced the size of the rooms. The circular entrance hall with its grand staircase and the alternating narrow and wide galleries were retained. Following Fowke's wishes, and taking a cue from the Kensington setting, Waterhouse continued to use terracotta, the material for which he is best known.[54]

Two interior perspective drawings may have accompanied the letter. One looks down a transverse gallery (Figure 5.12). Waterhouse's letter described a gallery 'lit from the haunches of the vault,' which may have referred to this drawing.[55] Waterhouse had imagined this gallery as a paleontology and general osteology gallery, and the wall-cases are packed with skeletons.[56] At this point, the room is full of the bones of both living and extinct species (a giraffe and a mammoth can both be identified), although Richard Owen had wanted the displays divided between living and extinct species. The long rooms were broken up by sweeping half-round arches, and the gallery terminated with a slightly pointed arch in a rectangular frame. The all-over geometric patterning of the ceiling and arches suggests Byzantine as well as Romanesque precedents.

Figure 5.12 Alfred Waterhouse, Natural History Museum, interior perspective, *c.*1868. By permission of the British Architectural Library, RIBA, London, V13/6 2.

The companion drawing is more difficult to read (Figure 5.13). It suggests a view
of a transverse gallery toward the front of the building – the only part of the building
with windows as shown in the drawing.[57] The larger arch, and its surrounding beasts,
was the main feature of the drawing, and Waterhouse proposed the repetitive ornamental motifs that were easily manufactured from terracotta. A pair of deer stood on
plinths too high on the wall to allow inspection; beneath them Waterhouse imagined
places for two trophies. For these, as well as the gorilla and chimpanzee in active
poses on pedestals, Waterhouse drew relatively convincing depictions of stuffed
creatures. The three similar flattened figures, possibly seal skins, are decoratively
scattered, one on each wall. If Waterhouse's lively drawing was meant to capture the
spirit of a natural history museum, it leaned toward the depiction of the museum as
public entertainment rather than scientific research. These interior perspectives,
and the highly developed plan, show Waterhouse's progress in 1868, before the
project became side-tracked by a well-meaning but ill-fated scheme.

THE THAMES EMBANKMENT

When the Liberal Party returned to power under Gladstone in December 1868,
Henry Layard replaced John Manners as head of the Office of Works. Layard, the
archeologist responsible for major discoveries of Assyrian art, recommended moving
the museum from South Kensington to the centrally located Thames Embankment,
and thereby delayed the construction of the museum by a year and a half. The new
site lay between Charing Cross Station and Waterloo Bridge, on partly reclaimed
land. A Select Committee of Parliament met on May 3, 1869 to discuss the proposal,
and called upon an array of luminaries to give testimony. Three men of science,
Owen, Huxley and Sir Roderick Murchison (a geologist and the director of the
British Geological Survey) were asked whether naturalists in general would prefer

the Thames site to the South Kensington site. Alfred Waterhouse and Henry Cole were interviewed, too. Almost all of those giving opinions preferred the Thames – it was closer to central London, and the banks of the river offered an impressive location for a grand public edifice. Also, it was thought that the museum, never to be crowded by nearby buildings, would receive consistently high-quality light off the Thames. The site was smaller than that in South Kensington and thus raised questions about the number of storeys for the new building.

Although the meeting was ostensibly called to study the idea of moving the Natural History Museum to the Thames site, Huxley seized the opportunity to denounce Owen's encyclopedic museum. Huxley argued that before the committee could discuss the building, they must settle the question of whether it should display the entirety of its collections or be limited to didactic displays of selected specimens. Huxley had codified his theories of museum construction in a short pamphlet (published in January 1868) proposing a museum for the city of Manchester.[58] These ideas were closely related to those he espoused at the meeting to discuss the Thames Embankment site. In Huxley's ideal museum, a member of the public would have entered the building directly into a long gallery with natural historical exhibitions on either side, all behind glass. Carefully chosen type specimens – 'enough to illustrate all the most important truths of Natural History, but not so extensive as to weary and confuse ordinary visitors' – were to be the only items on display, while the rest of the museum's collections would be stored elsewhere.[59] Naturalists and students using his ideal museum could move about behind the glass, sharing space with the specimens. Huxley included a cross-section and an elevation of an interior wall in the pamphlet. The section diagram shows the 'curator's division,' also open to scientific students, at the far left; the 'public division' lies in the middle, with another curator's division on the right (Figure 5.14). A frontal view of a whale's skeleton dominates the case on the left side, while the elevation reveals the same skeleton from the side (Figure 5.15).

At the May 1869 meeting, Huxley argued that the public must be segregated from working men of science, and he insisted that all of his colleagues believed an encyclopedic exhibition would be an expensive nuisance:

> According to what Professor Owen has published, the demands for space which he makes are based upon the principle of exhibiting all specimens, of allowing everything to be seen by the public. I do not desire to dispute the weight which ought fairly to be attached to Mr. Owen's judgment, but as a matter of fact, all of us who are conversant with the organization of museums are on the other side; we maintain that the carrying out of that principle would involve an enormous unnecessary outlay, that it would make the collections wearisome, and of very little use to the public, and would at the same time, interfere with their usefulness to the working men of science.[60]

Layard agreed with Huxley on one question, indicating that there might be a way for naturalists to inspect the specimens without public interference:

> [I have had] the opportunity of speaking with you privately on this matter, and we discussed a plan to make the specimens accessible at the same time to the public and to students, by so arranging the cases that there should be a

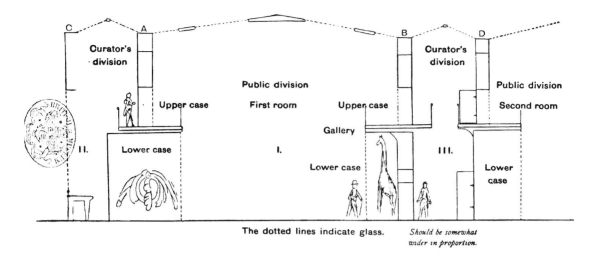

The dotted lines indicate glass.   *Should be somewhat
                                      wider in proportion.*

Figure 5.14 Thomas
H. Huxley, Proposed
museum for
Manchester, Section,
1858. *Suggestions for a
Proposed Natural
History Museum in
Manchester* ([1868]
reprint, London:
Report of the
Museums
Association, 1896)
fig. 1, p. 128. By
permission of the
British Library,
AC2672/9.

passage behind them in which students could remove and examine the
specimens.[61]

In spite of Huxley's strong claims, however, Layard supported Owen on the essential point of whether the entire collection should be on display. Even so, upon hearing that Layard had conferred with Huxley, Owen must have felt that Huxley had undermined his power. At the Thames Embankment meeting, Layard presented a plan quite close to Huxley's own Manchester Museum model: the same specimens could be on view to both the public and scientific students in two-sided cases, sealed on the public side only, so that students could handle and examine the specimens from their private corridors. One problem with this arrangement was that members of the public were likely to watch naturalists at work; naturalists saw this as a distraction, since they would become part of the display. Yet this would have been an improvement over the British Museum, where bystanders crowded around the men of science as they opened drawers and handled specimens.

Waterhouse brought only 'block plans' to the Thames Embankment meeting, but he later developed its elevation; a perspective sketch in pencil indicates his enthusiasm for the splendid site.[62] He added a basement level to the 1868 layout, heightened the structure, crowned the new composition with a central dome, and, rather daringly, curved the building to fit the contour of the river (Figure 5.16).[63] A visitor standing at one end of the long galleries at the front would have seen the myriad specimens gently disappearing from view. Waterhouse described the plan to Layard in 1869: 'in the present plan the Student's Rooms are all placed side by side with the Galleries, immediately behind and having direct access to the wall-cases of Specimens – an arrangement considered by Prof. Huxley and others as of the greatest importance.'[64] Waterhouse asserted the river's 'superiority as a Site for the effective display of a great Architectural Work,'[65] but a Romanesque Revival spectacle on the Thames was never to be seen. Layard's successor as first commissioner, a notoriously parsimonious Liberal, Acton Smee Ayrton, cut the Natural History Museum's budget, necessitating a move back to the South Kensington site. The drastic cut, from £500,000 to £330,000, forced Waterhouse to concentrate on the museum's

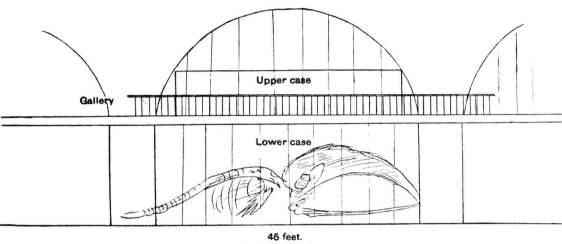

Gallery

Upper case

Lower case

45 feet.
Whale 50 feet long.

front facade. He temporarily ignored the building's back and sides, perhaps expecting to ornament them later. One of Waterhouse's most important changes, made some time around 1869, was to eliminate the round entrance hall and theatre, which he replaced with a spacious hall, similar to the nave of a Romanesque church. In a large perspective of the interior, Waterhouse depicted this hall as the Index Museum (Figure 5.17). The contrast to the earlier interior perspective drawings is clear: this is not a cluttered ensemble of architectural ornament, bones and stuffed animals. In fact, Waterhouse omitted specimens where they should have been; Owen had expected the Index Museum to contain a number of large stuffed animals and skeletons, including a whale, elephant, megatherium, giraffe, moa, and giant Irish deer, which would have been placed on the floor in the central space.[66] In Waterhouse's drawing, however, the central space is empty, emphasizing its quiet, somber, church-like quality. Type specimens, elephants and camels among others, are tucked neatly into the side chapels.[67]

Figure 5.15 Thomas H. Huxley, Proposed museum for Manchester, Elevation of interior wall, 1858. *Suggestions for a Proposed Natural History Museum in Manchester* ([1868] reprint, London: Report of the Museums Association, 1896) fig. 2, p. 130. By permission of the British Library, AC2672/9.

THE NATURAL HISTORY MUSEUM AS BUILT

The Natural History Museum, as finally constructed, was covered inside and out with shiny buff-coloured terracotta, accented in blue (Figures 5.18 and 5.19). Waterhouse approved of Fowke's plan to use terracotta to face the entire building, but since large, uniformly coloured blocks of terracotta were difficult to manufacture, a classical facade would be difficult to produce: the surface would have too many different hues and the blocks would be too small to evoke the massive quality of classical architecture. Terracotta was better suited to medieval revival styles because subtle gradations of colours and small blocks were common in the original historical sources.[68] He curtly described the style as 'the round-arched style common in Southern Germany so late as the 12th century,' asserting that it would 'afford both the grandeur and simplicity which should characterise a building of this description.'[69] By grandeur and simplicity, he was probably alluding to its symmetry and frontality. But he never spoke extensively about theoretical matters, and it is perhaps not surprising that he left historians with so

Figure 5.16 Alfred Waterhouse, Natural History Museum, exterior perspective for the Thames Embankment site, *c.*1869. By permission of the British Architectural Library, RIBA, London, WATA [41] 7.

few hints about his choice of German over any other round-arched medieval style.[70]

Victorian visitors to the museum entered the Great Hall, Owen's Index Museum, finding the British natural history collection directly behind it, on the far side of a grand staircase (Figure 5.20). Waterhouse's plan, like Fowke's and Owen's earlier versions, placed the Index Museum and British natural history collection at the core of the building; visitors saw those highly decorated rooms first, centrality indicating their importance. In Owen's arrangement of the Index Museum, the visitor would have seen humankind represented in the human skeletons which were to form the introductory ethnology display in the front western alcove, a mark of that collection's prominence as compared to other specimens. The final plan of the Natural History Museum, with perpendicular galleries arrayed like the spine and teeth of a comb, forced no linear path and frequently required retracing one's steps. The plan did not lend itself to linear processions, or to the unfolding of knowledge that might accompany such a procession.[71] The explanation for this comb-like plan lay in the Natural History Museum's dual character as public entertainment and scientific institution. The general public was supposed to look at the Index Museum and then browse the rest of God's creations, while scientific visitors and amateur naturalists would go directly to the gallery of their personal interest. These galleries, perpendicular to the facade, were not the lofty rooms with balconies Fowke had originally proposed (Kerr's bazaars), but lower galleries with windows at the haunches of the vault (Figures 5.21, 5.22, and 5.23).

THE ORNAMENT

Waterhouse's ornamental program for the Natural History Museum, like Woodward's in the Oxford Museum, depicted the natural world through illustrative detail.[72] On both the interior and exterior, extinct species were the models for ornament on the east side of the building, while living species were represented in the

Figure 5.17   Alfred
Waterhouse, Natural
History Museum,
watercolour drawing
by Waterhouse
showing interior
perspective of the
Index Museum,
*c.*1878. By
permission of the
British Architectural
Library, RIBA,
London, V13/6.

west and in the Index Museum. Waterhouse's drawings were transferred to clay by
the French sculptor Dujardin, from the firm of architectural modelers Farmer and
Brindley, who often worked with him on terracotta ornament.[73] Owen thought of
himself as responsible for the decorative program, telling the British Association for
the Advancement of Science that 'I took the liberty to suggest, as I had previously
done to Capt. Fowke, that many objects of natural history might afford subjects for
architectural ornament; and at Mr. Waterhouse's request I transmitted such as
seemed suitable for that purpose.'[74] Owen's scientific seal of approval was important
to Waterhouse, who encouraged him to visit the site to affirm the accuracy of the
depictions of extinct creatures. Waterhouse wrote 'I should feel greatly obliged if
you would take some early opportunity of calling at our Works at South Kensington
and looking at some models which Du Jardin [the sculptor] has prepared of Extinct
Creatures. Until you have seen them I hardly like to perpetuate them in Terra
Cotta.'[75]

   Although it is difficult to know what pictures of extinct creatures Owen gave
Waterhouse, scientific journals and books, including Owen's own publications,
included simple illustrations. Waterhouse was then free to shape the animals as he
wished. For example, the illustration of the paleotherium (an extinct tapir) in
Owen's *History of British Fossil Mammals and Birds* is a line drawing of the animal
in a simple pose (Figure 5.24). Waterhouse's terracotta paleotherium is similar but
more striking – its well-defined brow ridge gives its face a stern expression, and
it turns its head dramatically to look over its shoulder (Figure 5.25). Another

Figure 5.18 Alfred Waterhouse, Natural History Museum, exterior photograph. The Natural History Museum, London.

Figure 5.19 Alfred Waterhouse, Natural History Museum, exterior perspective, 1879–81. *Graphic*, 27 March 1880.

artistic transformation of a scientific source is seen in the pterodactyl on the cornice of the museum; the torso appears almost human, if not Michelangelesque, in musculature (Figure 5.26).

Men of science had studied prehistoric animals since the late eighteenth century, and the public was widely familiar with certain extinct mammals, especially the mastodon and mammoth. Dinosaurs were not as well known. When Owen coined the term 'dinosaur' in 1842, only four different species were recognized.[76] Owen did help popularize dinosaurs at the Sydenham Crystal Palace in 1854, the first large-

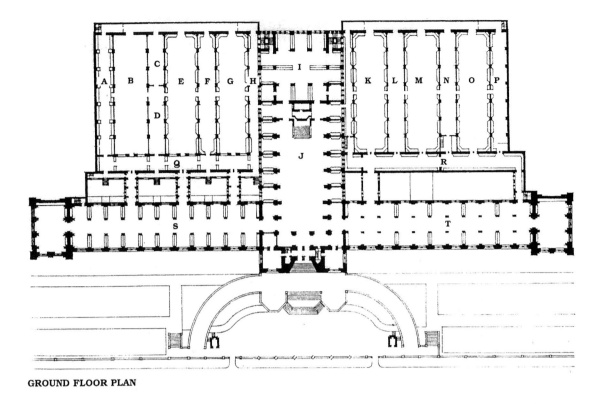

GROUND FLOOR PLAN

A. BIRD GALLERY   **B**. SHELL GALLERY   **C**. STUDENTS   **D**. STAR FISH GALLERY
E. REPTILE GALLERY **F**. INSECT GALLERY **G**. FISH GALLERY **H**. RESERVE GALLERY **I**. BRITISH
NATURAL HISTORY MUSEUM (ZOOLOGY) **J**. CENTRAL HALL **K**. FOSSIL FISHES **L**. GEOGRAPHICAL
COLLECTIONS   **M**. FOSSIL GASTEROPODA & CONCHIFERA **N**. GALLERY FOR STUDENT USE
O. FOSSIL CORALS, SPONGES, ETC. **P**. STRATIGRAPHICAL SERIES **Q**. CORAL GALLERY **R**. FOSSIL
REPTILIA **S**. BIRD GALLERY **T**. GEOLOGY & PALAEONTOLOGY

scale three-dimensional reconstructions of extinct animals. In a wonderful publicity stunt, we see Owen in one of his finest moments, hosting a dinner for fellow scientists inside an iguanodon made by sculptor Benjamin Waterhouse Hawkins (no relation to the architect). The *Illustrated London News* shows the outline of the heavy-set beast (Figure 5.27), but the dinner was actually held in a less glamorous mold.[77] In a gesture similar to the columns at the Museum of Practical Geology and the Oxford Museum, the specimen has become the display, science is the architecture. Owen and his naturalist friends try to inhabit science, but it eludes them: Huxley later denounced Owen's four-legged rhino-like iguanodon, and replaced it with a reconstruction in which the dinosaur stands on two legs like a kangaroo. In 1996 the iguanodon was reconstructed yet again as a four-legged animal, not exactly like Owen's but closer to his than Huxley's. Attempts to materialize science are our best record of changing scientific truths, and, in a wise decision, the Natural History Museum in London exhibited two different reconstructions to show these shifting notions.[78]

Owen helped Hawkins design ancient reptiles for a permanent exhibition at the

Figure 5.20 Alfred Waterhouse, Natural History Museum, final plan, 1879–81. Drawn by Naama Ferstenfeld, based on a plan that appeared in the *Builder* 44 (19 May 1883) 671.

Figure 5.21 Alfred Waterhouse, Natural History Museum, interior, Central hall with whale skeleton. The Natural History Museum, London, photograph taken in 1895.

Figure 5.22 Alfred Waterhouse, Natural History Museum, interior, Fossil Fish Gallery, showing original cases. The Natural History Museum, London, photograph taken in 1923.

Sydenham Crystal Palace Park, in which models were placed on an island in an artificial swamp (Figures 5.28 and 5.29). Given this earlier experience collaborating with artists, it is highly likely that Owen suggested that Waterhouse study Hawkins' sculptures.[79] Formal evidence also suggests that Waterhouse looked closely at a series of wall posters that Hawkins designed for the Department of Science and Art; Waterhouse seems to have copied the smallest pterodactyl (second from the left in

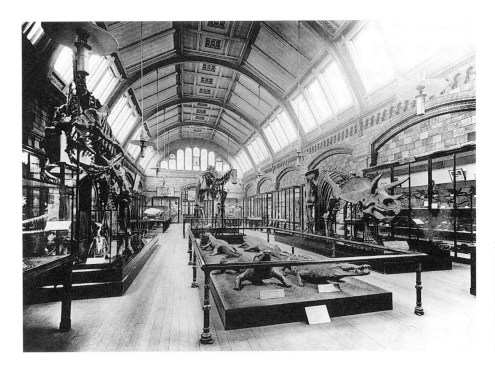

Figure 5.23 Alfred Waterhouse, Natural History Museum, interior showing diplodocus skeleton installed in a rear gallery. The Natural History Museum, London, photograph taken after 1905.

Palæotherium magnum.

Figure 5.24 Illustration of *Paleotherium magnum.* Richard Owen, *A History of British Fossil Mammals and Birds* (London: John Van Voorst, 1846) fig. 119.

the flock of four perched on the rock in the background of the drawing) in his designs for the facade ornament (see Figure 5.26) (Figure 5.30; detail, Figure 5.31). Both beasts, which the Victorians called 'prehistoric bats,' sit with their wings tucked behind their shoulders and their long jaws turned sharply to the right.[80] Waterhouse took some liberties with the depiction of each species, but Owen's approval still gave the ornamental representations scientific legitimacy. For less exotic animals, Waterhouse needed neither research nor Owen's primatur, and he depicted even the most familiar animals with a playful artistic flair. The domestic cat he showed enveloped with vines, with a stylized ruff around her neck, minding a mischievous kitten (Figure 5.32). The ornamental program of the Natural History Museum, and

Figure 5.25 Alfred
Waterhouse, Natural
History Museum,
drawing of
paleotherium, 1876.
Alfred Waterhouse,
'Pencil Sketches for
the Terracotta
Decoration of the
Natural History
Museum', vol. 1, fol.
58. The Natural
History Museum,
London.

Figure 5.26 Alfred
Waterhouse, Natural
History Museum,
exterior detail,
pterodactyl
ornament.
Photograph by the
author.

Figure 5.27 'Dinner in the iguanodon model at the Crystal Palace, Sydenham.' *Illustrated London News* 24 (7 January 1854) 22.

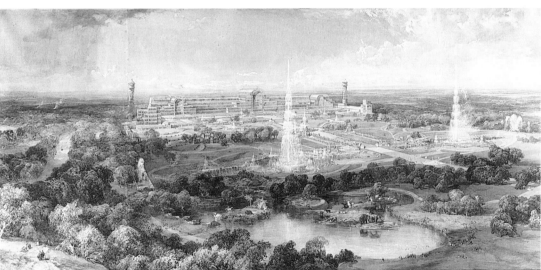

Waterhouse's artistic contribution, typify Victorian culture: buildings needed ornament to communicate and ornament was meant to teach.

Figure 5.28 Sydenham Crystal Palace, watercolour showing the second and larger Crystal Palace in the background, several fountains in the middle ground, and, in the foreground, the artificial swamp with its sculptures of extinct reptiles and mammals. British Architectural Library, RIBA, London.

THE CONTEMPORARY RECEPTION OF THE NATURAL HISTORY MUSEUM

The museum opened to the public on Easter Monday 1881. Because the communicative character of Victorian architecture was often specific and local, the reception of architecture is especially helpful in analyzing how contemporary audiences understood the meaning of buildings. Accounts of the Natural History Museum can be found in the architectural press, the scientific press, newspapers and travel guides; these accounts reveal how the architecture acted as a mediating force between science and its varied publics. The Easter Monday Bank Holiday was a

Figure 5.29
Benjamin
Waterhouse
Hawkins, sculptures
in the Sydenham
Crystal Palace Park
as they appeared in
1998. Photograph by
the author.

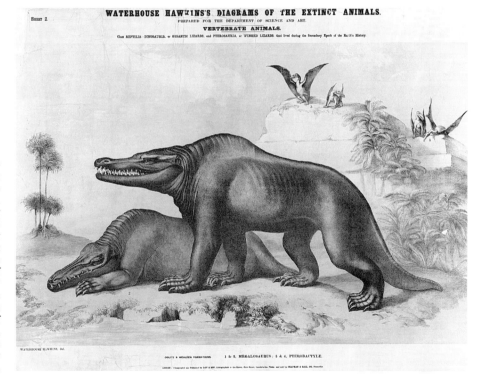

Figure 5.30
Benjamin
Waterhouse
Hawkins,
'Dinosauria, or
gigantic lizards, and
pterosauria, or
winged lizards, that
lived during the
secondary period of
the earth's history.'
Wall posters
commissioned by the
Department of
Science and Art,
sheet 2, *c*.1862. The
Natural History
Museum, London.

popular day for Victorian family outings, and a logical time to unveil the new building. Newspaper articles on opening day were probably compiled from a press release written by museum officials, since the articles tend to contain the same basic information about the building's size and style. If dinosaurs are the publicity draws for today's natural history museums, in the nineteenth century large stuffed mammals stole the show.[81] As disappointed reporters noticed, the mammals and birds had not yet been moved from Bloomsbury when the new museum opened.[82] Although there were several important fossils on display in South Kensington in 1881, none of these

Figure 5.31 Detail of pterodactyls in Figure 5.30.

Figure 5.32 Alfred Waterhouse, Natural History Museum, drawing of house cat, 1876. Alfred Waterhouse, 'Pencil Sketches for the Terracotta Decoration of the Natural History Museum', vol. 2, fol. 7. The Natural History Museum, London.

were mentioned in the daily newspapers on opening day.[83] Instead, newspapers focused on Waterhouse's decoration, which may have acted as the most immediate communication of the form of extinct animals – even more than fossilized skeletons – because, for the unscientifically trained, Waterhouse's artistic interpretations of the flesh, skin and countenance of extinct animals were more informative. One reviewer described Waterhouse's ornament with enthusiasm, concentrating on the extinct creatures:

> the vast monsters which dwelt in the dim twilight of prehistoric time look
> grimly down unconscious of any world but that of vast steaming swamps and

shallow lagoons, bordered by gigantic plants of species now embedded in the strata from which we extract heat and power. Great fish lizards and the strange bird lizard, whose misunderstood figure may have originated the fable of the dragon, are there, as well as the colossal armoured beast of South America and the hairy-elephant of that shadowy world which lived out its life ages before men dwelt in lake villages and made themselves weapons of stone.[84]

At first this ambivalent author made the ornament seem exotic with his evocations of dragons and steaming swamps, but he then assured readers that the form of the animals had been 'secured by scientific supervision':

> Such is the line of distinction to be rigidly maintained between extant and extinct organisms – a system of classification not easy to reconcile perhaps with many existing theories, but entitled to respect more on account of the scientific rank of those who have devised it than for any advantages apparent on the surface. One success has already been secured by scientific supervision. The animals and plants sculptured in terra cotta are like the organisms they profess to represent – the scientific mind of Professor Owen having rejected any images so modelled as to leave doubt as to their species.[85]

The reporter was aware that the division of the ornament into extant and extinct was difficult to 'reconcile with many existing theories,' a reference, of course, to evolution. He seems to be saying, in fact, that although the ornamental program might mislead the viewer by showing animals strictly divided into extant and extinct (with transitions ignored) Owen's 'scientific rank' superseded, or sidestepped, theoretical controversy.

The architectural press admired Waterhouse's efforts because he chose a style which suited the museum's purpose and because he successfully used terracotta. This view was summed up by the *Builder* in a preview of the building in 1878:

> But taking the building as a whole, its architect is to be congratulated on having produced a remarkable work, eminently suited to its intended purpose, and presenting, in the interior especially, unusual architectural interest both of *ensemble* and detail, and forming a very fine illustration of what can be done with terra-cotta as a material for architectural embellishment on a great scale.[86]

The phrase 'suited to its intended purpose,' typical praise for Victorian buildings, did not imply that the building would be perfectly adapted to the daily needs of the keepers, independent naturalists and students. Indeed, men of science like Huxley had been objecting to the building's plan since the 1850s. The important issue for this architectural critic was that the building's naturalistic ornament was suited to its purpose in an abstract sense: the form expressed the *concept* of a natural history museum. The *Magazine of Art* wrote similarly: 'The purpose and end of the building is disclosed by its design, which says, plain as a whisper in the ear, that this can be no other than a Museum of Natural History.' The analysis hinged in the end on religion:

> Glancing upwards over the whole field of its varied and orderly scheme of
> enrichment, the eye rests upon the consummation of the whole in the figure
> which terminates appropriately the highest gable. There standing erect, is
> seen the 'quintessence of nature,' with outstretched arms and upward gaze
> directed towards a still higher power.[87]

This 'quintessence of nature' was a statue of Adam at the peak of the gable. An
editorial in *The Times* compared the Natural History Museum to Noah's Ark, and
said the museum would restore an appreciation of the vastness of nature to city-
dwellers. Biblical references and spiritually tinged language were commonplace in
coverage of the Natural History Museum – in both art journals and newspapers, but
not in the scientific press. All would have agreed that the architecture should express
the concept of a natural history museum, but the concept was never fixed.

One of the most important publications for professional men of science was
Nature; *Nature* was not a general magazine, then, but the key journal for one 'party'
within science – those who actively followed Huxley. The first article on the
museum in *Nature*, from the week the museum opened, is a straightforward description of where collections were housed in the new museum; this location guide was a
practical necessity for naturalists who needed to find individual specimens. But after
more specimens had been transferred to the new building, the journal conducted a
critical review of the architecture:

> The first point which strikes a visitor at the present time is that a serious
> mistake has been made in the erection of a building with such elaborate and
> ornate internal decorations for museum purposes. Now that the cases are
> nearly all in position and the specimens are gradually being arranged in them,
> this incongruity between the style and objects of the building becomes more
> and more apparent.[88]

Nature also complained that the plan forced the display cases into dark corners, and
that the floor space was ill-used:

> On the one hand, it is clear that the form, position, and illumination of the
> cases has in many instances been sacrificed to a fear of interfering with the
> general architectural effect; and on the other hand it is equally manifest that it
> will be impossible to make full use of the floor space, and especially the best-
> lighted portion of it, without seriously detracting from the artistic effects
> designed by the architect . . . Again and again we find massive columns, beau-
> tiful in themselves perhaps, breaking up a line of cases, or throwing their
> contents into deep shade.[89]

Some of *Nature*'s complaints were rather vague – for instance that curators had been
afraid to interfere with 'general architectural effect.' But other complaints, such as
those about the shadows cast across cases, may have been recognitions of genuine
design flaws certain to emerge in a building of this scale. Another charge against the
museum was that the buff terracotta was too close in colour to the bone specimens:
'The peculiar tint of the terra-cotta, too, is far from being suitable for making the
objects of the Museum stand out in relief, and this is particularly manifest in the case
of the palaeontological collections, where a great majority of the specimens have a

very similar colouring.' The scientific audience found the architectural decoration to be unrealistic and baffling to the ordinary viewer:

> Nor is the wisdom apparent of bringing into close proximity natural-history objects with the conventional representations of them adopted by architects. The crowding together, on the same column or moulding, of representations on the same scale of microscopic and gigantic organisms, of inhabitants of the sea and of the land, and of the forms of life belonging to the present and those of former periods of the earth's history, seems to be scarcely warrantable in a building designed for educational purposes.[90]

The general complaint was that Waterhouse's building had too much character, which deflected attention from the scientific collection. Natural scientists, whose work relied heavily on the visual scrutiny of natural objects, apparently feared that visitors would look at Waterhouse's representations rather than the actual natural objects. The fabric of the building itself was to be educational, or at least not deceptive; if the ornament confused the visitors it was sure to offend the naturalists. Unlike the mainstream newspapers which appreciated the religious connotations of the architecture, *Nature* disapproved of the religious associations: 'Greatly as we admire the spacious hall, the grand staircase, the long colonnades, and the picturesque colouring of the whole building, we cannot but feel that the adoption of such a semi-ecclesiastical style was a mistake.'[91] *Nature* hoped the building would present science as accessible and secular, rather than exotic and religious.

Owen himself did not comment directly on the architecture's natural theological undertones, but he did admire Waterhouse's artistry, especially his choice of a Romanesque style, saying, 'No style could better lend itself to the introduction, for legitimate ornamentation, of the endless beautiful varieties of form and surface-sculpture exemplified by the animal and vegetable kingdoms.'[92] The phrase 'endless beautiful varieties' resonates with natural theological writings dating back to Paley, and it echoes Lord Wrottesley's exaltation of providential nature at the British Assocation meeting at Oxford in 1860: 'the beauties and prodigies of contrivance which the animal and vegetable world display, from mankind downwards to the lowest zoophyte, from the stately oak of the primeval forest to the humblest plant which the microscope unfolds to view.'[93] Owen, fortified by his personal philosophy based on natural theology, probably found the religious imagery of the central hall to be appropriate for the national natural history collections, which had been collected and displayed to show the diversity of Creation.

THE EXPRESSION OF ANTIQUATED SCIENCE IN THE MUSEUM'S PLAN AND ORNAMENT

When the museum opened in 1881, both the division of the ornamentation (into extinct and living species) and the encyclopedic planning were physical manifestations of antiquated science – almost none of Owen's contemporaries approved of the scientific concepts behind those two design decisions. When Owen retired in 1883 at the age of 79, he was one of last of his generation of scientific men; even his retirement notice in the London *Times* said so: 'It is possible that in dealing with such questions as now perplex and divide biologists, Professor Owen, who is a naturalist of the pre-Darwinian epoch, may be regarded by some of his junior contemporaries, who have sat at the feet of more adventurous teachers, as somewhat behind the age,'[94] and since Huxley thought Owen was old fashioned in the 1850s, he must have been desperate to see new leadership at the museum in the 1880s. Owen's successor was William Henry Flower, a friend of Huxley's and part of the mainstream of British science. Flower's accession to the directorship at the museum indicates that eventually Huxley's museum theory prevailed over Owen's. The idea that a museum should be comprised of carefully selected educational exhibitions, promoted by Huxley and others, is now almost taken for granted in museum practice.

Flower, at a meeting of the Museums Association in 1893, complained about the architecture of the new Natural History Museum, which he found unsuited to its function: 'Though [it is] a building of acknowledged architectural beauty, and with some excellent features, it cannot be taken structurally as a model museum, when the test of adaptation to the purpose to which it is devoted is rigidly applied.'[95] For Flower, the building's major flaw was that it was designed, following Owen's master plan, to display every specimen of the national collection, which for Flower was an absurdity similar to asking the British Library to display every page of every book, behind glass or hung on walls. Huxley and Flower are often represented as progressive middle-class men of science who rose in the ranks of Victorian society and ousted aristocratic naturalists from their chairs at universities and the directorships of major museums. This is indeed what happened when Flower took over the Natural History Museum at Owen's retirement.

Flower also denounced the museum's architecture for failing to recognize evolution, or at any rate, for doing nothing to break down the false, 'ancient' division between biology and paleontology, unmistakably represented on the facade of the building:

> For the perpetuation of the unfortunate separation of palaeontology from biology, which is so clearly a survival of an ancient condition of scientific culture, and for the maintenance in its integrity of the heterogenous compound of sciences which we now call 'geology,' the faulty organisation of our museums is in a great measure responsible. The more their rearrangement can be made to overstep and break down the abrupt line of demarcation which is still almost universally drawn between beings which live now and those which have lived in past times, so deeply rooted in the popular mind and so hard to eradicate even from that of the scientific student, the better it will be for the progress of sound biological knowledge.[96]

The museum's plan, which assigned living and extinct species to opposite sides of the central hall, enforced this demarcation. By the end of the nineteenth century, most biologists considered their science to be the study of the behaviour of organisms, not merely the study of form. Similarly, paleontologists reconstructed ancient plants and animals, categorized and named them – but paleontologists too sought to relate the extinct animals to the behaviour of living organisms. Therefore, the strict separation of extinct and living species did not accurately reflect the philosophy behind contemporary biology and paleontology. Flower felt compelled to reorganize the museum along more up-to-date lines, using carefully selected specimens to teach visitors lessons about nature. This was not merely an adjustment of Owen's encyclopedic concept, but an entirely new scheme erected within Waterhouse's walls.

CONCLUSION

Ironically, Owen's powerful leadership, coupled with the political obstacles and complex construction of any large public institution, insured that, as the decades passed, the museum's architecture lagged behind the visions of secular, evolutionist science. There are several disjunctions between the form of the natural history museum and its scientific currency in 1881 – its encyclopedic aims, the separation of living and extinct species, and its religious imagery were decades out-of-date in the opinion of most working men of science. Waterhouse and Owen worked together on a building which stood as a physical manifestation of early – not late – Victorian science. At the time of its opening, no working naturalist believed it was necessary or even valuable to exhibit every collectible natural specimen, nor did they believe in the separation of zoology from paleontology on the facade, a denial of decades of natural historical research showing the inter-relationship of extinct and living species. And the plan of the museum, which relegated living and extinct species to opposite sides of the Index Museum, showed nature cleaved in two. The Natural History Museum in London was an architectural spectacle, a grand public building, a break-through for terracotta decoration, and much more; but it was not a building which answered the needs of cutting-edge science. The development of the Natural History Museum in London encompasses more than decisions about site, program and style: the oppositions in its story prove that definitions of natural history ranged from the study of glorious Creation to the hard-headed advancement of secular science.

chapter 6

Still Life

Natural History Museums Today

The exhibition features dramatic moving models of a chimera, dragon, cyc-
lops, yeti, and an alien. Replicas of unique specimens from the Natural History Museum's collections help unravel fact from fiction and reveal the true
origins of these extraordinary creatures. (Web Site for temporary exhibition,
'Myths and Monsters,' Spring 1998, Natural History Museum, London)[1]

Richard Owen would have cringed at the thought of an exhibition titled 'Myths and
Monsters' at his beloved Natural History Museum. In 1998 the twin evils of superstition and showmanship are used to attract crowds to a museum that now must turn
in a profit. Even though the monster exhibition attempts to convince visitors that
mermaids and dragons are myth, not fact, the playful manipulation of the audience
within the walls of Waterhouse's building is ironic: the fun and freedom of world's
fairs have entered the hallowed rooms of the Natural History Museum after all.

Designing a permanent building for ever-changing science has never been easy.
Owen, Huxley and Flower were all seeking organic truth. But the architecture of
science stands as a reminder of the elusiveness of that truth – the buildings remain
fixed, but science moves on. The interiors of all the previously discussed buildings
were surprisingly inflexible; if a museum were broken up into small rooms, it would
be difficult for future curators to readjust the collections to fit the galleries. And if the
interiors were large and lofty, they carried associations with exhibitions and world's
fairs. Nineteenth-century naturalists sought to establish the study of the natural
world as a vital profession by lobbying for government sponsorship, academic societies, and permanent jobs at museums and universities. Professional science, from
the nineteenth century to the present, is mandated to constantly produce new knowledge. Delayed construction is common in the history of public institutions, but the
resulting awkwardness is all the more pronounced in a natural history museum,
because science depends upon currency for its legitimacy. This paradox arises in
almost any kind of architecture for science: one can hardly imagine a science
museum in a thatched cottage, with 'Ye Olde Exploratorium' posted over the door –
not even in Poundbury, the quaintly historical revivalist suburban town supported
by Prince Charles. Nostalgia – which has become the key design element in
suburban planning, housing, shopping malls and other building types – has no place
in the architecture of science.

DISPLAY STRATEGIES, THEN AND NOW

Owen was an opponent of Darwinism; and yet, in an event symbolic of scientific shifts, shortly after his retirement a statue of Darwin was installed on the landing of the grand staircase of the Natural History Museum. 'Darwin's Bulldog,' T. H. Huxley, gave a speech honoring his brilliant colleague at the unveiling of the sculpture, and the *Graphic* captured the moment, with Huxley standing at the foot of the statue while Darwin's stern likeness sits poised overlooking the museum's Great Hall – the space Owen had set aside for an Index Museum which would guide visitors in their exploration of Creation (Figure 6.1). In the 1920s, another shift occurred when museum officials replaced the Darwin statue with one of Owen. Today it is a material reminder that just as science constantly changes, so does the historical understanding of science. Darwin now sits in the café around the corner from the grand stair, in the area formerly the British natural history collection. Owen is once again revered, as he was during most of his lifetime, as a dedicated museum director and an effective leader. Since historians of science have begun to value the practice of ordinary or normal science, rather than individual men who made discoveries, a figure like Owen has re-emerged as historically central, even though his intellectual work was eclipsed by later biology.

Among historians, Owen now commands such respect, even though by the turn of the twentieth century his encyclopedic aims for the imperial natural history museum in London were out of fashion. In place of Owen's scheme, almost all museums switched to display techniques in which specimens were selected to illustrate a point, and visitors were taught lessons at each display. This didactic approach is now fundamental to museological practice, but it was by no means obvious in the eighteenth or nineteenth centuries. In fact, it did not take hold until the 1890s. A telling measure of Owen's defeat (and Huxley and Flower's success) is that today's natural history museums display only a portion of their collections and all have storage vaults. These perennially crowded basements and warehouses are, of course, the result of continuous collecting and a hesitancy to insult donors, but the *existence* of storage is a fact of museology.

One might wonder why there has been so little discussion of storage space in a

Figure 6.1 Huxley at the installation and dedication of the statue of Darwin on the grand stair of the Natural History Museum, London. *Graphic* (June 20, 1885).

book dedicated to the architecture of natural history museums. The answer is that Victorian architects and curators seldom discussed storage. For the 28 years of his directorship, Owen maintained that an overview of all of nature was necessary. Owen, who concerned himself with natural theology, nationalistic fervor, and (probably) his own ego, wanted to show everything. Ironically, Huxley, who devoted himself to the education of the working class, wanted the displays to be simple and clear. This suggests that an uneducated visitor to Owen's museum would have visual access to thousands of specimens, and assumes a greater level of competency on the part of the viewer. Owen's massive displays allowed visitors to construct their own meanings, and the vast collections preserved a sense of discovery. Museum professionals now call this type of display 'visible storage.' Usually these collections have minimal labels, but in some museums visitors can type a number into a nearby computer to get further information. Owen's idea, therefore, was a reasonably good one. Storage *is* rather wasteful: warehouses for objects that almost no one gets to see are expensive to build or rent. One could even argue that Huxley, and his supposedly class-sensitive colleagues, wanted to limit and control the public's access to natural science, whereas Owen allowed more freedom to explore.

SPECTACLE OR SCIENCE, REVISITED

Many issues presented in modern-day museum discourse were also present in the nineteenth century: do museums entertain or teach? are they primarily for scientists or primarily for the public? is it better to present a fossil sitting on a shelf or as part of a reconstructed skeleton? is it better to present stuffed animals standing calmly in boxes, or jumping about in an illusionistic diorama? This paradox (science versus spectacle) dates at least as far back as the invention of taxidermy in the eighteenth century – an invention that served two distinct purposes: some specimens were mounted for aesthetic enjoyment as household objects and trophies, while others were stuffed and kept in cabinets for scientific scrutiny. Bullock and Peale exhibited spectacular taxidermy in the 1820s, but serious museums usually presented stuffed animals mounted very simply, enough to prevent them falling over, and lined up in cases. Dramatic taxidermy did not enter the national museums (as opposed to the popular museum, where it had always been) until 1880, and it did so in the United States. William Hornaday, the chief taxidermist at the National Museum of Natural History in Washington DC, championed staged groupings of animals in front of painted backdrops at the very end of the nineteenth century. Complaining that 'museum managers the world over are too conservative by half,' he wrote in 1891 that

> as yet the museums will have no painted backgrounds. Ten years ago they would have no groups, and no birds with painted legs and beaks. They have all come to the two latter, and they will all come to painted backgrounds also, in due time, and it will be a good thing for them when they do.

Hornaday rhapsodized about the potential beauty of museums:

> Twenty-five years hence the zoological museums of this country will be as attractive and pleasing as the picture galleries, and they will teach ten times as

many object-lessons as they do now. To-day the average museum is as lifeless as a dictionary; but the museum of the future will be life itself.[2]

Historian Sophie Forgan has observed that sober nineteenth-century museums acted as analogies to the library, with specimens lined up in vitrines like books on shelves, and Hornaday's denigrating remark about lifeless dictionaries proves her point.

Hornaday saw himself as a professional scientist, not a showman. He maintained that while earlier taxidermized groups (like the tiger and snake at Bullock's) 'represented animals in theatrical attitudes, usually fighting,' these displays were of 'interest for certain purposes, [but] they were of little value to persons desiring to study typical forms of the species which were represented.'[3] Just as the *Wunderkammer's* freaks and mutants did not belong in the first natural history museums, sensational animal groups were too spectacular for the turn-of-the-century museum. World's fairs were at one end of a conceptual spectrum, while museums were at its other end. The most dramatic exhibition groups, Hornaday wrote, 'are valuable for great expositions, for show-windows, fairs and crystal palaces, and the like.'[4] But for natural history museums, the rules of composition were different: one animal in each group needed to be placed on flat ground in a conventional pose, so that its form and back outline could be studied by zoologists: 'Having done this much for pure science, we [taxidermists] are at liberty to vary the attitudes of the remaining specimens of the group.' (Incidentally, the expert taxonomist recommended against including humans in mammal groups, excepting Eskimos enveloped in thick furs.)

Henry A. Ward, who ran a taxidermy company in Rochester, New York, promoted more glamorous displays of animals, which he sold both to private collectors and museums. The most elaborate of these animal displays presented a narrative of two male orangutans fighting over a female in the Bornean forest. Ward showed it at the 1879 meeting of the American Association for the Advancement of Science, and later that year the American Museum of Natural History (AMNH) in New York purchased a similar tableau of orangutans battling in the tree tops; the apes dangle by their long arms and bare their teeth (Figure 6.2). The American museum also purchased a moose group and a bison group, in 1887 and 1888; these were thought to illustrate relations between the animals, in addition to animals' activity.

In the period from 1900 to 1935, full-scale dioramas (scenic arrangements in which life-like stuffed animals and plants were displayed in accurate environments, often with a curved back wall to represent illusionistic space) became the most prominent form of display in the natural history museum.[5] The art critic Rebecca Solnit has characterized the chief differences between an accumulation of animals in cases (the typical Victorian strategy, which is wonderfully preserved at the Dublin Museum of Natural History) and the diorama (the typical early twentieth-century design), arguing that dioramas try to rationalize vision:

> The kind of modern natural history museum I grew up with tries to rationalize our fascination with animals by placing each stuffed beast in a painted diorama accompanied by helpful plaques of scientific information. These displays belie our real reasons for looking at animals and push us towards a rational version of why we ought to look at them. But Dublin's Natural History Museum is itself a fossil, with displays that have hardly changed [since the nineteenth century] . . . The collection doesn't try to disguise the

Figure 6.2 William Hornaday, 'A fight in the tree tops,' group of taxidermized orangutans, plate XVII in *Taxidermy and Zoological Collecting* (London, 1891). This group was displayed in the American Museum of Natural History, New York.

seductions of collecting, of trophies, accumulations, abundances, and most of all, the forms of animals.[6]

Animals wrestling with each other cannot be studied by naturalists; and row upon row of dead stuffed things bores the public. Theorist Donna Haraway has written a scathing critique (1989) of the American Museum of Natural History's Africa Hall, engineered by the naturalist and big-game hunter Carl Akeley in the 1910s, with taxidermy assistance from Ward in Rochester.[7] Finding racism replete in primatology, Haraway finds violent, masculinist and imperialist motives in the Africa Hall. Museums like the AMNH and the Natural History Museum in Los Angeles used hunting trips as fund-raisers; men of leisure would travel to Africa with animal trackers, professional hunters, cooks and drivers, donating the game they bagged for museum displays. The enthusiasm for these hunts seems vulgar now – African natural habitats ravaged so that they could be re-created in deadly displays in American and European cities.[8]

Spectacle and commodification are currently closely linked, as they were in the nineteenth century. The sort of degeneration that Robert Kerr worried about in 1854 – that if a museum looked like a bazaar then the character of the displays would 'sink from that of science to that of show,' – has arrived. Commodities are present not only on the main floors of museums, but gallery space is given over to thematic, miniature gift shops scattered throughout the museums. There is a clear spatial meaning here:

profit is essential to the survival of a museum, and the space taken from galleries to sell rubber dinosaurs can be easily defended on economic grounds. The Chicago Field Museum's marketing blitz for the 'Man-eaters of Tsavo' shows that the temptation to create a spectacle can outstrip the goals of education (not to mention good taste). The Field Museum possesses the skulls of two lions who ate nearly 140 railroad workers in East Africa in March 1898; these feline skulls are displayed next to stuffed lions (similar to the man-eaters, but not the exact beasts) with a small historical photograph and a description of their misbegotten fame and the hunter who shot them. The display is surprisingly bland, considering the subject matter, and some visitors might reasonably be offended by the lack of sympathy for the dead African workers. Such soft-hearted visitors will be even more distressed at the gift shop, where 'Man-eaters of Tsavo' mugs, T-shirts and baseball caps are on sale. One might reasonably wonder how the relatives of the railroad workers feel about this publicity act, a stunt which gives credence to the worries of nineteenth-century naturalists who feared that museums would become commodifications of science and spectacles of capitalism.

SCIENCE: PRODUCT OR PROCESS?

Another controversy in contemporary museum practice that dates back to the nineteenth century is the question of whether to present scientific facts as a completed body of knowledge, or to show the process by which scientists work. If Owen's encyclopedic plans had been carried out, nineteenth-century naturalists would have become part of the display. Since there was no storage, a zoology student seeking a particular animal, or a foreign entomologist looking for that one special insect, would have to conduct his research in the galleries. Visitors would have seen the process of science, although the working naturalists might not have liked it. Similarly, in Huxley's ideal museum (described in Chapter 5), the work of scientific students and amateur naturalists scrutinizing, measuring and drawing specimens would have been clearly visible to the visitors. This is not generally the case today, when exhibitions tend to be presented as 'unequivocal statements rather than as the outcome of particular processes and contexts. The assumptions, rationales, compromises and accidents that lead to a finished exhibition are generally hidden away from public view.'[9] At present, taxonomists are hidden in the back rooms of most museums, but paleontology (now a much more popular branch of science than taxonomy) has taken up visible space. At the Field Museum, paleontology technicians chisel the fossil bones of 'Sue' (the remarkably complete Tyrannosaurus Rex skeleton) out of the rocks in which she was found; this painstaking work takes place in a glass laboratory, sponsored by McDonald's fast food restaurants, in the exhibition area, supposedly so that visitors can see the process. A similar glass laboratory is installed at the Page Museum at the La Brea Tar Pits in Los Angeles, but these are small gestures that cannot really introduce visitors to the complex ways in which new knowledge is produced.

'OBSERVING POWERS': VISUALITY AND INTERACTIVITY

Whether nineteenth-century visitors were looking at mounted specimens or dioramas, they were nonetheless *looking*, because there was not much else to do. In a lecture delivered by Edward Forbes in 1853, this museum enthusiast proclaimed that 'One of the great advantages of museums was that they stimulate the *observing powers*, a part of education which [has] been too long neglected' (emphasis added).[10] However, by 1881 the London *Times* was lamenting that the skills of observation were in decline among city folk:

> Nature, however, forces herself upon us, and compels attention. She does this by her endless variety of colour, form, action, and ways. The observant rustic eye notices and remembers every green thing, every flower, every feather, every singularity of form, every trick of flying, perching, or feeding, and, alas for the poor birds, every sort of nest ... Well, our poor Londoners and our townspeople generally have lost all this. Botany they have learned in gardens, or in shop windows. All the minerals they know are what they see in the pavement, the walls, and the fireplace. As for geology, the town covers and hides the earth it is built on. Cats and dogs, horses and sparrows, with a few caged birds, are all their living examples of the boundless animal world.[11]

This writer's claim that rustic folk were more observant than city-dwellers strikes a Romantic note, but the act of looking does seem to have diminished gradually from Victorian days to 1999. One current-day teacher remarked that her students look less carefully at the Natural History Museum in London now that audiophones are installed, which play a tape-loop about the exhibitions. Schoolchildren pick up the handset, listen for a moment, then move along to the next phone, every bit as uninformed as they were a few seconds earlier.

Stephen Jay Gould, natural history's most widely read author and a professor at Harvard University, has championed Victorian museums and their crowded, visually overwhelming displays. While he is open-minded about exploratoria and dazzling contemporary science museums, he also admires Victorian display practices:

> The display of organisms in these museums rests upon concepts strikingly different from modern practice, but fully consonant with Victorian concerns. Today, we tend to exhibit one or a few key specimens, surrounded by an odd mixture of extraneous glitz and more useful explanation, all in an effort to teach (if the intent be maximally honorable) or simply to dazzle (nothing wrong with this goal either). The Victorians, who viewed their museums as microcosms for national goals of territorial expansion and faith in progress fueled by increasing knowledge, tried to stuff every last specimen in their gloriously crowded cabinets – in order to show the full range and wonder of global diversity.[12]

Gould supports different types of displays, but he prefers the plenitude of the Victorians, saying 'nothing thrills me more than the raw diversity of nature.'

Gould continues 'You can put one beetle in a cabinet (usually an enlarged model and not a real specimen), surround it with fancy computer graphics and push-button whatsits, and then state that no other group maintains such diversity. Or you can fill the same cabinet with real beetles representing a thousand species – of differing colors, shapes, and sizes – and then state that you have tried to display each kind in the county.'[13] Like Gould, Solnit is besotted by the Natural History Museum in Dublin, in which shelves are overloaded with specimens and there are almost no labels (Figure 6.3):

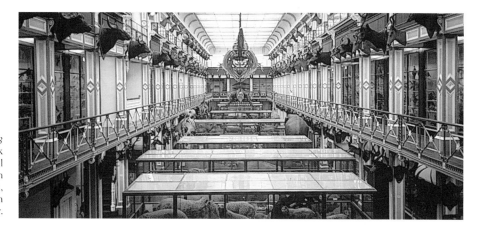

Figure 6.3
Frederick
Clarendon, Natural
History Museum
(Ireland), Dublin,
1856–57. Photograph
by the author.

> In this jumble was a survey of the whole natural world in terms of faded fur
> and yellowed bone and glassy eyes. It offered a pleasure unlike the shifty one
> of zoos. In a zoo one hopes to catch a glimpse of Life and often misses it, or
> sees prison rather than real animal life, but here one came to see Form, and it
> was absolutely utterly available, overwhelmingly so. The animals served as
> images of themselves, like a book that had come to life, although the cham-
> bers were collections of deaths.[14]

A visit to Dublin suggests that Victorian natural history museums would be better off
not even trying to update themselves. They could just be as they are: old, historical,
irrational, value-laden, even religious.

The Dublin Museum of Natural History manifests a simple assumption, common
to the nineteenth century: people learn by looking. This object-based epistemology
is partly lost now that museum curators assume that visitors need audiophones,
touch-sensitive computer screens, and buttons to press. Observation can be active,
as Barbara Maria Stafford argues. Recently, science museums have shunned observation as the primary activity, and they have tried to embed scientific knowledge in
friendlier media.[15] Museum officials introduced 'interactivity' (as it is called) to
enhance learning, but unfortunately 'activities' have almost replaced learning. Stafford bemoans the loss of critical vision: 'Educated seeing is precisely about recognizing that information cannot be separated from the manner and style of its display.'[16]
Stafford's is not an anti-technology position: the rise of computers and the internet
(in museums or at home) offers an opportunity for people to criticize what they see –
for people to recognize that the manner of display affects their perception of the
information. The natural history museum of the future could become the ideal
setting to encourage such 'educated seeing.'

'DINOMANIA' AND THE NATURAL HISTORY MUSEUM

Today natural history museums are able to attract large numbers of visitors, especially to see dinosaurs. Dinosaurs were present in nineteenth-century museums, but
these were different beasts altogether. Some (like the ichthyosaur or iguanodon)
could be represented by almost complete skeletons, and their bones alone created
enough of a spectacle to capture the attention of museum visitors. Steven Conn

believes that the hadrosaurus was the single most important item for drawing crowds to the Academy of Sciences in Philadelphia, but newspaper coverage of the Natural History Museum in London (for example) did not emphasize any one fossil.[17] Besides, many specimens, such as skeletons folded on themselves, were difficult to read. Other bones did not add up to complete skeletons. Gould used the word 'dinomania' to describe the craze for dinosaurs which has erupted since the 1950s. Some observers have claimed that children's fascination for dinosaurs is explicable because while dinosaurs are large and fierce, they are also extinct, and therefore pose no ultimate threat to the child. But Gould recognizes that dinosaurs were large, fierce and extinct in the 1940s, too, and yet were not so popular. Therefore, without anyone actually knowing its exact origin, the love of dinosaurs can best be explained by the commercialization of the extinct reptiles. At present dinosaurs are the most popular displays at any natural history museum. Old-fashioned dinosaur displays (partial fossils and reconstructed skeletons of either fossil bones or plaster casts) have been superseded by robotic dinosaurs at many museums, as Gould describes:

> consider the plight of natural history museums in the light of commercial dinomania. In the past decade, nearly every major or minor natural history museum has succumbed (not always unwisely) to two great commercial temptations: to sell many scientifically worthless, and often frivolous, or even degrading, dinosaur products in their gift shops, and to mount, at high and separate admission charges, special exhibits of colorful robotic dinosaurs that move and growl but (so far as I have been able to judge) teach nothing of scientific value about these animals. Such exhibits would be wonderful educational aids, if properly labeled and integrated with more traditional material; but I have never seen these robots presented for much more than their colors and sound effects (the two aspects of dinosaurs that must, for obvious reasons, remain most in the realm of speculation).[18]

Gould's complaint against museums is that they are veering toward theme parks: not that he dislikes theme parks – that's not his point – instead he argues that dinomania reveals 'a conflict between institutions with disparate purposes – the museums and theme parks.' He goes on to state that 'theme parks are ... the antithesis of museums,' and even more emphatically, that 'museums exist to display the authentic objects of nature.'[19] This absolute faith in authenticity rejects academic postmodernism and the current enthusiasm for simulation, the copy, and reproduction. Ultimately Gould is a scientist, not a cultural theorist, and his belief that the display of real specimens will save the natural history museum is a wishful leap across the decades that links him to the nineteenth-century natural historians he so admires.

James A. Secord, historian of science at Cambridge University, has argued, in contrast, that there is no 'aura' for dinosaur bones; even the original specimens have to be 'carefully chiselled out of their matrix and soaked in artificial preservative before they can be studied.'[20] Still, Secord prefers specimens to robots, because when fossilized bones or plaster casts are displayed, the public is asked to admire the same object the paleontologist studies. When motorized models fill museum galleries, clumsily lowering their necks and groaning at unsuspecting toddlers, visitors experience nothing of the process by which scientists work. In the Victorian museums described in this book, museums first began to present science as a set of tangible products rather than a social and intellectual process. It is no wonder, then, that today's natural history museums are bursting with gift shops and growling Tyrannosaurs – such is the legacy of the late Victorian secular museum.

ENVIRONMENTALISM AND CONSERVATION

'It is paradoxical, but no real surprise, that natural history is today both hugely popular and at the bottom of the scientific hierarchy,' writes Secord.[21] Environmentalism is the subject of international conferences, an oil spill – and general outrage over it – will always make the top story on the evening news, and the potential demise of a species is now enough to stop a superhighway or a housing development. The endangered status of many of the most-loved big mammals (rhinoceroses, tigers, pandas, gorillas) touches the hearts of many people. There is an obvious irony in the fact that natural history museums are full of dead beasts, many of them shot for sport by game hunters, at the same time museums promote conservation. One hundred years ago, at the opening of London's Natural History Museum, a reporter remarked that 'a living dog is better than a dead lion,' an observation that many present-day viewers would affirm.[22] Certainly a living *lion* is better than a dead lion, and that is why many visitors choose zoos over museums. Systematics and morphology were the two main facets of nineteenth-century natural history; most scientists studied the categorization and form of animals, not their behavior. Around 1900, however, the biological sciences expanded and diversified, so that natural history came to be 'just one of several orientations that a biologist could pursue.'[23] Although biology did not simply replace natural history, experimental biology (practiced in university laboratories) was valued above the usual museum practices. At present the study of the 'life sciences' is normal, while systematics and morphology are marginalized. Some non-scientists might assume that most of the classification has been done, there are few new species, and that the work of taxonomists is nearing completion. In fact, nearly 90 per cent of existing species are still undescribed,[24] and the work of taxonomists could be put to good use in preserving biodiversity. One needs to know what is out there before one protects it. Since biologists tend to study living organisms in the laboratory or in the field, they do not need museums as nineteenth-century paleontologists and taxonomists did. Nineteenth-century natural history museums served systematics and morphology well, but when that method of examining the natural world began to fade, natural history museums faded as well. Scientists determined the way their discipline was presented to the public and, not surprisingly, museums represented the interests of science. Rather than admit their obsolescence (or their possible estrangement from the biological sciences), natural history museums have shifted their focus to educating the public about conservation. Their role in research has been pushed, literally, to the back room.

The environmentalist movement, which has its roots in 1960s radical politics, offers yet another in a long line of historically specific definitions of nature – no longer the savage wilderness of the eighteenth century, or God's second book, or natural resource, or secular data: today's nature is fragile, a sickly child in need of care. Museum expert Peter Davis argues that the natural history museum has moved 'from collecting for its own sake to collecting with a conservation aim; from capturing specimens to capturing and interpreting data.'[25] This relatively new identity – endangered nature – might in the end help save the equally endangered natural history museum.

The practice of natural history has changed, but the buildings are reminders of the past, ghosts of former truths. In some cases, Victorian identities still persevere within Victorian walls. The Museum of Practical Geology was demolished in the 1930s because of structural flaws. The Hunterian, rebuilt after it was bombed in World War II, retains the aura of an inner sanctum for physicians. The Oxford University Museum also remains somewhat aloof, not particularly receptive to the public. Since the hours are not posted on the large wooden pointed-arched door, the museum is hardly inviting, even when it is open. The interior and exterior are much the same in 1999 as they appear in historic photographs. In the 1850s some scientists claimed the displays should be – if not encyclopedic – at least representative of nature. To have a university museum that was an eclectic cobbling-together of specimens was of little value for teaching. But the Oxford Museum, like many nineteenth-century museums, reflected the contingencies of history that shaped its collection; it had more bugs than beasts. It need hardly be pointed out that the theme 'nature as Creation' is currently completely absent from the displays. But is it absent from the museum? No. The portal over the door and the cloister still offer an earlier reading of nature to a handful of historically minded and observant visitors. Scholars have compared the skeletal quality of the roof to the skeletons of extinct animals sheltered beneath it, although this comparison was certainly not intended by the patrons or the architects: 'Standing beside one of the gigantic dinosaur skeletons, the visitor might alternatively have the sense of being inside the body of some great creature, the iron structure itself a kind of skeleton ... In a building crammed full of skeletons, such a correspondence would have been hard to escape.'[26] A major textbook on architecture makes a similar claim, that the 'iron was forged to fit a Rationalist vision of Gothic, and even to echo the skeletons of the creatures on display.'[27] This analogy is a twentieth-century perception which could occur only after the glorification of industrial architecture via modernism. The love of iron and glass and honestly expressed construction (promulgated by Sigfried Giedion in *Space, Time, and Architecture*, first published in 1941, and countless other authors) makes the link between the building and its bones compelling, yet ultimately anachronistic. These shifts in meaning are typical of architectural history; the building may be read in several ways and its multivalence celebrated.

As it did from its inception, the imperial Natural History Museum (NHM) still scrambles for public attention. The architectural fortunes of the Natural History Museum recapitulate the conditions of its opening, when the building was the main attraction because the objects had not yet been transferred from Bloomsbury. In 1881 a reporter enthused 'there is ... a great deal to see at South Kensington – the building itself first of all.'[28] The rising affection for Victorian architecture makes the building appealing to visitors, an added incentive to visit the museum. Lavish colour photographs of the building appear in publicity brochures and on the museum's web page. Professional museum directors like William Flower rejected Waterhouse's building, and in the modernist tastes of the mid-twentieth century the Natural History Museum was the worst of Victorian excess: applied ornament, colour, specific (as opposed to universal) communication. But a taste for postmodernism in architecture has developed alongside a renewed appreciation for old colourful, ornamental, elaborate buildings. But, because of its Victorian history, the museum cannot shed the imperial messages that were overt in the nineteenth century.

The museum's current stated goal is to promote 'biodiversity, environmental quality, mineral resources, agricultural resources, human evolution and human health.'[29] When the British National Lottery was launched in November 1994, many cultural institutions battled for grant funds. In that year, the Natural History Museum was successful in obtaining a grant, in spite of the fact that the NHM already charged a hefty entry fee, and many critics thought the money might be better spent on museums that did not charge the public. The museum used the grant money to renovate the geology gallery by creating an underground high-tech interactive exhibition about the earth sciences, with sound effects and shuddering floors to simulate an earthquake. The London *Times* quoted the exhibition designer as saying that 'he hoped to show that the earth sciences were not dull.'[30] This is a far cry from showing Owen's Creation or Huxley's progressive science. At the end of the twentieth century, museum officials start from the position that most people find science boring – so it is no wonder that the staff comes up with increasingly spectacular exhibitions. Museums faced this same identity problem in the nineteenth century: were they to entertain or educate? And if the answer is 'to entertain,' why are they subsidized by government funds, as they were in the nineteenth century, and as they are now with lottery funding?

Conclusion

The Role of Architecture in the Social Construction of Knowledge

Museum scholars have often noted that museums present themselves as neutral, when in fact they are politicized: Sherman and Rogoff write that 'The museum, in other words, while seemingly representing objectivity and empirically located contexts for the objects it displays, actually participates in the construction of these categories and in the numerous internal shifts and differentiations they are held to contain,' and, similarly, Sharon MacDonald claims:

> Museums which deal with science are not simply putting science on display; they are also creating particular kinds of science for the public, and lending to the science that is displayed their own legitimizing imprimatur. In other words, one effect of science museums is to pronounce certain practices and artefacts as belonging to the proper realm of 'science,' and as being science that an educated public ought to know about.[1]

The goal of this book has been to insert architecture into this discourse on science museums. How does a museum claim objectivity via its architecture? Since the 1930s, the pure forms, lack of ornament, and rejection of historical reference represented universality, so that modernist design (which encompassed entire museum buildings, their plain white walls and simple glass vitrines) came to be symbolically objective. Victorian architecture legitimated particular versions of science *without* any attempt to appear neutral. In fact, the Oxford museum's cloister and angel over the door, and the Natural History Museum's main hall and statue of Adam over the gable, were highly specific references which did not attempt to disguise the context in which objects should be viewed.

Nature's museums presented knowledge in the form of discrete specimens; the objects of nature were captured, stuffed, pinned down and categorized, sheltered beneath iron and glass canopies or Romanesque towers. These displays are historical evidence of our relationship to the natural world, and the museum buildings evidence of historical assumptions about what architecture can and cannot do. I have argued that 'nature' held different meanings for different audiences, and that its meaning was largely contextual. Natural history and architecture were products of society, and natural history museums were influenced by intellectual debates in science as well as aesthetic debates in architecture. The educational role of museums was under contestation, the availability of natural knowledge to the public was expanding, and science became a widely respected paying profession. It should come as no surprise that natural history museums took many different forms in the nineteenth century.

I have also argued that architecture participated in the local construction of knowledge. In the period when cabinets of curiosities were common, there was no concept of 'science' anything like our present definition, but the early cabinets established collecting as a means of interpreting the natural world. Charles Barry's Hunterian Museum of the Royal College of Surgeons (1837) was a significant step toward purpose-built architecture for display: its lighting (from the haunches of the vault) was copied by later designers. At the start of the 1800s, natural science was not yet an official part of Oxford or Cambridge's curricula, thus science had no architectural presence at either university. Things began to change at Cambridge with the competitions for a university library, but, even then, scientific objects would only have been displayed on the ground floor – a less-desirable space than that given to books. At Oxford, the construction of the University Museum in the 1850s not only heralded the acceptance of science at Britain's elite universities, but did so with a bold modern building in the Gothic Revival style. Deane and Woodward's museum legitimated natural theology, the study of nature as revelatory of Creation. The diversity of the natural world was not re-created in the displays, because Oxford's collections were not encyclopedic; but the ornamentation, which attempted to celebrate the diversity of Creation, illustrated a common Victorian moral about the essential goodness of nature. The architecture, even more than the incomplete displays, defined Oxford science as natural theology. The physical placement of natural history at Oxford – in an inspiring new building – announced the ascent of science in the intellectual life of the university.

Popular shows, the Museum of Practical Geology, and the Edinburgh Museum of Science and Art defined nature for a less-educated or more practically minded audience. At the geology museum, the mineral wealth of the British Empire was arranged stratigraphically in the collections, which were wrapped around the curved balconies beneath the skylight. The architecture of the Edinburgh Museum of Science and Art returns to the theme born at the Museum of Practical Geology. The iron, timber and glass interior and *Rundbogenstil* facade offered visitors a lesson in economic geology. In attaching the modifier 'economic' to the sciences of geology, zoology and sometimes botany, Victorians indicated that part of the role of nature was to be profitable, for it was widely accepted that animals, plants and rocks existed for the good of humans, and that they were meant to be capitalized. As social historian David Elliston Allen wrote of Victorian natural history:

> The moral and the useful became, increasingly, intertwined: pursuits like geology could be justified, in the self-same flickering of conscience, as a means of revering the earthly grandeurs of Creation – the Natural Theology as re-enunciated by Paley and now taken up as a ceaseless chant in every preface – and as a means of prospering materially.[2]

Allen identified a significant theme for all of Victorian culture: the moral and useful were equated. That is the reason it was such a clever trick to convince the Victorians that the Great Exhibition of 1851 which encouraged trade (shopping, by another name) was a moral, valuable enterprise. The most renowned ferrovitreous structure in the world, the Crystal Palace, then became associated with commodification, which Francis Fowke certainly knew when he used iron and timber to roof the Edinburgh Museum's lofty Great Hall.

Historians typically seek justification for their labors by claiming relevance to current debates. Secord believes that the cultures of natural history have had direct bearing on the current climate in science: endangered animals, shrinking habitats and global warming:

> the cultures of natural history have always been embedded in settings particular to time and place; thus 'curiosity' was not originally a psychological attribute, but part of an early modern practice of collecting and display. The roots of our contemporary situation are to be found in a material history of practices and any understanding will have to emerge from a recognition of the historical depth of current dilemmas . . . We have inherited not just our institutions and practices, but our problems: and these can only be understood as products of history.[3]

Natural history museums are among the science institutions we have inherited from the nineteenth century, and their preservation will help record not only practices, but the sources of our currently troubled relationship to the natural world.

Obviously, nature needs preservation. But, ironically, natural history needs to be preserved as well. It is through the story of natural history, best seen in museums, that we can trace the different definitions of nature that led to our relationship with the natural world. I have tried to argue that natural history museums are part of history; therefore they should not compete with zoos and wildlife movies, because they cannot win. They should be historical. They have the ability to show us nature as morphology and to relay an earlier representational schema for the natural world. Museums capture the history of nature, not natural history. For this they are a profoundly moving part of the cultural heritage of Europe and the United States. It is almost impossible to talk about nineteenth-century architecture and architectural theory without referring to nature; there are countless ways to define nature, and countless places to look for built responses to those meanings. This study of natural history museums in Victorian Britain offers a glimpse into the contested world of naturalists, as it offers a vision of an architecture that tried, perhaps vainly, to serve elusive and ever-changing ideals.

Epilogue

Two More Arks – The Museum of Creation and the Museum of Jurassic Technology

The display strategies of natural history museums speak a language separate from content: science displays speak of truth. So when creationists in California decided to place so-called 'creation science' on display, they used the same display techniques as other recent museums to sell their ideas.

The Museum of Creation and Earth History sits near the highway in a dusty suburb of San Diego, and its long, low lines are typical of commercial architecture (Figure E.1). Its exhibitions are arranged by each of the days of Creation, followed by galleries with information on Noah's Ark, the Biblical Flood, and the Ice Age. The Ice Age gallery is small, blue, and purposely refrigerated. After the Ice Age, visitors encounter a room on the civilization at Babel, which includes wall-cases on dinosaurs and Neanderthals. The Neanderthal bones are not presented as proof of evolution. The Neanderthal skull is explained in the following way: some people

Figure E.1
Museum of Creation and Earth History, Santee, California (near San Diego), exterior. Photograph by the author.

have pronounced brows, old people have protruding lower jaws because their teeth are missing, and Eskimos have flat noses; therefore, since folks in the Bible are described as living to be hundreds of years old, the Neanderthal skulls do not represent a separate species at all but just the remains of really old Eskimos.

The next three rooms, after Babel and the old Eskimos, focus on written history: the Greeks are singled out for special derision (they concentrated too much on mankind and had all those extra gods); a pause in the display celebrates the life of Christ, and there are wall displays on the Dark Ages and the Renaissance. The next sequence, like the entire museum, is carefully choreographed. Visitors are funneled through a narrow room representing the nineteenth century, with creationist worthies on the right, and evolutionist un-worthies on the left (Figures E.2 and E.3) Charles Darwin is the key villain on the evolutionist wall, although Karl Marx does not fare much better. Darwin's theory of evolution is presented as the precursor for many twentieth-century evils, including Nazism. In the next room, after the comparison of creationists and evolutionists, we face a key concept stated in a wall label above a photograph of Hitler. It reads 'Racism: The Fruit of Evolution.' It is the secondary title of Darwin's magnum opus which is emphasized – not *On the Origin of Species by Natural Selection*, but *The Preservation of Favoured Races in the Struggle for Life*. Since Darwin assumed that animals struggled continuously, and that evolution occurred concurrently, by extension humans also evolved. Therefore, Darwin must have believed that races within the human species were vying for superiority. The logic goes further: Creationists teach that all human beings are equal – the Bible does not mention races – while evolutionists teach racism, and therefore evolutionary theory ultimately brought about the Holocaust.

According to the museum's video guide (which can be purchased at the museum book store) the Noah's Ark room is a favourite among visitors. The tour guide tells us that so many visitors stumbled into the *trompe l'oeuil* painting of the Ark's interior,

Figure E.2
Museum of Creation and Earth History, Santee, California (near San Diego). Wall showing scientists who believed in Creation; Linnaeus and Faraday are the most celebrated on this wall. Photograph by the author.

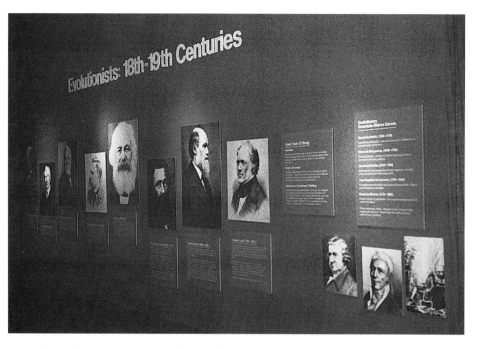

lovingly depicted on the far wall, that the museum had to install a rope; now a rustic and biblical equivalent of the modern velvet swag separates the viewer from the potentially dangerous painting. The painting shows hundreds of stalls (carefully measured in cubits, no doubt) with only the heads of the tallest animals visible. In the foreground, an ostrich stares imperiously at the visitor. A model of Noah's Ark, along with accounts of explorers who have seen the Ark's remains, fills an exhibition case on one side of the room. As Henry M. Morris, president of the Institute for Creation Research, argues (again in the video guide), the Flood was a significant geological event. He comments 'because [the Flood] so restructured the surface of the earth, any attempt to reconstruct history without using Noah's flood, is doomed to failure. How can you succeed if you deny truth?'

In one respect, the Museum of Creation and Earth History is the logical extension of the Oxford University Museum. The content of both museums is the same: a display of God's second book. At the Museum of Creation, however, the designers steer clear of any architectural religious imagery. To imitate the architecture of churches would defeat their purpose. In order to prove to their public that the Museum of Creation's displays are truthful, its keepers must use the strategies of mainstream evolutionist science. Therefore it maintains its gift shop to the left of the entrance and its logical sequence of didactic displays with simply written labels and colourful images. Everything is carefully executed with a high level of craftsmanship. Every design decision says, 'This is the truth.'

At the other end of the truth-seeking spectrum is the Museum of Jurassic Technology. This museum occupies an infill building in the middle of a block in Los Angeles; the architectural style is Italianate, and gold letters and a banner announce the museum's title as if were self-explanatory (Figure E.4). The museum has been described by its founder, David Wilson, as 'a small natural history museum, with an emphasis on curiosities and technological innovation . . . We're definitely interested in presenting phenomena that other natural history museums seem unwilling to

Figure E.4
Museum of Jurassic
Technology, Los
Angeles, California,
exterior. The banner
advertises the
exhibition titled 'No
one may ever have
the same knowledge
again.' Courtesy of
the Museum of
Jurassic Technology.

present.'[1] Although he is somewhat coy about it, Wilson's creation myth for his Museum of Jurassic Technology is clearly derived from the founding of the Ashmolean Museum, but he changed the locale from England to Nebraska. The Ashmolean collection had been originally gathered by two botanists, a father and son (John Tradescant the Elder and Younger); but their collection, called Tradescant's Ark, was taken over by Elias Ashmole when the younger Tradescant's wife (Hester Pookes Tradescant) drowned mysteriously in her backyard pond. Supposedly the collections at the Museum of Jurassic Technology came from Owen Thum the Elder and Younger, gardeners who put together a collection which later fell to a wily neighbor named Billius, when coincidentally the younger Thum's unfortunate wife (Hester Boxbutte Thum) drowned mysteriously in her backyard pool.[2] The exhibition 'Tell it to the Bees,' on old wives' tales and their meanings, includes a plastic model showing mice (toes up) on toast. In the 1830s the Oxford geologist William Buckland served this exact delicacy to his guests, along with other rare edibles. David Wilson knows the history of science and the history of collecting, and every detail of the Museum of Jurassic Technology (MJT) shows it. The displays are impeccable – beautifully crafted, with cleverly written labels (some taken almost word-for-word from other museums) and visually stunning items. It is a new museum that somberly pretends to be old. The museum makes manifest the key issues of both museum studies and the social constructionist[3] history of science: how do displays legitimize knowledge? What is real? What is fake? Where does truth begin and end? Is fact really stranger than fiction?

Lawrence Weschler's *Mr. Wilson's Cabinet of Wonder* (1995) describes an encounter with the museum and its founder in an appreciative study of this awesome work of

Figure E.5 Model
of Noah's Ark,
Museum of Jurassic
Technology, Los
Angeles, California,
1998. Courtesy of the
Museum of Jurassic
Technology.

installation art. The idea of wonder carries within it a sense of surprise: one does not feel 'wonder' at the supermarket or the department store. As Wilson says, 'Part of the assigned task is to reintegrate people to wonder.'[4] At the Museum of Jurassic Technology, wonder becomes surprise, which becomes disbelief. But the disbelief occurs slowly. The MJT blends belief and disbelief into a continuum of reality. Weschler's book describes one of Wilson's most charming natural history displays, the history and discovery of the *deprong mori*, a bat that flies through lead. Donald R. Griffin (author of *Listening in the Dark: The Acoustic Orientation of Bats and Men*, Yale University Press, 1958) laughed at the notion of such a creature, but then explained to Weschler, 'It's funny, fifty years ago when we were first proposing the existence of something like sonar in bats, most people thought that idea no less preposterous.'[5] (In a class of twelve art history majors to whom I assigned Weschler's book, six believed there was a bat that could fly through lead. One announced herself as a creationist.)

Like the curators at the Museum of Creation, the Museum of Jurassic Technology's director, David Wilson proudly exhibits a model of the Ark at his museum, and labels it 'the first natural history museum' (Figure E.5). There is more to this analogy than the gathering of animals – the Ark's purpose was preservation and conservation, a theme which has returned to the natural history museum of the twentieth century. The model is based on the drawing from Athanasius Kircher's book (see Figure 1.1) and brings us full circle: in the western world, the natural history museum cannot escape a culture which connects museums and ships as vessels that house the whole natural world. There is no nature outside culture; the natural history museum is Noah's legacy.

Notes

Introduction

1. This diary is now lost, unfortunately, but it is quoted extensively by the Owens' son, the Rev. Richard Owen, in *The Life of Richard Owen* (Westmead: Gregg International, reprinted 1970) 9. Dorinda Outram has written about the role of wives in the making of scientific careers. She suggests that women were deeply involved in the 'real-world maintenance of scientific organization, such as the handling of protégés, thus preserving intact the claims of her husband to exert his "scientificness" entirely outside the tainted world of career-making, patronage, and advantage.' Pnina G. Abir-Am and Dorinda Outram, *Uneasy Careers and Intimate Lives: Women in Science* (New Brunswick, NJ: Rutgers University Press, 1987) 21. We can speculate that Mrs Owen's role in her husband's success was greater than often supposed, and that her good humor about the rhinoceros was in keeping with her support of his enterprises.

2. Adi Ophir and Steven Shapin, 'The place of knowledge: a methodological survey,' *Science in Context* 4 (1991) 11.

3. David E. Allen, *The Naturalist in Britain: A Social History* (London: Allen Lane, 1976). The separation of natural history from medicine and agriculture is discussed in N. Jardine, J. A. Secord and Emma Spary (eds) *Cultures of Natural History* (Cambridge and New York: Cambridge University Press, 1996) part I.

4. Paula Findlen, *Possessing Nature: Museums, Collecting and Scientific Culture in Early Modern Italy* (Berkeley: University of California Press, 1994) 393.

5. The word 'scientist' was seldom used until the end of the nineteenth century, although it was coined by William Whewell in the 1830s. See Richard Yeo, *Defining Science: William Whewell, Natural Knowledge and the Public Debate in Early Victorian Britain* (Cambridge: Cambridge University Press, 1993) 5, 24. In this book I have tried not to use the anachronistic 'scientist,' opting for 'man of science' or 'naturalist' instead.

6. J. Morrell and Arnold Thackray, *Gentlemen of Science: Early Years of the British Association for the Advancement of Science* (Oxford: Clarendon, 1981) 36; and Frederick O'Dwyer, *The Architecture of Deane and Woodward* (Cork University Press, 1997) 211.

7. Science historian Sally Gregory Kohlstedt has called natural history museums 'symbols and centers for science,' but has also noted that, 'to date [1995] relatively little attention has been paid to the scientific institutions most visible to the general public and most essential to those involved in the exploration and ordering of the world's natural phenomena throughout the nineteenth century.' Sally Gregory Kohlstedt, 'Museums: revisiting sites in the history of natural sciences,' *Journal for the History of Biology* 28 (1995) 151–166.

8. Sophie Forgan, 'The architecture of display: museums, universities, and objects in nineteenth-century Britain,' *History of Science* 32, no. 96 (June 1994).

9. There are obviously other historians who continue to argue that the intellectual history of science consists of a series of discoveries in the search for universal truths, and these historians are opposed to the social constructivist position. For a detailed critique of the academic left's attitude toward science, see Paul R. Gross and Norman Levitt, *Higher*

Superstition: The Academic Left and Its Quarrels with Science (Baltimore: Johns Hopkins University Press, 1994) 45.

10. Jan Golinski, *Making Natural Knowledge: Constructivism and the History of Science* (Cambridge: Cambridge University Press, 1998) 6.

11. Mieke Bal, 'Telling, showing, showing off,' *Critical Inquiry* 18 (Spring 1992) 557–94.

12. There were hundreds of these clubs by the 1880s. Karen Wonders, 'Exhibiting fauna – from spectacle to habitat group,' *Curator* 32, no. 2 (1990) 136.

13. P. D. Lowe, 'Values and institutions in the history of British nature conservation,' in A. Warren and F. B. Goldsmith (eds) *Conservation in Perspective* (New York and Chichester: John Wiley, 1983) 329–52.

14. Paula Young Lee, 'The logic of the bones: architecture and the anatomical sciences at the Museum d'Histoire Naturelle, 1789–1889,' PhD diss., University of Chicago, 1998.

15. Donna Haraway, *Primate Visions: Gender, Race, and Nature in the World of Modern Science* (New York: Routledge, 1989); Mary Winsor, *Reading the Shape of Nature: Comparative Zoology at the Agassiz Museum* (Chicago: University of Chicago Press, 1991), and Steven Conn, *Museums and American Intellectual Life* (Chicago: University of Chicago Press, 1998).

16. Neil Levine, in Arthur Drexler (ed.) *Architecture of the École des Beaux-Arts* (New York: Museum of Modern Art and Cambridge: MIT Press, 1977) 327.

17. In 'Of other spaces,' (1967) Foucault proposes that utopias are 'fundamentally unreal,' leaving most of the built environment as heterotopias. He claims that the heterotopias of the western world are places of deviance – conflicted, multivalent spaces that resist easy analysis. Although museums are not spaces of obvious deviance (like mental hospitals or prisons), in several other ways museums clearly fit his complex definition of the heterotopia. Museums contain within themselves incompatible spaces and different time-frames. Foucault points out that some heterotopias are linked to 'time in its more futile, transitory, and precarious aspects,' and in this category he places fairgrounds, those liminal spaces which fill up once or twice a year with rickety rides and snake women, and then are suddenly empty of meaning and spectacle for the rest of the year. Temporary museum exhibitions have a similar, though less dramatic, effect. Eilean Hooper-Greenhill used a Foucauldian analysis throughout her book, *Museums and the Shaping of Knowledge*. In architectural history, Thomas Markus's *Buildings and Power: Freedom and Control in the Origins of Modern Building Types* (London and New York: Routledge, 1993) is a thorough example of Foucauldian theory brought to bear on the built environment.

18. Michel Foucault, *Power/Knowledge: Selected Interviews and Other Writings, 1972–1977* (New York: Pantheon, 1981) 149.

19. Daniel J. Sherman and Irit Rogoff, *Museum Culture: Histories, Discourses, Spectacles* (Minneapolis: University of Minnesota Press 1994) xi.

20. Tony Bennett, *The Birth of the Museum: History, Theory, Politics* (London and New York: Routledge, 1995) 19. See also Bennett, 'The exhibitionary complex' in Reesa Greenberg, Bruce W. Ferguson and Sandy Nairne (eds) *Thinking About Exhibitions* (London and New York: Routledge, 1996).

21. Bennett, *Birth of the Museum*, 28.

22. Bennett, *Birth of the Museum*, 52.

23. Although looking was the primary act, it was not necessarily looking as self-policing. The open room ringed with balconies was used for private museums like the Hunterian in addition to public museums; this therefore contradicts Bennett's theory that the open space of later public museums encouraged 'self-policing' whereas the 'warren-like layout of Sir John Soane's museum . . . provided no mechanism for inhibiting the visitor's conduct.' The Hunterian was an exclusive museum for the Royal College of Surgeons whose membership of wealthy physicians presumably did not require the threat of scopic power to behave. There is certainly an affinity between these nineteenth-century building types and the Familistère, but it is only an affinity (Bennett, *Birth of the Museum*, 53ff).

24. Conn, *Museums and American Intellectual Life*, 13.

25. Duncan and Wallach's article, in spite of certain flaws, was one of the most important arguments in art history about politicized museums. Later scholars have rejected their somewhat unidirectional analysis, and have observed that museum visitors could have constructed their own meanings from the displays. (This underscores the importance of the reception study put forth in Chapter 5 of *Nature's Museums*.) Duncan and Wallach's 1980 model might

serve well for interpreting a museum with a singular purpose, or perhaps for a museum that had a rather homogeneous audience. The Museum of Modern Art in New York was begun by a group of men who promoted one set of ideas; they had a clear vision of modern art and the goal of introducing European modernism to the United States. This is an excellent example of local knowledge presented as general, and their message of abstraction and universality was projected by the facade and interior of Edward Durrell Stone and Philip Goodwin's 1939 museum design. But this is an exceptional case in the history of museums: most museums emerge from conflicting sets of values, and their buildings understandably reflect that conflict.

26. Peter Bowler, *The Eclipse of Darwinism: Anti-Darwinian Evolutionary Theories in the Decades around 1900* (Baltimore: Johns Hopkins University Press, 1983) 44.

27. Adrian Desmond, *Huxley: From Devil's Disciple to Evolution's High Priest* (Reading, MA: Addison-Wesley, 1997) xvii.

28. John V. Pickstone, 'Museological science? The place of the analytical/comparative in nineteenth-century science, technology and medicine,' *History of Science* 32 (1994) 114.

29. Pickstone, 'Museological science,' 118.

30. James A. Secord, 'Introduction' to Robert Chambers, *Vestiges of the Natural History of Creation and other Evolutionary Writings* (Chicago: University of Chicago Press, 1994) xii.

31. Ophir and Shapin, 'The place of knowledge,' 3–21.

32. Ophir and Shapin, 'The place of knowledge,' 4.

33. Chapter 5 of this book is most successful in discussing different audience responses to a building, because there was simply more newspaper coverage of the Natural History Museum than of any other Victorian museum.

34. Nelson Goodman, 'How buildings mean,' *Critical Inquiry* (June 1985) 652.

35. Sophie Forgan, ' "But indifferently lodged": perception and place in building for science in Victorian London,' in Crosby Smith and Jon Agar (eds) *Making Space for Science: Territorial Themes in the Shaping of Knowledge* (London: Macmillan, 1998) 214.

1 Museum Vision: 'Sights Unseen Before'

1. Michel Foucault, *The Order of Things: An Archaeology of the Human Sciences* (New York: Vintage, 1994) xv.

2. Eilean Hooper-Greenhill, *Museums and the Shaping of Knowledge* (London and New York: Routledge, 1992) 5.

3. 'The Natural History Museum,' Memorandum of the Royal Dublin Society, May 1862, National Archives of Ireland, CSORP 1858/11098.

4. Mario Baglioli, 'Confabulating Jurassic science,' in George Marcus (ed.) *Technoscientific Imaginaries: Conversations, Profiles, and Memoirs* (Chicago: University of Chicago Press, 1995).

5. Mieke Bal, 'Telling, showing, showing off,' *Critical Inquiry* 18 (1992) 556–594.

6. Janet Browne, *The Secular Ark: Studies in the History of Biogeography* (New Haven: Yale University Press, 1983) 9.

7. Krzysztof Pomian, *Collectors and Curiosities: Paris and Venice, 1500–1800*, trans. Elizabeth Wiles-Portier (Cambridge, UK: Polity, 1990) 69.

8. Pomian, *Collectors and Curiosities*, 77.

9. Stephen Bann has analyzed the cabinet owned by John Bargrave as a kind of material portrait of the collector. See *Under the Sign: John Bargrave as Collector, Traveler, and Witness* (Ann Arbor: University of Michigan Press, 1994).

10. Pomian, *Collectors and Curiosities*, 78.

11. Pomian, *Collectors and Curiosities*, 99.

12. Paula Findlen, *Possessing Nature: Museums, Collecting, and Scientific Culture in Early Modern Italy* (Berkeley and London: University of California Press, 1994) 199.

13. Findlen, *Possessing Nature*, 9.

14. Findlen, *Possessing Nature*, 192.

15. James A. Secord, 'Crisis of Nature,' in N. Jardine, J. A Secord and Emma Spary, (eds) *Cultures of Natural History*, 457. See article by Katy Whitaker in the same volume.

16. Hooper-Greenhill, *Museums and the Shaping of Knowledge*, 192.

17. Svetlana Alpers, 'The museum as a way of seeing,' in Ivan Karp and Steven D. Lavine (eds) *Exhibiting Cultures: The Poetics and Politics of Museum Display* (Smithsonian Institution Press, 1991) 26.

18. Hooper-Greenhill, *Museums and the Shaping of Knowledge*, 10.

19. Douglas Crimp, *On the Museum's Ruins* (Cambridge, MA: MIT Press, 1993) 225.

20. Crimp, *On the Museum's Ruins*, 234.

21. Findlen, *Possessing Nature*, 407.

22. Richard D. Altick, *The Shows of London* (Cambridge, MA: MIT Press, 1978) 10. For an illustration of Tradescant's house, see page 11.

23. Arthur MacGregor, *Tradescant's Rarities: Essays on the Foundation of the Ashmolean Museum, 1683* (Oxford: Clarendon, 1983) 21.

24. P. B. Duncan, *A Catalogue of the Ashmolean* (Oxford: Collingwood, 1836) v.

25. Altick, *The Shows of London*, 12.

26. R. F. Ovenell, *The Ashmolean Museum 1683–1894* (Oxford: Clarendon, 1986) 20–1. Ovenell believes Wood to be the architect, but R. T. Gunther attributed the building to Wren. The attribution debate is beyond the scope of the present study.

27. Zacharias Conrad von Uffenbach, *London in 1710*, trans. W. H. Quarrell and Margaret Ware (London, 1934) 203. Quoted in Findlen, *Possessing Nature*, 147.

28. Findlen, *Possessing Nature*, 148.

29. Edward P. Alexander, *Museums in Motion* (Nashville, TN: American Association of State and Local History, 1979) 44.

30. John Henry Parker, *The Ashmolean Museum: Its History, Present State, and Prospects: A Lecture given to the Oxford Architectural Society* (Oxford, 1870) 4.

31. Findlen, *Possessing Nature*, 150.

32. Barbara Maria Stafford, *Good Looking: Essays on the Virtue of Images* (Cambridge, MA: MIT Press, 1996) 33.

33. Stafford, *Good Looking*, 40.

34. Findlen, *Possessing Nature*, 403.

35. Altick, *The Shows of London*, 25.

36. *Repository of the Arts, Literature, and Commerce* (London: R. Ackermann) vol. 3 (1810) 388.

37. *A Companion to Mr. Bullock's Museum*, 8th edn (London, 1810) 82ff.

38. *Repository of the Arts*, vol. 3 (1810) 388.

39. *Repository of the Arts*, vol. 3 (1810) 388.

40. Thomas Greenwood, *Museums and Art Galleries* (London: Simkin, Marshall, 1888) 41–2.

41. Peter Davis, *Museums and the Natural Environment: The Role of Natural History Museums in Biological Conservation* (London and NY: Leicester University Press, 1996) 65.

42. E. G. Hancock, 'One of those dreadful combats: a surviving display from William Bullock's London Museum 1807–1818,' *Museums Journal*, 79/1: 172–5.

43. Sharon MacDonald (ed.) *The Politics of Display: Museums, Science, Culture* (New York and London: Routledge, 1998) 1–24.

44. Karen Wonders, *Habitat Dioramas: Illusions of Wilderness in Museums of Natural History* (Uppsala: Acta Universitatis Upsaliensis, 1993) 30.

45. Steven Conn, *Museums and American Intellectual Life* (Chicago: University of Chicago Press, 1998) 34.

46. W. S. W. Ruschenberger, *A Notice on the Origin, Progress, and Present Constitution of the Academy of Natural Sciences of Philadelphia* (Philadelphia: T. K. and P. G. Collins, 1852) 45. Cited in Appel (see Note 48). Ruschenberger figures prominently in Steven Conn's analysis as well.

47. Greenwood, *Museums and Art Galleries*, 6.

48. Toby Appel, 'Science, popular culture, and profit: Peale's Philadelphia Museum,' *Journal of the Society for the Bibliography of Natural History* 9, no. 4 (1980) 626.

49. Wonders, *Habitat Dioramas*, 29.

50. Charlotte Porter, 'Natural history in the twentieth century: an oxymoron?' in *Natural History Museums: Directions for Growth* (Lubbock: Texas Tech. University, 1991) 225.

51. J. Britton and Augustus C. Pugin, *Illustrations of the Public Buildings of London* (London: J. Taylor, 1825) vol. 2: 2.

52. John M. MacKenzie, *The Empire of Nature: Hunting, conservation and British Imperialism* (Manchester: Manchester University Press, 1988) 30–31.

53. C. J. Wright, 'Holland House and the fashionable pursuit of science: a nineteenth-century cabinet of curiosities,' *Journal of the History of Collections* 1, no. 1 (1989) 97.

54. Lindy Brewster, 'The Harpur Crewe collection of natural history at Calke Abbey, Derbyshire,' *Journal of the History of Collections* 9, no. 1 (1997) 132.

55. Samuel Scudder, 'In the laboratory with Agassiz,' *Every Saturday* (4 April 1874) 369–70. Quoted in Winsor, *Reading the Shape of Nature*, 14.

56. Winsor, *Reading the Shape of Nature*, 14.

57. [Rennie, James] *Insect Architecture*, 4th edn (London: Nattali & Bond, [1830]) 16.

2 Displays of Natural Knowledge in the 1830s and 1840s

1. Adrian Desmond, *Huxley: From Devil's Disciple to Evolution's High Priest* (Reading, MA: Addison-Wesley, 1997) 162.

2. Roy Porter, 'Gentlemen and geology: the emergence of a scientific career, 1660–1920,' *Historical Journal* 21, no. 4 (1978) 809–36.

3. The idea of professionalization in science does not equate with progress, nor was such professionalization inevitable. See Jan Golinski, *Making Natural Knowledge: Contructivism and the History of Science* (Cambridge: Cambridge University Press, 1998) 68.

4. William Paley, *Natural Theology, or Evidences of the Existence and Attributes of the Deity, Collected from the Appearances of Nature* (1805 edition) 585.

5. The Zoological Society of London established a zoo at Regent's Park in 1828.

6. Additional illustrations may be found in J. P. F. Deleuze, *Histoire et Description du Museum Royal d'Histoire Naturell* (Paris, 1823) 2 vols.

7. Paula Young Lee, 'The Musaeum of Alexandria and the formation of the museum in eighteenth-century France,' *Art Bulletin* 79, no. 3 (September 1997) 384.

8. P. B. Duncan, *A Catalogue of the Ashmolean Museum* (Oxford: Collingwood, 1836) i. Duncan confuses the issue somewhat by implying that the library was part of the museum.

9. Camille Limoges, 'The development of the Museum d'Histoire Naturelle,' in Robert Fox and George Weicz (eds) *The Organization of Science and Technology in France, 1808–1914* (Cambridge University Press, 1980) 212–13.

10. Limoges, 'The development of the Museum d'Histoire Naturelle,' 226.

11. Nicolaas A. Rupke, *Richard Owen: Victorian Naturalist* (London and New Haven: Yale University Press, 1994) 24.

12. Robert Willis and J. W. Clark, *An Architectural History of the University of Cambridge* (Cambridge: Cambridge University Press, 1886) vol. 3 100.

13. [George Peacock], *Observations on the Plans for the New Library, etc. By a Member of the First Syndicate* (Cambridge: J Smith, 1831) 11.

14. A Syndicate was a special committee appointed by the faculty Senate; it submitted reports to the Senate, and when the time came to make final decisions, the members of the Senate voted. William Whewell and George Peacock were both members of the three Syndicates (1829, 1830 and 1836) that dealt with the competition for the University Library.

15. Willis and Clark, *An Architectural History*, vol. 3: 97.

16. The history of the University Library is recounted in more detail in Willis and Clark, *Architectural History*, vol. 3: 97–128, and in David Watkin, *The Life and Work of C. R. Cockerell* (London: Zwemmer, 1974) 183–96.

17. Peacock, *Observations*, 10.

18. Peacock, *Observations*, 1.

19. Watkin, *C. R. Cockerell*, 184.

20. David Watkin, *The Triumph of the Classical: Cambridge Architecture, 1804–1834* (Cambridge: Cambridge University Press, 1977) 9.

21. Letter, William Whewell to Dawson Turner, 23 July 1834, Whewell Papers, O.4.13/20, Trinity College Library, Cambridge.

22. Watkin surmised that Cockerell added these staircases after the competition, because they do not appear in the competition plan. David Watkin, 'Newly discovered drawings by C. R. Cockerell for Cambridge University Library,' *Architectural History* 26 (1983) 89. Watkins's article also contains illustrations of Cockerell's second entry, which was a richer composition that would have transformed the immediate surroundings of the new library by creating, in effect, two courtyards (plates 47a and 47b).

23. C. R. Cockerell to the Syndics, 31 October 1829. 'C. R. Cockerell, 1830–1836,' Add. 6630 AAA, Cambridge University Library.

24. In Cockerell's plans from 1829 he placed three lecture rooms outside the quadrangle on the north side, in a location far-removed from the museums. See Watkin, 'Newly discovered

drawings,' plates 46a and 46b. Wilkins's surviving entry, also classical, was typical of his crisp personal aesthetic and more characteristic of the archeological Greek Revival than Cockerell's imaginative synthesis. In the plan, Wilkins pushed the museums into the northwest corner, making access from the museums to the two lecture theatres inconvenient.

25. Willis and Clark, *Architectural History*, vol. 3: 159.

26. Watkin, *C. R. Cockerell*, 185.

27. In 1830 Rickman's partner Hutchinson complained that Cockerell's designs were Roman, not Grecian, which was indeed a fair point, but it was later agreed that the Syndics only meant 'not Gothic,' and did not care whether the designs were Greek or Roman.

28. *History of the Library*, vol. 1, fol. 381. University Archives, Cambridge University Library.

29. Peacock, *Observations*, 40.

30. Peacock, *Observations*, 24–7. The Royal Institute of British Architects has in its drawings collection seven drawings by Rickman and Hutchinson for the 1829 competition, but the RIBA does not have any drawings for the 1830 or 1836 competition. Rickman's plans for the 1830 competition are at the Cambridge University Library.

31. Peacock, *Observations*, 40.

32. Watkin's account of the history of the University Library makes the decision in favour of Rickman sound like an inexplicable lapse of judgment: 'What Cockerell must have suffered on learning that the banal and clumsy designs of Rickman and Hutchinson were now preferred to his own, we can only imagine' (185). However clumsy Rickman's designs were, his plans followed the competition guidelines and served the clients.

33. John Willis Clark used Robert Willis's notes to complete Willis's book on Cambridge architecture; in 1886 Clark wrote of the delay: 'the whole scheme was once more laid aside, for reasons which it is impossible to discover.' Willis and Clark, *Architectural History*, vol. 3: 113.

34. The drawings submitted by Wilkins and Rickman are either lost or their location is unknown.

35. Watkin, 'Newly discovered drawings,' 90.

36. Willis and Clark, *Architectural History*, vol. 3: 117.

37. In 1863–65, the architect Anthony Salvin built a simple red-brick Italianate building near the Botanical Garden which included natural science museums (only geology and mineralogy were in the University Library) as well as up-to-date laboratories. It was later demolished. Willis and Clark, *Architectural History*, vol. 3: 171–80. An interior photograph may be found at the Cambridge University Library, Map Room, Views X.2, figs 80 and 81.

38. Willis and Clark, *Architectural History*, vol. 3: 155. '[In 1829] the Instructions to Architects for the [University Library] . . . directed them to provide Museums and Lecture-Rooms for Geology, Mineralogy, Zoology, and Botany . . . This scheme . . . was not carried out, Geology and Mineralogy alone being accommodated in Cockerell's building, nor had the wants of Anatomy and Chemistry been so much as recognised' (155). In 1853, the ground floor of the new university library was considered too small: 'The Mineralogy Museum is now arranged in a room under the new wing of the University Library, which is by no means sufficient for the display of the collection' (161).

39. Richard Yeo, *Defining Science: William Whewell, Natural Knowledge and the Public Debate in Early Victorian Britain* (Cambridge: Cambridge University Press, 1993) passim.

40. Jess Dobson, 'The architectural history of the Hunterian Museum,' *Annals of the Royal College of Surgeons of England* 29 (August 1961) 117.

41. Rupke, *Richard Owen*, 24.

42. Mary P. Winsor, *Reading the Shape of Nature: Comparative Zoology at the Agassiz Museum* (Chicago and London: Chicago University Press, 1991) 11.

43. Rupke, *Richard Owen*, 13.

44. Dobson, 'Architectural history of the Hunterian Museum,' 120.

45. Richard Owen, *Report of the British Association for the Advancement of Science* (1881) 657.

46. John Weale, *The Pictorial Handbook of London* (London: H. G. Bohn, 1854) 718. 'The stone portico of the present building remains from an older one, but the rest was rebuilt in 1835 from a competition design by C. Barry, RA. It is composed of "artificial stones," i.e. cast blocks of concrete and stucco.' Since the original building was destroyed in World War II, it is difficult to know much more about the construction of Barry's museums.

47. Rupke, *Richard Owen*, 12–13.

48. Rupke, *Richard Owen*, 13.

49. Adrian Desmond and James Moore, *Darwin* (London: Michael Joseph, 1991) 223. See also Dobson, 'Hunterian Museum,' 121.

50. *Illustrated London News* 7 (4 October 1845) 210.

51. Roy Porter, 'Gentlemen and geology: the emergence of a scientific career, 1660–1920,' *Historical Journal* 21, no. 4 (1978) 822.

52. Porter, 'Gentlemen and geology,' 825.

53. In addition to Porter's 'Gentleman and geology,' see also J. Morrell and Arnold Thackray, *Gentlemen of Science: Early Years of the British Association for the Advancement of Science* (Oxford: Clarendon, 1981); Anne Secord has conducted research on naturalists, especially botanists, who were artisans rather than gentlemen. 'Corresponding interests: artisans and gentlemen in nineteenth-century natural history,' *British Journal for the History of Science* 27 (1994) 383–408.

54. Roy Porter, 'Gentlemen and geology,' 825.

55. P. S. Doughty, 'Museums and geology,' in Susan Pearce (ed.) *Exploring Science in Museums*, New Research in Museum Studies Series (London and Atlantic Highlands, NJ: Athlone, 1996) 6.

56. Quoted in Doughty, 'Museums and geology,' 5.

57. Geoffrey Tyack, *Sir James Pennethorne and the Making of Victorian London* (Cambridge: Cambridge University Press, 1992) 179.

58. The Museum of Practical Geology was called the Museum of Economic Geology from 1836 to 1848; its later, permanent name will be used here.

59. Rupke, *Richard Owen*, 62.

60. Tyack, *Pennethorne*, 317.

61. Sophie Forgan, ' "But indifferently lodged": perception and place in building for science in Victorian London' in Crosbie Smith and Jon Agar, *Making Space for Science: Territorial Themes in the Shaping of Knowledge* (London: Macmillan, 1998) 205.

62. Doughty, 'Museums and geology,' 6.

63. The fact that the colourful stones of the Museum of Practical Geology pre-date the more famous Oxford Museum has been noted by Sophie Forgan, in 'Bricks and bones' in Peter Galison and Emily Thompson (eds) *The Architecture of Science* (MIT Press: 1999) and Yanni, 'Building natural history: constructions of nature in British Victorian architecture and architectural theory,' PhD dissertation, University of Pennsylvania, 1994.

64. *The Times* (London), 27 March 1858.

65. Doughty, 'Museums and geology,' 7.

66. Desmond, *Huxley*, 189.

67. Desmond, *Huxley*, 201.

68. John W. Papworth, *Museums, Libraries and Picture Galleries, Public and Private, Their Establishment, Formation, Arrangement, and Architectural Construction* (London: Chapman and Hall, 1853) 68.

69. Bernard H. Becker, *Scientific London* (1874; reprint, London: Frank Cass, 1968) 251–2.

70. Forgan, 'Bricks and bones,' 197.

71. Forgan, 'Bricks and bones,' 197–200.

72. 'The Museum of Practical Geology: its uses to architects,' *Builder* 18, no. 885 (21 Jan 1860) 33.

73. Becker, *Scientific London*, 252.

3 Nature as Creation: The Oxford University Museum

1. 'British Association, The President's Address,' *Athenaeum* (June 30, 1860) 891. Also quoted in J. Vernon Jensen, 'Return to the Wilberforce–Huxley debate,' *British Journal of the History of Science* 21 (June 1988) 179. See also the *Report of the British Association for the Advancement of Science* (1860) lxxv.

2. *Athenaeum* (June 30, 1860) 891.

3. As described by J. Morrell and Arnold Thackray, *Gentlemen of Science: Early Years of the British Association for the Advancement of Science* (Oxford: Clarendon, 1981): 'natural theology was the favoured genre of the clerical leaders within the BAAS,' (227). And 'Natural theology thus blunted criticism while serving to rebut the allied charge that science led inexorably to impiety and atheism. Design arguments also fulfilled a further function, in claiming for natural

philosophers a valuable freedom of activity within their chosen fields. If the study of nature led to nature's God, then the fullest and freest scientific enquiry was entirely proper' (229).

4. As Adrian Desmond writes '[In 1870] . . . the English public schools and universities shunned science as useless and dehumanizing. Their world was of character-forming Classics and Theology. Oxford and Cambridge were finishing schools for prosperous Anglicans.' Adrian Desmond, *Huxley: From Devil's Disciple to Evolution's High Priest* (Reading, MA: Addison-Wesley, 1994) xvii. In the 1850s, when the Oxford museum was commissioned, practical science was shunned even more than in 1870.

5. In addition to appearing in many textbooks on architectural history, the Oxford Museum has been closely studied by several historians. The most complete account may be found in Frederick O'Dwyer, *The Architecture of Deane and Woodward* (Cork University Press, 1997); O'Dwyer's work is remarkably detailed, nuanced and documented. Michael W. Brooks, *John Ruskin and Victorian Architecture* (Thames and Hudson, London: 1987) placed the museum in the context of Ruskin's career. Trevor Garnham's *Oxford Museum: Deane and Woodward* (London: Phaidon, 1992) offers a well-written essay with beautiful illustrations. One of the first serious archival studies of the museum was published in Eve Blau, *Ruskinian Gothic: The Architecture of Deane and Woodward, 1845–1851* (Princeton: Princeton University Press, 1982). My work differs from these earlier authors in its concentration on natural theology, although Garnham also addresses the issue. It is my modest hope that the Oxford Museum looks different in the context of earlier and later British museums. Other sources include Howard Colvin, *Unbuilt Oxford* (New Haven and London: Yale University Press, 1983); Birkin Haward, 'The Oxford University Museum,' *Architect's Journal* (September 27, 1989) 41–63, reprint, Oxford: Oxford University Museum, 1991; and Peter Ferriday, 'The Oxford Museum,' *Architectural Review* (December 1962) 408–16.

Earlier accounts of the museum include: Reverend William Tuckwell, *Reminiscences of Oxford* (London: Cassell, 1901); Horace Middleton Vernon and K. Dorothea Vernon, *A History of the Oxford Museum* (Oxford: Clarendon, 1909); E. T. Cook and A. Wedderburn, *The Works of John Ruskin* (London: G. Allen, and New York: Longmans, 1905–12), vol. 16, xli–liv, 207–44; and, most importantly, Henry Acland's personal account, *The Oxford Museum* (London: George Allen, 1859). Acland revised and enlarged his book for three later editions: 1860, 1861 and 1893.

6. Colvin asserts two standard dichotomies, which are perhaps more derived from twentieth-century intellectual history than nineteenth-century thought, when he writes: 'This double victory – of Science over obscurantism, and of Gothic over classic – was not easily won' (*Unbuilt Oxford*, 128). It is true that the 'battles' were not easily won, which is why historians have much to learn from studying Barry's classical design and from understanding that the scientific culture of the day cannot be characterized by the phrase 'science over obscurantism.' Brooks wrote, 'It is remarkable, in retrospect, that a competition should have been required to select Woodward as the architect of the Oxford Museum' (Brooks, *John Ruskin and Victorian Architecture*, 117).

7. Michael Sanderson, *The Universities in the Nineteenth Century* (London and Boston: Routledge & Kegan Paul, 1975) 5.

8. Victorian terminology may be misleading because the word 'museum' was sometimes used to refer to an entire structure and sometimes only to a display space within a larger building. Even more confusingly, 'museum' sometimes had no spatial connotation at all – for example, 'Hope's Museum' referred to the entomology collection that Frederick William Hope (1797–1862) donated to Oxford in 1849; it did not matter whether the insects were on display or in boxes – the *collection* was called 'Hope's Museum.' On the Oxford Museum as a science centre, see also Colvin, *Unbuilt Oxford*, 125.

9. Vernon and Vernon, *A History of the Oxford Museum*, 40. Greswell's plans are reproduced in O'Dwyer, *The Architecture of Deane and Woodward*, fig. 5.1.

10. Acland, *Oxford Museum*, 110.

11. Morrell and Thackray, *Gentlemen of Science*, 225–30.

12. Colvin noted that Wilberforce supported the establishment of an honours school for science, writing that Acland was 'supported not merely by medical and scientific colleagues, but by influential churchmen, some of whom (including Bishop Wilberforce) recognized that nature was the work of God, and its study therefore an eminently Christian activity, while others (such as Dr Pusey) were, like the scientists, challenging an

established order that was equally hostile to change whether theological or scientific' (Colvin, *Unbuilt Oxford*, 125).

13. Richard Greswell, *Memorial on the (Proposed) Oxford University Lecture Rooms, Library, Museums &c. Addressed to Members of Convocation* (Oxford: Beaumont Street, May 20, 1853) 7–8. Papers concerning the Oxford Museum, 1849–53, NW/2/1/8, Oxford University Archives, Oxford University. All emphases in the following quotations are Greswell's.

14. Greswell, *Memorial*, 11.

15. The convocation, or the House of Convocation, was the administrative body that formed university policy and controlled university funds. The museum delegacy was appointed by the convocation to plan the new science building – delegates had to choose a site, hold a competition, select an architect and raise money. When the museum delegacy came to a decision, the delegacy presented its conclusions to the convocation, and the members of the convocation voted on whether to approve the delegacy's decisions. James J. Moore, *The Historical Handbook and Guide to Oxford embracing a Succinct History of the University and City* (Oxford: Thomas Shrimpton, 1878) 61.

16. Notice of Meeting of Convocation, May 9, 1849. MSS Acland, d. 95, fol. 71, Bodleian Library, Oxford (hereafter cited as MSS Acland).

17. *Report of the Delegates for the Oxford University Museum*, February 17, 1853, p. 6. Papers concerning the University Museum, 1849–53, NW/2/1/7, Oxford University Archives.

18. Greswell, *Memorial*, 8.

19. *Report of the Delegates for the Oxford University Museum*, February 17, 1853. Papers concerning the University Museum, 1849–53, NW/2/1/7, Oxford University Archives.

20. O'Dwyer, *The Architecture of Deane and Woodward*, 166. Some accounts say 32 drawings were submitted.

21. O'Dwyer, *The Architecture of Deane and Woodward*, 174.

22. Oxford Museum Delegates, vol. 1, UM/M/1/1, May 2, 1856, fols. 114, and May 3, 1856, fol. 118.

23. *Athenaeum*, November 11, 1854, 1374.

24. *Jackson's Oxford Journal* reported on October 21, 1854, that the designs would be 'open to public inspection,' but on November 4, 1854, it clarified this statement, reporting that 'Members of Convocation, and persons introduced by them will be enabled to inspect' the drawings. The *Oxford Chronicle and Berks and Bucks Gazette* (November 18, 1854) covered the story after the drawings had been on display for two weeks and explained that members of the public could inspect the drawings only after 'production of a card from Dr. Acland.'

25. *Jackson's Oxford Journal*, December 16, 1854.

26. O'Dwyer, *The Architecture of Deane and Woodward*, 178.

27. Based on his discovery of side elevations found in the Horwood Collection, Archives of Ontario, Toronto, O'Dwyer maintains that the designs for the competition were considerably different from these 1855 drawings. I defer to O'Dwyer's impressive research on this matter. See O'Dwyer, *The Architecture of Deane and Woodward*, fig. 5.14.

28. See Blau, *Ruskinian Gothic*, fig. 55.

29. George Edmund Street, *An Urgent Plea for the Revival of the True Principles of Architecture in the Public Buildings of the University of Oxford* (Oxford and London: John Henry Parker, 1853) 4.

30. Street, *Urgent Plea*, 4.

31. Street, *Urgent Plea*, 17.

32. Two architectural historians have claimed a direct correspondence between the naturalism of the Gothic style and the natural history museum building type. Blau wrote in *Ruskinian Gothic* (p. 52) that Street's 'reasoning' was 'so in sympathy with Deane and Woodward's own,' that it 'possibly had some influence on their design. It had perhaps an even greater influence on the governing bodies of the University, and may have been instrumental in weighing the balance in favour of Deane and Woodward's Gothic and "naturalistic" design.' Colvin agreed with Blau, writing in *Unbuilt Oxford* that given the shortcomings of classical architecture, it was 'the moral and symbolical superiority of Gothic that won the day.' He continues: 'First, in trying to understand why Deane and Woodward's foreign-looking Gothic should have been regarded as more suitable for the purposes of nineteenth century science than . . . [a] grand parade of Roman columns, we may wonder whether it was partly because the orders were, after all, so closely associated with the dead hand of classical learning from which the scientists

were trying to liberate themselves. It was certainly to some degree because Gothic was a style in which Nature was supposed to find expression in a way that the established conventions of classical architecture could hardly permit' (Colvin, *Unbuilt Oxford*, 132). I think Colvin is correct that the Gothic style allowed for more variety in the ornament, which I argue is a reflection of the desire to show the diversity of nature – a key theme in natural theology. It is unlikely that men of science like Acland, Phillips and Burgon would even think of an idea like 'the dead hand of classical learning.' But obviously Phillips and Burgon, who liked the classical design, did not see it that way. These men were, after all, professors at Oxford – they were part of a world where the classics were taken for granted as a basis for learning. Britain had its share of radical thinkers who did reject classical learning, but they would more likely be found at a liberal institution like the University of London.

33. *Builder*, 12 (1854). The list of entries, arranged by style, is reprinted in Colvin, *Unbuilt Oxford*, 126.

34. Ruskin to Acland, December 11, 1854. MSS Acland, d. 72. fol. 44. 'Acland from John Ruskin *c.*1840–86,' Oxford University Archives.

35. Ruskin to Acland, December 11, 1854. MSS Acland, d. 72. fol. 44. 'Acland from John Ruskin *c.*1840–86,' Oxford University Archives.

36. Ruskin to Acland, December 11, 1854. MSS Acland, d. 72, fol. 11. A thorough description of the museum's meaning for John Ruskin may be found in Kristine Garrigan, *Ruskin on Architecture* (Madison, WI: University of Wisconsin Press, 1973) 122–33.

37. Oxford Museum Delegates, vol. 1, UM/M/1/1, October 18, 1855, fol. 82, Oxford University Archives. The first appearance of Ruskin's name in the official minutes of the delegates was ten months after the competition, when he donated £300.

38. 'ΕΡΓΑΤΗΣ,' published anonymously but written by Acland. Papers concerning the University Museum, 1849–53, NW/2/1/21. Also filed in the Oxford University Museum archives, History of the Building of the Museum, HBM 5/2.

39. For more on the Gothic as a modern style suitable for university science buildings, see Sophie Forgan, 'The architecture of science and the idea of a university,' *Studies in the History and Philosophy of Science* 20, no. 4 (December 1989) 430.

40. Eve Blau also reported that the 'competition released a deluge of pamphlets'; and, like Clark, she assumed that the debate was polarized, arguing that '[t]he opposing factions of Classicists and Gothicists were thus once again polarised in a competition for the most important commission of the day.' Blau, *Ruskinian Gothic*, 7. Earlier, Kenneth Clark described the Gothic and Classical styles as juxtaposed, implying strictly divided opinions, and noted that the competition 'resulted in the usual storm of pamphlets.' Kenneth Clark, *The Gothic Revival: An Essay in the History of Taste*, 3rd edn (London: J. Murray, 1962) 205.

41. Colvin, *Unbuilt Oxford*, 131–2.

42. Oxford Museum Delegates, vol. 1, December 4, 1854. UM/M/1/1, fol. 47, Oxford University Archives.

43. Colvin, *Unbuilt Oxford*, 132.

44. Phillips arranged the fossils at the York Museum before his appointment as professor of geology at King's College in London in 1834. King's was the Tory Anglican alternative to London's University College, which was a secular university allied with the Whig Party.

45. Morrell and Thackray, *Gentlemen of Science*, 386.

46. Oxford Museum Delegates, vol. 1, December 4, 1854, UM/M/1/1, fols. 49–50, Oxford University Archives.

47. I thank Simon Bailey, archivist of the Oxford University Archives, for answering this tricky question of the convocation's vote. According to Bailey, the information is contained in a note of a meeting from the convocation of December 12, 1854, inserted in the minute book of the Museum delegacy between the meetings of December 4 and 15. UM/M/1/1, fol. 51.

48. O'Dwyer, *The Architecture of Deane and Woodward*, 172.

49. Blau, *Ruskinian Gothic*, 53–4. Shortly after its vote, the convocation requested a modified plan, which Deane and Woodward submitted on February 23, 1855.

50. Original Plans, UM/P/3/#1–9. Papers of the Oxford University Museum, Oxford University.

51. Garnham, *Oxford Museum*, 20.

52. Blau discovered one of Woodward's sketchbooks, now in the National Gallery in Dublin (Woodward Sketchbook 7387), and by comparing this pocket-sized private book to the

published illustration in the *Builder*, Blau showed how and when Woodward altered the design. Blau, *Ruskinian Gothic*, 54.

53. *Building News* 5 (January 21, 1859) 59.

54. Oxford Museum Delegates, vol. 1, UM/M/1/1, May 28, 1858, fol. 5, Oxford University Archives.

55. Greenwood, *Museums and Art Galleries*, 137.

56. Garnham has noted that the cloister at the Oxford Museum bears the exact dimensions of the cloister at Westminster Abbey. Garnham, *Oxford Museum*, 7.

57. I thank Dietrich Neumann for this observation.

58. Acland, *Oxford Museum*, 21.

59. Tuckwell, *Reminiscences*, 49. Quite possibly, the historian Tuckwell confused Street's fantasy, written before the competition, with the actual circumstances of the O'Sheas.

60. Ruskin to his father John James Ruskin, March 6, 1859, cited in Brooks, *John Ruskin and Victorian Architecture*, 127 and O'Dwyer, *The Architecture of Deane and Woodward*, 175.

61. Oxford Museum Delegates, vol. 1, UM/M/1/1, February 1854, fol. 89. Oxford University Archives.

62. Sophie Forgan, 'Bricks and bones,' in Peter Galison and Emily Thompson (eds) *Science and Architecture* (Cambridge, MA: MIT Press, 1999) 181–208.

63. Brooks points out that wrought iron (as opposed to cast iron) was more in keeping with Ruskin's principles because it was a medieval craft which required handiwork. Brooks, *John Ruskin and Victorian Architecture*, 128.

64. Oxford Museum Delegates, vol. 1, UM/M/1/1, April 24, 1856, fol. 109, Oxford University Archives. Of course, iron had been used in mill buildings since the end of the eighteenth century. The delegate probably meant that glass roofs were a new invention.

65. Oxford Museum Delegates, vol. 1. UM/M/1/1, April 24, 1856, fol. 114, Oxford University Archives.

66. As described by Morrell and Thackray, Daubeny believed that the 'virtue of science not only resided in its practical applications to the arts, but in its affording the higher gratification of moral and intellectual improvement.' Morrell and Thackray, *Gentlemen of Science*, 261. Section G of the British Association for the Advancement of Science was established in 1836 for mechanical science, that is, theoretical aspects of engineering rather than industrial practice. Morrell and Thackray, *Gentlemen of Science*, 260.

67. Nicolaas Rupke, *Richard Owen: Victorian Naturalist* (London and New Haven: Yale University Press, 1994) 61.

68. Garnham, *Oxford Museum*, 1. Garnham conflates science and engineering when he writes: '[The Oxford Museum's] unique contribution resides in its attempt to reconcile science and religion – the iron of the "Crystal Palace" and the Christian Gothic – through an integration of form and content where natural history slides easily from display to ornament, and echoes of faith reverberate through the structure.' Some nineteenth-century writers saw the museum's architecture as the Crystal Palace transformed into the Gothic style, but this still does not imply a 'reconciliation' between technology and art, or science and religion, because there were architects and theorists who refused to believe the Gothic style was more 'Christian' than classicism. (C. R. Cockerell and Alexander 'Greek' Thomson are two examples.)

69. I respectfully disagree with Caroline Van Eck on this particular point, because I think it creates confusion to assume the ascendancy of secular science at this early date, on the basis of the Huxley – Wilberforce exchange. Van Eck writes 'On the one hand, as the result of the collaboration between Ruskin, Acland, and Woodward, it is the culmination of romantic organicism . . . but on the other hand, as the first building in Oxford for the natural and medical sciences, built at the time of the publication of Darwin's *The Origin of Species* (1859), it announces the ascendancy of a concept of nature that is scientific rather than religious or metaphysical.' I would argue that it does not announce the ascendancy of the new science, because Acland was firmly rooted in natural theology; furthermore, Acland's concept of nature was both scientific and religious. Caroline Van Eck, *Organicism in Nineteenth-Century Architecture* (Amsterdam: Art and Natura Press, 1994) 203.

70. Acland, *Oxford Museum*, 7.

71. John Hedley Brooke, *Science and Religion: Some Historical Perspectives* (Cambridge, UK: Cambridge University Press, 1991) 310ff.

72. Acland, as quoted by Vernon and Vernon, *A History of the Oxford Museum*, 84–5. Cook and Wedderburn (*Works*, vol. 16, li, and quoted in O'Dwyer, *The Architecture of Deane and Woodward*, 222) summarized the iconography of the portal differently. The angel is described as 'bearing in his right hand a book – the open book of Nature – and in his left, three living cells – typical of the mysteries of life.' I find that visual analysis to be less accurate than Vernon's quotation from Acland, in which he refers to 'a nucleated cell.' The term 'to nucleate' means to form a nucleus or cluster, which describes the activity occuring in the center of the angel's cell: it is one cell with a two-lobed organelle in the middle, thus it is one cell in the process of forming a nucleus. Three living cells would appear as separate forms with distinct cell walls, and they would not be encased within another circular shape.

73. Vernon and Vernon, *A History of the Oxford Museum*, 84.

74. Darwin himself did not use the word 'evolution' until a later edition of *The Origin of Species* was published.

75. Less well-educated Protestants (not Oxbridge intellectuals) were more likely to reinforce their religious identity by opposing evolution, and therefore take offense at *The Origin of Species*. John Hedley Brooke, *Science and Religion*, 282.

76. Not surprisingly, there are numerous interpretations of the event. O'Dwyer narrated the customary tale: 'The museum was to be the scene, at its inauguration in June 1860, of the celebrated debate on evolution between the Bishop of Oxford, Dr Samuel Wilberforce, and "Darwin's Bulldog," T. H. Huxley,' *The Architecture of Deane and Woodward*, 283. Before the benefit of Jensen's research, Michael Brooks read the so-called debate as a watershed – proof that the museum's religiosity was soon to be obsolete: 'The first major public dispute over Darwin's theories . . . took place at the Museum in 1860. It is very awkward to put a sermon on God and nature into stones if it will need instant revision,' *John Ruskin and Victorian Architecture*, 142; and Morrell and Thackray saw Huxley as the victor: 'Like Daubeny and Phillips, Acland had envisaged the museum as a place in which the study of the material works of the Great Artificer would necessarily reinforce Christianity. In 1860 Huxley showed the rashness of that assumption, as if in defiance of the angel carved on the keystone of the arch at the entrance to the museum,' *Gentlemen of Science*, 386.

77. J. Vernon Jensen, *T. H. Huxley: Communicating for Science* (Newark, DE: University of Delaware Press, 1991) 79.

78. Jensen, 'Return to the Wilberforce–Huxley debate,' 164; Morrell and Thackray, *Gentlemen of Science*, 395.

79. *Athenaeum*, July 7, 1859, also quoted in Jensen, *T. H. Huxley*, 71.

80. Jensen, 'Return to the Wilberforce–Huxley debate,' 177.

81. Tuckwell, *Reminiscences*, 52.

82. Huxley, letter to Dyster, September 9, 1860, Huxley papers, vol. 15, fols. 117–18. Also cited in Jensen, *T. H. Huxley: Communicating for Science*, 73–4.

83. Acland to Owen, October 4, 1862, fol. 6, Acland MSS, d. 220, Letters to Professor Owen.

84. Owen to Acland, March 23, 1855, Acland MSS, d. 81, fol. 101. 'Misc Letters to Acland'. This letter clearly contradicts Howard Colvin's remark that Victorian scientists sought to 'liberate themselves' from the 'dead hand of classical learning.' Colvin, *Unbuilt Oxford*, 132. Owen's comments also undermine the security of O'Dwyer's statement that 'As the prayers dedicating the great secular cathedral to be were read out, it must have seemed entirely appropriate to supporters of Acland's arguments for the associations of Gothic that 'Christian architecture' should have triumphed over pagan Barryan Palladianism,' 186. Owen was a religiously minded anatomist who admired Barry's entry and saw classical philosophers as his predecessors.

85. John Ruskin, rough draft for *The Stones of Venice*, vol. 3; quoted in Cook and Wedderburn (eds) *Works*, vol. 11, xvii. Also quoted in David B. Brownlee, *The Law Courts* (Cambridge, MA: MIT Press, 1984) 21.

4 Nature as Natural Resource: The Edinburgh Museum of Science and Art

1. The Edinburgh Museum has received less scholarly attention than it deserves, but there have been a few published accounts of the museum's history, to which I am indebted. These include Douglas A. Allan, *The Royal Scottish Museum: Art and Ethnography, Natural History, Technology, Geology, 1854–1954* (Edinburgh: Oliver & Boyd, 1954); Jenni Calder, *The Wealth of a*

Nation in the National Museums of Scotland (Edinburgh: Royal Museums of Scotland, 1989); Sophie Forgan, 'The architecture of display: museums, universities, and objects in nineteenth-century Britain,' *History of Science* 32, no. 96 (June 1994) 139–62; and R. G. W. Anderson, 'Connoisseurship, pedagogy, or antiquarianism?' *Journal of the History of Collections* 7, no. 2 (1995) 211–25.

2. The museum has been popularly called the Royal Museum of Scotland or Royal Scottish Museum since about the turn of the century, but its nineteenth-century name, the Edinburgh Museum of Science and Art, will be used here. For a brief period, from 1854 to 1861, before the industrial collections and natural history collections were combined, it was planned to build a home for an institution to be called the Industrial Museum of Scotland. In 1985 the Royal Museum of Scotland joined with the National Museum of Antiquities of Scotland (founded in 1780), and their official name is The National Museums of Scotland.

3. Bruce Lenman, *Integration, Enlightenment, and Industrialization: Scotland, 1746–1832* (Toronto and Buffalo: University of Toronto Press, 1981) 1.

4. James Scotland, *The History of Scottish Education, Vol. 1: From the Beginning to 1872* (London: University of London Press, 1969) 332.

5. Matthew Arnold, *Complete Prose Works*, ed. R. H. Super, *Vol. 4: Schools and Universities on the Continent* (Ann Arbor, MI: University of Michigan Press, 1964) 287–288. Also cited in Scotland, *History of Scottish Education*, 332.

6. Calder, *Wealth of a Nation*, 12.

7. *Daily Scotsman* (Edinburgh), June 10, 1858.

8. Tony Bennett, *Birth of the Museum: History, Theory, Politics* (London: Routledge) 41.

9. *The Times* (London), March 27, 1858.

10. F. H. W. Sheppard (ed.) *Survey of London, Vol. 38: The Museums Area of South Kensington* (London: Athlone, 1975) 74.

11. Jonathan Crary, *Techniques of the Observer: On Vision and Modernity in the Nineteenth Century* (Cambridge, MA: MIT Press, 1996) 18.

12. Thomas Richards, *The Commodity Culture of Victorian England: Advertising and Spectacle, 1851–1914* (Stanford: Stanford University Press, 1990) 3–4.

13. James A. Secord, 'Dining in the iguanodon: the anatomy of a meal,' paper delivered at the Cambridge University Cabinet of Natural History, Department of History and Philosophy of Science, November 1992.

14. R. G. W. Anderson, ' "What is technology?": Education through museums in the mid-nineteenth century,' *British Journal for the History of Science* 25 (1992) 174.

15. Adam White, *Four Short Letters: The First and Fourth Addressed to the Late and to the Present Lord Provosts of Edinburgh, on the Subject of An Open Museum in the Scottish Capital* (Edinburgh: Edmonston and Douglas, 1850) 4.

16. The Department of Art was formed in 1837 as a part of the Board of Trade. In 1853, Science was added to the department, and the name was changed to the Department of Science and Art. Also in 1853, the Department of Science and Art took over the administration of the Geological Survey and the Museum of Practical Geology (previously under the Board of Ordnance). In 1856 the Department of Science and Art joined the Privy Council on Education, became a subdivision of the newly named Department of Education, and therefore was removed from the Board of Trade. Playfair was appointed Secretary of Science in 1853, at the same time Cole was made Secretary of Art, but in 1855 Playfair took charge of both Science and Art. When Playfair resigned in 1858 to take the professorship of chemistry at Edinburgh University, Cole took command of both Science and Art.

17. Calder, *Wealth of a Nation*, 9.

18. John V. Pickstone, 'Museological science? The place of the analytical/comparative in nineteenth-century science, technology, and medicine,' *History of Science* 32 (1994) 121.

19. Allan, *The Royal Scottish Museum*, 7.

20. George Wilson, *On the Relation of Ornamental to Industrial Art: A Lecture Delivered in the National Galleries at the Request of the Art-Manufacture Association* (Edinburgh: Edmonston and Douglas, 1857) 5–6. The lecture was delivered on Christmas Eve 1856.

21. George Wilson, *The Industrial Museum of Scotland in its Relation to Commercial Enterprise: Delivered at the Request of the Company of Merchants of the City of Edinburgh* (Edinburgh: R. & R. Clark, 1857) 21.

22. Wilson, *Industrial Museum of Scotland*, 53.

23. Meeting Agenda, Science and Art Department Minute Books, April 15, 1857. United Kingdom Public Record Office (PRO), ED 28/7, fol. 3.

24. Meeting Agenda, April 15, 1857, fol. 3.

25. Meeting Agenda, April 15, 1857, fol. 3.

26. Fowke's association with Cole was of great benefit to his career. Their affiliation was personal as well: in 1870, five years after Fowke's death, his son Frank married Henry Cole's daughter Isabella. Elizabeth Bonython, *King Cole: A Picture Portrait of Sir Henry Cole, 1808–1882* (London: Victoria and Albert Museum, 1982) 45.

27. Sheppard, *Survey of London*, vol. 38: 101.

28. *Builder* 22 (April 23, 1864) 290.

29. Meeting Agenda, Science and Art Department Minute Books, April 15, 1857, PRO, ED 28/7, fol. 3. These rather utilitarian drawings are in the collection of the Scottish Record Office, RHP 6524/30, parts 1, 2, 3, and 4; they are signed 'Francis Fowke Capt. R.E. 25 Mar. 1857.'

30. Science and Art Department of the Committee of Council on Education. 'Annual Report of the Director of the Industrial Museum of Scotland' (January 1, 1858) in *Directory of The Industrial Museum of Scotland and of the Natural History Museum, Edinburgh* (London: George E. Eyre, 1858) 149.

31. Drawing signed 'Francis Fowke, Capt. R. E., March 1859,' Scottish Record Office, RHP 6524/36.

32. *Daily Scotsman* (Edinburgh), October 24, 1861.

33. *Daily Scotsman* (Edinburgh), October 24, 1861.

34. Later in his career, in 1865, he designed the Royal Albert Hall, the philharmonic hall in South Kensington named in Albert's honor, in a red-brick and round-arched style that was again close to contemporary German sources.

35. 'Edinburgh,' *London Journal* (1862) 72.

36. *Daily Scotsman* (Edinburgh) October 24, 1861.

37. Natural History Museum Archives, O.DES/2. Robert Kerr, 'Kensington museums competition of architectural designs.'

38. Bennett, *Birth of the Museum*, 51.

39. I thank Sophie Forgan for this observation.

40. Adam White, *Four Short Letters*, 4.

41. *Evening Courant* (Edinburgh), October 24, 1861.

5 Nature in Conflict: The Natural History Museum in London

1. Steven Shapin and Simon Schaffer, *Leviathan and the Air-Pump: Hobbes, Boyle, and the Experimental Life*, (Princeton, NJ: Princeton University Press, 1985) 7.

2. Published accounts of the Natural History Museum's history include Colin Cunningham and Prudence Waterhouse, *Alfred Waterhouse, 1830–1905: Biography of a Practice* (Oxford: Clarendon, 1992); Mark Girouard, *Alfred Waterhouse and the Natural History Museum* (London: British Museum–Natural History, 1981); Kenneth Hudson, *Museums of Influence* (Cambridge: Cambridge University Press, 1987); John Olley and Caroline Wilson, 'The Natural History Museum,' *Architects' Journal* 181, no. 13 (March 27, 1985) 32–50, 55; Nicolaas A. Rupke, 'The road to Albertopolis: Richard Owen (1804–92) and the founding of the British Museum of Natural History,' *Science, Politics, and the Public Good: Essays in Honor of Margaret Gowing* (London: Macmillan, 1988); Rupke, *Richard Owen: Victorian Naturalist* (New Haven and London: Yale University Press, 1994); F. H. W. Sheppard (ed.) *Survey of London, Vol. 38: The Museums Area of South Kensington* (London: Athlone, 1975); William Stearn, *The Natural History Museum at South Kensington: A History of the British Museum (Natural History)* (London: Heinemann, 1981). Colin Cunningham and Prudence Waterhouse placed the museum in the context of Waterhouse's life's work. Girouard's book celebrated the centennial of the museum's opening as did Stearn's; Stearn concentrated on the many influential men of science who worked at the museum. Rupke's article provided a thorough analysis of the political context for establishing separate quarters for the British Museum's natural history collections, in which he paid close attention to the adversarial action of Thomas H. Huxley; chapters 'Museum politics I' and 'Museum politics II' of Rupke's *Richard Owen: Victorian Naturalist* extend this discussion.

3. Richard Greswell, founder of the Ashmolean Society in Oxford, had three years earlier made the less-than-prophetic claim that Owen had 'determined for ever the principles on

which all future Museums are to be built.' Richard Greswell, *Memorial on the (Proposed) Oxford University Lecture Rooms, Library, Museums &c. Addressed to Members of Convocation* (Oxford: Beaumont Street, 1853) 19.

4. Owen and Huxley had opposite opinions on many issues, and their disagreements over museum theory were only a minor issue in their well-known rivalry. Between 1859 and 1862 Huxley published a series of articles attacking Owen's scientific position that the human skull was essentially distinct from the skulls of higher apes. Huxley eventually proved Owen wrong, and consequently called into question Owen's objectivity, because Owen's religious views were seen to have influenced his anatomical conclusions.

Even so, Victorian naturalists cannot be divided into neat camps of religious and evolution-ary thinkers, and the polarity of Huxley and Owen's museum philosophy, which is in fact related to religion, should not be extrapolated to all scientific debates. Indeed, many Victorian men of science reconciled their religious views with evolution. See Peter Bowler, *The Non-Darwinian Revolution* (London and Baltimore: Johns Hopkins University Press, 1988).

5. Adrian Desmond, *Huxley: From Devil's Disciple to Evolutions's High Priest* (Reading, MA: Addison-Wesley) 213.

6. Adrian Desmond's position on the professionalization of science in the nineteenth cen-tury stresses class conflict. He argues that a 'New Scientist' was emerging, and for this New Scientist the concept of progression was a fundamental law of nature. This in turn suggested that the class stratification of Britain was artificial, and that lower and middle-class people ought to be able to attain power and prestige in society. Desmond writes: 'As the materialists appealed to the increasingly-powerful bourgeoisie – the main benefactors of the industrial boom – so the Owenians, like their Cambridge contemporaries, were largely backed by cler-ical, landed and upper-class interests, in fact those destined to lose most from industrial expansion and the accompanying secular movement.' Adrian Desmond, *Archetypes and Ances-tors: Palaeontology in Victorian London, 1850–1875* (London: Blond & Briggs, 1982) 177. Owen himself was not born into money (Rupke, *Richard Owen*, 12) but he did represent the interests of the scientific establishment.

7. The 'typical or popular' and 'scientific' collections were the two main categories pro-posed in this memorial. Additionally, the naturalists recommended an 'economic museum,' which would display commercial goods derived from natural substances, and zoological and botanical gardens, for the display of living specimens. Charles Darwin, *The Correspondence of Charles Darwin, Vol. 7: 1858–1859*, edited by Frederick Burckhardt and Sydney Smith (Cam-bridge: Cambridge University Press, 1991) 526, 'Memorial Addressed to the Right Honour-able Chancellor of the Exchequer,' November 18, 1858. An earlier memorial, from July 1858, written by geologist Roderick Murchison, proposed that the collections stay in Bloomsbury, but this was apparently abandoned because naturalists soon realized the move was imminent, thus they prepared the second memorial in July to have influence over the impending re-categorization of specimens. the *Correspondence of Charles Darwin*, vol. 7: 523–4. John Edward Gray, keeper of zoology at the British Museum, was another proponent of dividing natural history into a 'study-series' and 'exhibition-series.' See John Edward Gray, 'On museums, their use and improvement, and on the acclimatization of animals,' *Report of the British Associ-ation for the Advancement of Science* (1865) 75–86. See also Mary P. Winsor, *Reading the Shape of Nature: Comparative Zoology at the Agassiz Museum* (Chicago and London: University of Chicago Press, 1991) 121.

8. In this letter, Huxley described the ideal (but unlikely) locations for these two collec-tions, whereas in the November 1858 memorial, the men of science proposed that the popular and study museums be housed in the same building. Thomas H. Huxley, *Life and Letters of Thomas Henry Huxley*, ed. Leonard Huxley (New York: Appleton, 1900) vol. 1: 172.

9. *Correspondence of Charles Darwin*, vol. 7: 177.

10. T. H. Huxley, *Life and Letters*, vol. 1: 172.

11. Leonard Huxley (ed.) *Life and Letters of Joseph Dalton Hooker* (London: John Murray, 1918) vol. 1: 380–1.

12. At the end of 1859, museum trustees compared sites in Bloomsbury and South Ken-sington, and deemed the smaller Bloomsbury site to be too costly. The site in South Kensing-ton was at the southern end of the Horticultural Society Gardens, on which the International Exhibition of 1862 had been constructed. Sheppard, *Survey of London*, vol. 38: 202.

13. Rupke, *Owen*, 37.

14. Richard Owen, *On the Extent and Aims of a National Museum of Natural History* (London: Saunders, Otley, 1862) 23.

15. Richard Owen, *Report of the British Association for the Advancement of Science* (1858) 48.

16. Owen, *Extent and Aims*, 123.

17. Desmond, *Huxley*, 246.

18. Owen's peculiar brand of natural theology, as evidenced by his reaction to Robert Chambers's anonymously published *Vestiges of the Natural History of Creation* (London: J. Churchill, 1844) has been debated extensively by historians of science. See Eveleen Richards, 'A question of property rights: Richard Owen's evolutionism reassessed,' *British Journal for the History of Science* 20, part 2, no. 65 (April 1987) 127–71.

19. Owen, *Report of the British Association* (1881) 652.

20. The length of the plot is inscribed on the drawing itself. Plan, Richard Owen, Proposed Natural History Museum, 1859. Natural History Museum Library and Archives.

21. *Building News* 11 (April 22, 1864) 297; *Art Journal* (April 1862) 47.

22. This ratio of architects was quite high for the Victorian period. The Royal Institute of British Architects had been lobbying for many years to increase the participation of professional architects on public juries.

23. 'Richard Owen: Miscellaneous Manuscripts,' vol. 4, fol. 40. Natural History Museum Library and Archives.

24. Competition announcement: 'Public Buildings (South Kensington)' p. 1, Public Record Office, Work 17, 16/2 (hereafter abbreviated PRO). British Museum trustees objected to the inclusion of Owen and Hunt's plan with the instructions for architects, because they felt they had not been consulted about space requirements. PRO, Work 17, 16/1, fols. 1–2.

25. Competition announcement: 'Public Buildings (South Kensington)' p. 2, PRO, Work 17, 16/2.

26. Competition announcement, p. 2, PRO, Work 17, 16/2.

27. In this and other early plans, Owen placed ethnology close to the centre, and mammals and birds were given a great deal of space compared to the other departments (botany, geology and paleontology). The number of specimens in the existing bird collection and the physical size of some of the mammals demanded extra space.

28. *Builder* 22 (April 23, 1864) 290.

29. *Building News* 11 (April 29, 1864) 313.

30. *Building News* 11 (April 29, 1864) 313.

31. Sheppard, *Survey of London*, vol. 38: 203.

32. James Fergusson, 'The new Law Courts,' *MacMillan's Magazine* 25 (November 1871 to April 1872) 250–6.

33. Waterhouse to Office of Works, May 4, 1868, PRO, Work 17, 16/2.

34. *Builder* 22 (May 14, 1864) 359. An associate of Fowke's, John Liddell, later claimed to have completed the exterior design. After Fowke died, Liddell requested to be hired to replace him, but the Office of Works refused. Sheppard, *Survey of London*, vol. 38: 205.

35. Jacques Androuet du Cerceau, *Les Trois Livres d'Architecture* (Paris, 1559, 1561 and 1582). See especially *L'elevation du bastiment et contenu du cloz*, Plate V. I thank John Paoletti for recognizing the similarity.

36. George Hamilton (for the British Museum trustees) to the Treasury, January 13, 1864, PRO, Work 17, 16/1.

37. When Victorian naturalists referred to 'students' or the need for 'student galleries,' they did not mean schoolchildren. It is more likely that they meant students of natural history, in a general sense. This would have included professional men of science, some amateur naturalists, and advanced students, many of them working toward medical degrees, who would have had references from other known men of science which allowed them to work with the specimens.

38. British Museum Trustees to Office of Works, March 27, 1865, PRO, Work 17, 16/1.

39. *Builder* 22 (June 25, 1864) 473.

40. Robert Kerr, 'Kensington Museums: competition of architectural designs,' Natural History Museum Library and Archives, O.DES/2.

41. *Builder* 22 (June 25, 1864) 473.

42 Michael Darby and David Van Zanten, 'Owen Jones's iron buildings of the 1850s,' *Architectura* (1974) 60.

43. Francis Fowke, 'Remarks on the plans for the proposed new buildings at South Kensington in connection with the British Museum,' (December 7, 1865) 1. Victoria and Albert Museum, National Art Library.

44. Fowke, 'Remarks,' 1.

45. Fowke, 'Remarks,' 4.

46. Fowke, 'Remarks,' 4.

47. Girouard, *Alfred Waterhouse*, 17–18; Cunningham and Waterhouse, *Alfred Waterhouse*, 73; and Sheppard, *Survey of London*, vol. 38: 206: 'as an executant of Fowke's elevational design his selection was implausible.'

48. Waterhouse to Commissioner of Works, February 27, 1866, PRO, Work 17, 16/2.

49. Waterhouse to Commissioner of Works, March 19, 1867, PRO, Work 17, 16/2.

50. Waterhouse to Commissioner of Works, August 2, 1869, PRO, Work 17, 16/2.

51. The Natural History Museum in Dublin was designed by Clarendon before Fowke began work on the National Gallery of Ireland; the two buildings have almost identical exteriors. Catherine De Courcy, *The Foundation of the National Gallery of Ireland* (Dublin: National Gallery of Ireland, 1985) 15. Waterhouse probably visited Deane and Woodward's museum for Trinity College, since he admired their University Museum at Oxford which he had seen in 1858. Waterhouse found the 'upper arcade very pretty,' the 'cornice above very simple,' and the 'window glass with bull's eyes very good.' Cunningham and Waterhouse, *Alfred Waterhouse*, 17.

52. Memorandum, Treasury to Office of Works, February 14, 1867, PRO, Work 17, 16/2.

53. This plan is in the collection of the Natural History Museum Archives. It has notes in Richard Owen's hand, and is dated 1868.

54. Waterhouse to Office of Works, May 4, 1868, PRO, Work 17, 16/2.

55. This location for the glazing was correctly attributed by Waterhouse to Charles Barry: '[the rooms] lit at an angle between the ceiling and the walls after the manner of the Museums at the College of Surgeons.' Waterhouse to Office of Works, May 4, 1868, PRO, Work 17, 16/2.

56. The Royal Institute of British Architects has published this drawing (RIBA V13/6 2) as a postcard with the caption 'Dinosaur Gallery.' This labelling is misleading, because the only dinosaur skeletons visible in the drawing are mounted on the wall. All of the other skeletons seem to be from extinct or living mammals.

57. The small arch at the left of the drawing does not correspond to any detail in the 1868 plan.

58. T. H. Huxley, *Suggestions for a Proposed Natural History Museum in Manchester* [1868] (reprint, London: Report of Museum Association, 1896). A closely related text, without illustrations, was reprinted in T. H. Huxley, *Life and Letters*, vol. 1: 146–7.

59. T. H. Huxley, *Suggestions*, 146.

60. 'First Report: Hungerford Bridge and Wellington Street Viaduct,' May 10, 1869, 111. Natural History Museum Library and Archives.

61. 'Hungerford Bridge,' 112.

62. 'Hungerford Bridge,' 116.

63. The effect is subtle in his perspective drawing, but a small plan for a curved museum, dated May 3, 1869, clearly shows his intention. Drawing, WATA [41] 10, Royal Institute of British Architects, Drawings Collection.

64. Waterhouse to Commissioner of Works, December 20, 1869, PRO, Work 17, 16/2.

65. Waterhouse to Commissioner of Works, December 19, 1869, PRO, Work 17, 16/2.

66. 'Richard Owen miscellaneous manuscripts,' vol. 4, p. 20. Natural History Museum Library and Archives.

67. The drawing may show the influence of Owen in the inclusion of four sculptures of female nudes on the staircase, one with a jug on her head. Although it is almost impossible to ascertain the meaning of the sculptures from this drawing alone, one possibility is that the four nude female figures were personifications of continents – perhaps an adept visual allusion to Owen's imperialistic goals for the institution.

68. E. Ingress Bell, 'The new Natural History museum,' *Magazine of Art* 4 (May 1881) 464.

69. Waterhouse to Office of Works, May 3, 1868, PRO, Work 17, 16/2.

70. Cunningham and Waterhouse, *Alfred Waterhouse*, 3: 'For most of the time he was too busy building to theorise, and has left little record of his thinking.'

71. Carol Duncan and Alan Wallach have described a visitor's walk through an art

museum as a ritual in which visitors 'unknowingly internalize universal values of citizenship.' As part of the ritualistic experience, visitors are compelled to walk through the museum in a sequential order. In the Natural History Museum, no such sequence existed. Carol Duncan and Alan Wallach, 'The universal survey museum,' *Art History* 3, no. 4 (December 1980) 452.

72. At the Oxford Museum, the ornament was carved and thus each detail is different. At the Natural History Museum, the use of molds for the terracotta enabled the architect to use the same ornamental detail in many places.

73. Alfred Waterhouse to Richard Owen, October 12, 1874, 'Richard Owen: miscellaneous manuscripts,' Natural History Museum Library and Archives. Little is known of Dujardin, but he may have been Auguste Dujardin, born in Paris in 1847, who showed a bas-relief medallion in marble at the Salon of 1866. Stanislas Lami, *Dictionnaire des Sculpteurs de L'École Française au Dix-Neuvième Siècle* (Paris, 1916) 238.

74. Owen, *Report of the British Association for the Advancement of Science* (1881) 658.

75. Alfred Waterhouse to Richard Owen, October 12, 1874, 'Richard Owen: miscellaneous manuscripts,' Natural History Museum Library and Archives.

76. For more on the date of the term's first use, see Hugh Torrens, 'When did the dinosaur get its name?' *New Scientist* 134, no. 4 (April 1992) 40–4.

77. James A. Secord, 'Dining in the iguanodon: the anatomy of a meal,' paper delivered at the Cambridge Cabinet of Natural History, Department of History and Philosophy of Science, Cambridge University, November 1992.

78. *The Times* (London) March 8, 1996.

79. Although the Sydenham Crystal Palace burned down in 1938, the dinosaur and extinct mammal sculptures are still in the park.

80. Waterhouse probably did not choose the species for the ornament: Owen did. But again it is difficult to determine why Owen chose some species and not others. Owen did include several creatures on which he had published articles, including the dodo and the pterodactyl, but he did not include the famous moa (*Dinornus maximus*) which signified Owen's precociousness as a reconstructive anatomist. (Owen had predicted the existence of an extinct giant flightless ostrich-like bird from a six-inch femur fragment, and soon after his prediction the discovery of whole skeletons proved him correct.) Both archeopteryx and moa fossils were displayed in the museum when it opened, even though neither appear in the decoration. There is no archeopteryx in the museum's ornament, which might be explained by Owen's conservatism: one can speculate that he would not want any transitional animals that offered some of the best evidence for evolution commemorated on his museum. *Nature* 23, no. 598 (April 14, 1881) 550.

81. Guidebooks to London corroborate this finding. Most noted that the stuffed mammals were the highlight of the museum, and that the hummingbird collection, mineralogy display (especially the diamond and ruby donated by John Ruskin) and British birds were worth viewing. Guidebooks usually gave the same description of the architecture that appeared in the newspapers: 'magnificent building in the Romanesque style, which prevailed in Lombardy from the tenth to the twelfth century,' *London and Fashionable Resorts* (London: J. P. Segg, 1894) 196.

82. *Daily News* (London) February 15, 1881.

83. *Nature* 23, no. 598 (April 14, 1881) 550.

84. *Daily News* (London) September 6, 1879.

85. *Daily News* (London) September 6, 1879.

86. *Builder* 36 (June 22, 1878) 635.

87. Bell, 'The new Natural History Museum,' 360.

88. *Nature* 27, no. 681 (November 16, 1882) 55.

89. *Nature* 27, no. 681 (November 16, 1882) 55.

90. *Nature* 27, no. 681 (November 16, 1882) 55.

91. *Nature* 27, no. 681 (November 16, 1882) 55.

92. Owen, *Report of the British Association of the Advancement of Science* (1881) 660.

93. *Athenaeum* (June 30, 1860) 891.

94. *The Times* (London) December 11, 1881.

95. William Henry Flower, *Essays on Museums and other Subjects connected with Natural History* (London: MacMillan, 1889) 42.

96. William Henry Flower, *Essays on Museums and Other Subjects Connected with Natural History* (London: Macmillan, 1889) 42.

6 Still Life: Natural History Museums Today

1. Quotation from the Natural History Museum's official web site, www:/http/nhm.ac.uk.

2. William T. Hornaday, *Taxidermy and Zoological Collections* (London: Kegan Paul, Trench and Trubner, 1891) 222.

3. Hornaday, *Taxidermy*, 229.

4. Hornaday, *Taxidermy*, 238.

5. Karen Wonders, 'Exhibiting fauna – from spectacle to habitat group,' *Curator* 32, no. 2: 142. These museum dioramas are obviously different from the diorama begun in the 1830s by Daguerre in Paris, which was more like the panorama buildings in Leicester Square and Regent's Park.

6. Rebecca Solnit, *A Book of Migrations: Some Passages in Ireland* (London and New York: Verso, 1997) 20.

7. For a critical reading of the American Museum of Natural History's African Hall, see Donna Haraway, *Primate Visions: Gender, Race, and Nature in the World of Modern Science* (New York: Routledge, 1989) 29–31.

8. Charlotte Porter, 'Natural history in the twentieth century: an oxymoron?' in Paisley S. Cato and Clyde Jones (eds) *Natural History Museums: Directions for Growth* (Lubbock, TX: Texas Tech. University Press) 233.

9. Sharon MacDonald, *Politics of Display: Museums, Science, Culture* (London and New York: Routledge, 1998) 2.

10. *Morning Chronicle* (London) October 3, 1853.

11. *The Times* (London) April 18, 1881.

12. Stephen Jay Gould, 'Cabinet museums revisited: jam-packed Victorian displays still contain up-to-date messages,' *Natural History* (January 1994) 16.

13. Gould, 'Cabinet museums revisited,' 16.

14. Solnit, *Migrations*, 20.

15. MacDonald, *Politics of Display*, 13.

16. Barbara Stafford, *Good Looking: Essays on the Virtue of Images* (Cambridge, MA: MIT Press, 1996) 40.

17. Steven Conn, *Museums and American Intellectual Life* (Chicago: University of Chicago Press, 1998) 45.

18. Stephen Jay Gould, 'Dinomania,' *New York Review of Books* (August 12, 1993) 51–6.

19. Gould, 'Dinomania,' 55.

20. James A. Secord, in N. Jardine, J. A. Secord and Emma Spary (eds) *Cultures of Natural History*, (Cambridge and New York: Cambridge University Press, 1996) 455.

21. Secord, in *Cultures of Natural History*, 450.

22. *The Times* (London) April 18, 1881: 'museums are, or, at least, have been hitherto, very dull and wearisome places. Most visitors are made to feel the force of the saying that "a living dog is better than a dead lion." '

23. Lynn Nyhart, 'Natural history and the "New" Biology,' in N. Jardine, J. A. Secord and Emma Spary (eds) *Cultures of Natural History*, 439. Nyhart argues that it is incorrect to assert, as many historians have, that biology superseded natural history. This latter version of history was written primarily by those championing the new biology. The practice of systematics and morphology continued in less glamorous settings than the university laboratory, and thus has been underestimated.

24. Secord, in *Cultures of Natural History*, 452.

25. Peter Davis, *Museums and the Natural Environment: The Role of Natural History Museums in Biological Conservation* (New York and London: Leicester University Press, 1996) 2.

26. Trevor Garnham, *Oxford Museum* (London: Phaidon, 1992) 17.

27. William J. R. Curtis, *Modern Architecture Since 1900*, 3rd edn (London: Phaidon, 1996) 38.

28. *The Times* (London) April 18, 1881.

29. Natural History Museum, Corporate Plan, 1900–1905, quoted by Secord, in *Cultures of Natural History*, 452.

30. *The Times* (London) July 18, 1996.

Conclusion: The Role of Architecture in the Social Construction of Knowledge

1. Daniel J. Sherman and Irit Rogoff, *Museum Culture: Histories, Discourses, Spectacles* (Minneapolis: University of Minnesota Press, 1994) xi; Sharon MacDonald, *Politics of Display: Museums, Science, Culture* (London and New York: Routledge, 1998) 2.

2. David E. Allen, *The Naturalist in Britain: A Social History* (London: Allen Lane, 1976) 74.

3. James A. Secord, in N. Jardine, J. A. Secord and E. Spary (eds) *Cultures of Natural History* (Cambridge and New York: Cambridge University Press, 1996) 457–9.

Epilogue: Two More Arks – The Museum of Creation and the Museum of Jurassic Technology

1. David Wilson, quoted in Lawrence Weschler, *Mr. Wilson's Cabinet of Wonder* (New York: Vintage, 1995) 26.

2. Billius was certainly bilious, so that etymology is clear. I personally choose to believe that the Owen Thums were named after Richard Owen.

3. Jan Golinski, *Making Natural Knowledge: Constructivism and the History of Science* (Cambridge: Cambridge University Press, 1998).

4. Weschler, *Mr. Wilson's Cabinet of Wonder*, 60.

5. Weschler, *Mr. Wilson's Cabinet of Wonder*, 38.

Select Bibliography

Archival Sources and Drawings

Acland, Henry, Acland MSS, Bodleian Library, Oxford.

Letters to John Ruskin, Letters to Richard Owen, and Miscellaneous Letters.

Barry, Edward M., Competition drawings for the Oxford University Museum. Royal Institute of
    British Architects, Drawings Collection.

Boisserée, Sulpiz, *Denkmale der Baukunst der Nieder Rhein*, Munich, 1833. British Library, Rare
    Books.

British Museum, Minutes of the Trustees of the British Museum, Sub-Committees on
    Natural History, Buildings, and Finance. Archives of the British Museum.

Cockerell, Charles R., Letters and drawings pertaining to the Cambridge University Library
    and Cambridge University Archives.

Daubeny, Charles, 'A Dream of a New Museum,' 1855. Oxford University Archives.

Duncan, P. B., *A Catalogue of the Ashmolean Museum*, Oxford: Collingwood, 1836. British
    Library.

'First Report: Hungerford Bridge and Wellington Street Viaduct' (May 10, 1869). Natural
    History Museum Archives.

Fowke, Francis, Drawings of the Edinburgh Museum of Science and Art. Scottish Record
    Office and Royal Scottish Museum, Edinburgh.

Fowke, Francis, 'Remarks on the plans for the Proposed New Buildings at South Kensington
    in connection with the British Museum.' National Art Library, Victoria and Albert
    Museum, 1865.

Huxley, Thomas H., Papers. Imperial College Archives, London.

Papers concerning the Oxford University Museum, NW/2/1. Oxford University Archives.

Oxford Museum Delegates, UM/M/1. Oxford University Archives.

Owen, Richard, Manuscripts. Natural History Museum Archives.

United Kingdom Public Record Office, Papers of the Office of Works, Work 17, 16/1, Work 17,
    16/2, Papers of the Department of Education, ED 28/2, ED 28/7.

Rickman, Thomas, Drawings. Royal Institute of British Architects, Drawings Collection.

Rickman, Thomas, Diaries. Royal Institute of British Architects, Library.

Waterhouse, Alfred, Drawings. Royal Institute of British Architects.

Waterhouse, Alfred, 'Pencil sketches for the terracotta decoration of the Natural History
    Museum.' Natural History Museum Archives.

Whewell, William, Papers. Trinity College Library, Cambridge.

Woodward, Benjamin, Drawings. Drawings department of the National Gallery of
    Ireland.

Woodward, Benjamin and Thomas Deane, Original plans. Oxford University Archives, UM/P/ 3/nos 1–9.

Newspapers and periodicals
Art Journal, 1862.
Athenaeum, 1860.
Builder, 1848, 1855, 1860, 1864, 1883.
Building News, vol. 11, 1864.
Chronicle and Berks and Bucks Gazette (Oxford) 1854.
Daily News (London) 1879.
Daily Review (Edinburgh) 1861.
Daily Scotsman (Edinburgh) 1858, 1861.
Evening Courant (Edinburgh) 1861.
Evening Standard (London) 1881.
Illustrated London News (London) 1845, 1851, 1852, 1854, 1858.
Jackson's Oxford Journal (Oxford) 1854.
London Journal (London) 1862.
Nature (London) 1881, 1882.
Punch (London) 1862.
Reports of the British Association for the Advancement of Science.
Repository of the Arts, Literature and Commerce (published by Rudolf Ackerman) 1810, 1815.
The Times (London) 1858.

Articles and books
Acland, Henry W. and John Ruskin, *The Oxford Museum*, 4th edn, London: George Allen, 1893 [1859].
Alexander, Edward P., *Museums in Motion*, Nashville, TN: American Association of State and Local History, 1979.
Alexander, Edward P., *Museum Masters: Their Museums and Their Influence*, Nashville, TN: American Association of State and Local History, 1983.
Allan, Douglas A., *The Royal Scottish Museum 1854–1954*, Edinburgh: Oliver & Boyd, 1954.
Allen, David E., *The Naturalist in Britain: A Social History*, London: Allen Lane, 1976.
Altick, Richard D., *The Shows of London*, Cambridge, MA: MIT Press, 1978.
Anderson, R. G. W., ' "What is technology?": Education through museums in the mid-nineteenth century,' *British Journal for the History of Science*, 25 (1992) 169–84.
Arnold, Matthew, *Complete Prose Works of Matthew Arnold*, ed. R. H. Super, Ann Arbor, MI: University of Michigan Press, 1964.
Bailey, P., *Leisure and Class in Victorian Britain: Rational Recreation and the Contest for Control, 1830–1885*, London, 1978.
Baglioli, Mario, 'Confabulating Jurassic science,' in George Marcus (ed.) *Technoscientific Imaginaries: Conversations, Profiles, and Memoirs*, Chicago: University of Chicago Press, 1995.
Barber, Lynn, *The Heyday of Natural History 1820–1870*, Garden City, NJ: Doubleday, 1980.
Beaver, Patrick, *The Crystal Palace, 1851–1936: Portrait of a Victorian Enterprise*, London: Hugh Evelyn, 1970.
Becker, Bernard H., *Scientific London*, London: Henry S. King, 1874.
Bell, E. Ingress, 'The new Natural History Museum,' *Magazine of Art* 4 (May 1881) 358–62, 463–5.
Bennett, Tony, *The Birth of the Museum: History, Theory, Politics*, London: Routledge, 1995.
Blau, Eve, *Ruskinian Gothic: The Architecture of Deane and Woodward 1845–1861*, Princeton: Princeton University Press, 1982.
Bonython, Elizabeth, *King Cole: A Picture Portrait of Sir Henry Cole, 1808–1882*, London: Victoria and Albert Museum, 1982.

Booth, Michael R., *Victorian Spectacular Theatre 1850–1910*, London: Routledge & Kegan Paul, 1981.

Bowler, Peter J., *The Eclipse of Darwinism: Anti-Darwinian Evolutionary Theories in the Decades around 1900*, Baltimore: Johns Hopkins University Press, 1983.

Bowler, Peter J., *The Non-Darwinian Revolution: Reinterpreting a Historical Myth*, Baltimore and London: Johns Hopkins University Press, 1988.

Brewster, Lindy, 'The Harpur Crewe collection of natural history at Calke Abbey, Derbyshire,' *Journal of the History of Collections* 9, no. 1 (1997) 131–8.

Briggs, Asa, *Victorian Things*, Chicago: University of Chicago Press, 1988.

Brooke, John Hedley, *Science and Religion: Some Historical Perspectives*, Cambridge: Cambridge University Press, 1991.

Brooks, Michael W., *John Ruskin and Victorian Architecture*, London: Thames and Hudson, 1987.

Brown, Thomas, *The Taxidermist's Manual, or the Art of Collecting, Preparing, and Preserving Objects of Natural History*, Glasgow: Archibald Fullarton, 1837.

Browne, Janet, *The Secular Ark: Studies in the History of Biogeography*. New Haven: Yale University Press, 1983.

Brownlee, David B., *The Law Courts: The Architecture of George Edmund Street*, Cambridge, MA, and London: MIT Press, 1984.

Brownlee, David B., 'The first High Victorians: British architectural theory in the 1840s,' *Architectura* 15, no. 1 (1985) 33–46.

Brownlee, David B., 'That regular mongrel affair: G. G. Scott's design for the government offices,' *Architectural History* 28 (1985) 159–97.

Burckhardt, Frederick, and Sydney Smith (eds) *The Correspondence of Charles Darwin*, 10 vols, Cambridge: Cambridge University Press, 1985–1997.

Calder, Jenni, *The Enterprising Scot: Scottish Adventure and Achievement*. Edinburgh: Royal Museums of Scotland, 1986.

Calder, Jenni, (ed.) *The Wealth of a Nation in the National Museums of Scotland*, Edinburgh: Royal Museums of Scotland, 1989.

Cannon, Susan F., *Science in Culture: The Early Victorian Period*, New York: Science History Publications, 1978.

Cato, Paisley S. and Clyde Jones, *Natural History Museums: Directions for Growth*, Lubbock, TX: Texas Tech University Press, 1991.

Checkland, Sydney and Olive, *Industry and Ethos: Scotland, 1832–1914*, Baltimore: Edward Arnold, 1984.

Clark, Kenneth, *The Gothic Revival: An Essay in the History of Taste*, 3rd edn, London: J. Murray, 1962.

Cole, Henry, *Fifty Years of Public Work of Sir Henry Cole, Accounted for in his Deeds, Speeches, and Writing*, London: G. Bell, 1884.

Cole, Henry, 'Brief notes on the career of the late Captain Francis Fowke, RE,' *Papers on Subjects Connected with the Royal Engineers* 15 (1866) xiii.

Colvin, Howard, (ed.) *The History of the King's Works*, London: Her Majesty's Stationery Office, 1963.

Colvin, Howard, *Unbuilt Oxford*, New Haven and London: Yale University Press, 1983.

Conn, Steven, *Museums and American Intellectual Life*, Chicago: University of Chicago Press, 1998.

Cook, Jeffrey, and Tanis Hinchcliffe, 'Designing the well-tempered institution of 1873,' *ARQ Architectural Research Quarterly*, Winter 1995.

Crimp, Douglas, *On the Museum's Ruins*, Cambridge, MA: MIT Press, 1993.

Crook, J. Mordaunt, *The British Museum*, New York: Praeger, 1972.

Cunningham, Colin, and Prudence Waterhouse, *Alfred Waterhouse, 1830–1905: Biography of a Practice*, Oxford: Clarendon, 1992.

Darby, Michael, and David Van Zanten, 'Owen Jones's Iron Buildings of the 1850s,' *Architectura* (1974) 53–75.

Davis, Peter, *Museums and the Natural Environment: The Role of Natural History Museums in Biological Conservation*, London and New York: Leicester University Press, 1996.

Dear, Peter, (ed.) *The Scientific Enterprise in Early Modern Europe: Readings from Isis*, Chicago: University of Chicago Press, 1997.

Desmond, Adrian, *Hot-Blooded Dinosaurs: A Revolution in Palaeontology*, London: Blond & Briggs, 1975.

Desmond, Adrian, *Archetypes and Ancestors: Palaeontology in Victorian London, 1850–1875*, London: Blond & Briggs, 1982.

Desmond, Adrian, *Huxley: From Devil's Disciple to Evolution's High Priest*, Reading, MA: Addison-Wesley, 1997.

Desmond, Adrian, and James Moore, *Darwin*, London: Michael Joseph, 1991.

Dixon, Roger, and Stefan Muthesius, *Victorian Architecture*, New York and London: Oxford University Press, 1978.

Dobson, Jess, 'The architectural history of the Hunterian Museum,' *Annals of the Royal College of Surgeons of England* 29 (August 1961) 113–26.

Douglas, Allan A., *The Royal Scottish Museum: Art and Ethnography, Natural History, Technology, Geology, 1854–1954*, Edinburgh: Oliver & Boyd, 1954.

Duncan, Carol, *Civilizing Rituals: Inside Public Art Museums*, London and New York: Routledge, 1995.

Duncan, Carol, and Alan Wallach, 'The universal survey museum,' *Art History* 3, no. 4 (December 1980) 448–69.

Elsner, John, and Roger Cardinal, *Cultures of Collecting*, London: Reaktion, 1994.

Fawcett, Jane (ed.) *Seven Victorian Architects*, London: Thames & Hudson, 1976.

Fergusson, James, *History of the Modern Styles of Architecture*, vol. 3, New York: Dodd, Mead, 1891.

Fergusson, James, 'The new Law Courts,' *MacMillan's Magazine* 25 (November 1871 to April 1872) 250–6.

Ferriday, Peter, 'The Oxford Museum,' *Architectural Review* (December 1962) 408–16.

Findlen, Paula, *Possessing Nature: Museums, Collecting, and Scientific Culture in Early Modern Italy*, Berkeley: University of California Press, 1994.

Flower, William Henry, *Essays on Museums and Other Subjects Connected with Natural History*, London: MacMillan, 1889.

Forgan, Sophie, 'Context, image and function: a preliminary enquiry into the architecture of scientific societies,' *British Journal for the History of Science* 19 (1986) 89–113.

Forgan, Sophie, 'The architecture of science and the idea of a university,' *Studies in the History and Philosophy of Science* 20, no. 4 (December 1989) 405–34.

Forgan, Sophie, 'The architecture of display: museums, universities, and objects in nineteenth-century Britain,' *History of Science* 32, no. 96 (June 1994) 139–62.

Forgan, Sophie, ' "But indifferently lodged": perception and place in building for science in Victorian London,' in Crosbie Smith and Jon Agar (eds) *Making Space for Science: Territorial Themes in the Shaping of Knowledge*, London: Macmillan, 1998.

Forgan, Sophie, 'Bricks and Bones: architecture and science in Victorian Britain,' in Peter Galison and Emily Thompson (eds) *The Architecture of Science*, Cambridge, MA: MIT Press, 1999.

Forgan, Sophie, and Graeme Gooday, 'Constructing South Kensington: the buildings and politics of T. H. Huxley's working environments,' *British Journal for the History of Science*, 29 (1996) 435–68.

Foucault, Michel, *Power/Knowledge: Selected Interviews and Writings, 1972–1977*, New York: Pantheon, 1981.

Foucault, Michel, *The Order of Things: An Archeology of the Human Sciences*, New York: Vintage, 1994.

Fox, Celina, (ed.) *London – World City*, New Haven and London: Yale University Press, 1992.

Friebe, Wolfgang, *Buildings of the World Exhibitions*, trans. Jenny Vowles and Paul Roper, Leipzig: Druckerei Volksstimme Magdeburg, 1985.

Galison, Peter, and Caroline Jones (eds) *Picturing Science, Producing Art*, New York: Routledge, 1998.

Garland, Martha McMackin, *Cambridge before Darwin: The Ideal of a Liberal Education, 1800–1860*, New York and Cambridge: Cambridge University Press, 1980.

Garnham, Trevor, *Oxford Museum: Deane and Woodward*, London: Phaidon, 1992.

Garrigan, Kristine, *Ruskin on Architecture*, Madison, WI: University of Wisconsin Press, 1973.

Girouard, Mark, *Alfred Waterhouse and the Natural History Museum*, London: British Museum – Natural History, 1981.

Golinski, Jan, *Making Natural Knowledge: Constructivism and the History of Science*, Cambridge: Cambridge University Press, 1998.

Goodman, Nelson, 'How buildings mean,' *Critical Inquiry* (June 1985) 642–53.

Grant, James, *Cassell's Old and New Edinburgh, Its History, Its People, Its Places*, London: Cassell, 1882.

Gray, John Edward, 'On museums, their use and improvement, and on the acclimatization of animals,' *Report of the British Association for the Advancement of Science* (1865) 75–86.

Greenwood, Thomas, *Museums and Art Galleries*, London: Simkin, Marshall, 1888.

Greswell, Richard, *Memorial on the (Proposed) Oxford University Lecture Rooms, Library, Museums &c. Addressed to Members of Convocation*, Oxford: Beaumont Street, 1853.

Gunther, A. E., *The Founders of Science at the British Museum, 1753–1900*, Halesworth, Suffolk: Halesworth, 1980.

Hall, James, *Essay on the Origin, History, and Principles of Gothic Architecture*, London: J. Murray, 1813.

Haraway, Donna, *Primate Visions: Gender, Race, and Nature in the World of Modern Science*, New York: Routledge, 1989.

Haward, Birkin, 'The Oxford University Museum,' *Architect's Journal* (27 September 1989) 41–63. Reprint, Oxford: Oxford University Museum, 1991.

Hawkins, Benjamin Waterhouse, 'On visual education as applied to geology,' *Journal of the Society of Arts* 2 (1854) 444–9.

Helsinger, Elizabeth A., *Ruskin and the Art of the Beholder*, Cambridge, MA and London: Harvard University Press, 1982.

Hersey, George, *High Victorian Gothic: A Study in Associationism*, Baltimore: Johns Hopkins University Press, 1972.

Hewison, Robert, *John Ruskin: The Argument of the Eye*, London: Thames and Hudson, 1976.

Hilton, Tim, *John Ruskin: The Early Years, 1819–1859*, New Haven: Yale University Press, 1985.

Hoage, R. J. and William A. Deiss (eds) *New Worlds, New Animals: From Menagerie to Zoological Park in the Nineteenth Century*, Baltimore: Johns Hopkins University Press, 1996.

Hobhouse, Christopher, *1851 and the Crystal Palace*, London: John Murray, 1937.

Hooper-Greenhill, Eilean, *Museums and The Shaping of Knowledge*, London and New York: Routledge, 1992.

Hornaday, William T., *Taxidermy and Zoological Collecting*, London: Kegan Paul, Trench and Trubner, 1891.

Hudson, Kenneth, *A Social History of Museums: What the Visitors Thought*, Atlantic Highlands, NJ: Humanities, 1975.

Hudson, Kenneth, *Museums of Influence*, Cambridge: Cambridge University Press, 1987.

Hunt, John Dixon, *A Wider Sea: A Life of John Ruskin*, New York: Viking, 1982.

Huxley, Leonard, *Life and Letters of Joseph Dalton Hooker*, [1918] 2 vols, New York: Arno, 1978.

Huxley, Thomas H., *Suggestions for a Proposed Natural History Museum in Manchester*, [1868] reprint, London: Report of the Museums Association, 1896.

Huxley, Thomas H., *Life and Letters of Thomas Henry Huxley*, ed. Leonard Huxley [1900] reprint, New York: AMS, 1979.

Impey, Oliver, and Arthur MacGregor, *The Origins of Museums: The Cabinet of Curiosities in Sixteenth- and Seventeenth-Century Europe*, Oxford: Oxford University Press, 1985.

Jackson, Peter, *George Scharf's London: Sketches and Watercolours of a Changing City, 1820–50*, London: John Murray, 1987.

Jardine, N., J. A. Secord and Emma Spary (eds) *Cultures of Natural History*, Cambridge and New York: Cambridge University Press, 1996.

Karp, Ivan, and Steven D. Lavine (eds) *Exhibiting Cultures: The Poetics and Politics of Museum Display*, Washington, DC: Smithsonian Institution, 1991.

Kenseth, Joy (ed.) *The Age of the Marvelous*, Hanover, NH: Hood Museum of Art, 1991.

Knott, Cargill G., (ed.) *Edinburgh's Place in Scientific Progress*, Edinburgh and London: W. & R. Chambers, 1921.

Lee, Paula Young, 'The logic of the bones: architecture and the anatomical sciences at the Museum d'Histoire Naturelle, 1789–1889,' PhD dis., University of Chicago, 1998.

Lee, Paula Young, 'The Musaeum of Alexandria and the formation of the museum in eighteenth-century France,' *Art Bulletin* 79, no. 3 (September 1997) 385–412.

Lefebvre, H., *The Production of Space*, trans. Donald Nicholson-Smith, Blackwell: Oxford, 1981.

Lenman, Bruce, *Integration, Enlightenment, and Industrialization: Scotland, 1746–1832*, Toronto and Buffalo: University of Toronto Press, 1981.

Lever, Jill, *Catalogue of the Drawings Collection of the Royal Institute of British Architects*, London: Gregg International, 1984.

Limoges, C. 'The development of the Museum d'Histoire Naturelle' in R. Fox and G. Weicz (eds) *The Organization of Science and Technology in France 1800–1914*, Cambridge and Paris: Cambridge University Press, 1980.

Liscombe, R. W., *William Wilkins, 1778–1839*, Cambridge: Cambridge University Press, 1980.

MacDonald, Sharon (ed.) *The Politics of Display: Museums, Science, Culture*, London and New York: Routledge, 1998.

MacGregor, Arthur, *Tradescant's Rarities: Essays on the Foundation of the Ashmolean Museum, 1683*, Oxford: Clarendon, 1983.

Markus, Thomas A., *Order in Space and Society: Architectural Form and its Context in the Scottish Enlightenment*, Edinburgh: Mainstream, 1982.

Markus, Thomas A., 'Domes of enlightenment: two Scottish university museums,' *Art History* 8, no. 2 (June 1985) 158–77.

Markus, Thomas A., *Buildings and Power: Freedom and Control in the Origin of Modern Building Types*, London and New York: Routledge, 1993.

Moore, James J., *The Historical Handbook and Guide to Oxford: Embracing a Succinct History of the University and City from the Year 912*, Oxford: Thomas Shrimpton, 1878.

Morrell, J. and Arnold Thackray, *Gentlemen of Science: Early Years of the British Association for the Advancement of Science*, Oxford: Clarendon, 1981.

O'Dwyer, Frederick, *The Architecture of Deane and Woodward*, Cork University Press, 1997.

Olley, John, and Caroline Wilson, 'The Natural History Museum,' *Architects' Journal* 181, no. 13 (27 March 1985) 32–50, 52.

Ophir, Adi, and Steven Shapin, 'The place of knowledge: a methodological survey,' *Science in Context* 4 (1991) 3–21.

Orosz, Joel J., *Curators and Culture*, Tuscaloosa and London: University of Alabama Press, 1990.

Outram, Dorinda, and Pnina G. Abir-Am (eds) *Uneasy Careers and Intimate Lives: Women in Science*, New Brunswick, NJ: Rutgers University Press, 1987.

Ovenell, R. R., *The Ashmolean Museum, 1683–1894*, Oxford: Clarendon, 1986.

Owen, Richard, *Geology and Inhabitants of the Ancient World, the animals constructed by B. W. Hawkins, FGS*, London: Crystal Palace Library/Bradbury & Evans, 1854.

Owen, Richard, *A History of British Fossils and Birds*, London: John Van Voorst, 1846.

Owen, Richard, *On the Extent and Aims of a National Museum of Natural History*, London: Saunders, Otley, 1862.

Owen, Richard, *Report of the British Association for the Advancement of Science* (1858) 49–60.

Owen, Richard, *Report of the British Association of the Advancement of Science* (1881) 651–61.

Owen, Richard, Rev., *The Life of Richard Owen*, Westmead: Gregg International, reprint, 1970.

Paley, William, *Natural Theology, or Evidences of the Existence and Attributes of the Diety, Collected from the Appearances of Nature*, London, 1802.

Papworth, John W., *Museums, Libraries and Picture Galleries, Public and Private, Their Establishment, Formation, Arrangement, and Architectural Construction*, London: Chapman Hall, 1852.

Parker, John Henry, *The Ashmolean Museum: Its History, Present State, and Prospects: A Lecture given to the Oxford Architectural Society*, Oxford, n.p., 1870.

[Peacock, George], *Observations on the Plans for the New Library &c. By a Member of the First Syndicate*, Cambridge: J. Smith, 1831.

Pearce, Susan M., *Museums, Objects and Collections: A Cultural Study*, Leicester and London: Leicester University Press, 1992.

Pearce, Susan M. (ed.) *Exploring Science in Museums*, New Research in Museum Studies Series, London and Atlantic Highlands, NJ: Athlone Press, 1996.

Peponis, J. and J. Hedin, 'The lay-out theories in the Natural History Museum,' *9H* 2, no. 3 (1982) 21–5.

Physick, John and Michael Darby, *Marble Halls: Drawings and Models for Victorian Secular Buildings*, London: Victoria and Albert Museum, 1973.

Pickstone, John V. ' "Museological science": the place of the analytical/comparative in nineteenth-century science, technology, and medicine,' *History of Science* 32 (1994) 113–32.

Pomian, Krzysztof, *Collectors and Curiosities: Paris and Venice, 1500–1800*, trans. Elizabeth Wiles-Portier, Cambridge: Polity Press, 1990.

Port, M. H., *Imperial London: Civil Government Building in London*, New Haven and London: Yale University Press, 1995.

Porter, C. M., 'The Natural History Museum,' in *The Museum – A Reference Guide*, M. S. Shapiro (ed.) New York: Greenwood, 1990.

Porter, Gaby, 'Alternative Perspectives,' *Museums Journal* 93: no. 11 (1993) 25–7.

Porter, Roy, 'Gentlemen and geology: the emergence of a scientific career, 1660–1920,' *Historical Journal* 21, no. 4 (1978) 809–36.

Preston, Douglas J., *Dinosaurs in the Attic: An Excursion into the American Museum of Natural History*, New York: St Martin's Press, 1986.

Prösler, M., 'Museums and Globalization,' in S. MacDonald and G. Fyfe (eds) *Theorizing Museums*, Oxford: Blackwell, 1996.

Rawle, Tim, *Cambridge Architecture*, London: Trefoil, 1985.

Richards, Eveleen, 'A question of property rights: Richard Owen's evolutionism reassessed,' *British Journal for the History of Science* 20, part 2, no. 65 (April 1987) 127–71.

Richards, Thomas, *The Commodity Culture of Victorian England: Advertising and Spectacle, 1851–1914*, Stanford: Stanford University Press, 1990.

Richardson, Albert, *Monumental Classic Architecture in Great Britain and Ireland* [1914] reprint, New York: W. W. Norton, 1982.

Rickman, Thomas, *An Attempt to Discriminate the Styles of Architecture in England, from the Conquest to the Reformation, with a Sketch of the Grecian and Roman Orders*, 7th edn, London: Parker, 1881.

Rudwick, Martin J. S., 'The emergence of a visual language for geological science, 1760–1840,' *History of Science* 14 (1976) 149–95.

Rudwick, Martin J. S., *Scenes from Deep Time: Early Pictorial Representations of the Prehistoric World*, Chicago: University of Chicago Press, 1992.

Rugoff, Ralph, 'Beyond belief: the museum as metaphor,' in Lynn Cooke and Peter Wollen (eds) *Visual Display: Culture Beyond Appearances*, Seattle: Bay Press, 1995.

Rupke, Nicolaas A., 'The road to Albertopolis: Richard Owen (1804–92) and the founding of the British Museum of Natural History,' in *Science, Politics, and the Public Good: Essays in Honor of Margaret Gowing*, London: Macmillan, 1988.

Rupke, Nicolaas A., *Richard Owen: Victorian Naturalist*, London and New Haven: Yale University Press, 1994.

Ruskin, John, *The Works of John Ruskin*, ed. E. T. Cook and A. Wedderburn, (Library Edition) London: George Allen, 1903.

Sanderson, Michael, *The Universities in the Nineteenth Century*, London and Boston: Routledge and Kegan Paul, 1975.

Schepelern, H. D. 'The museum wormianum reconstructed: a note on the illustration of 1655,' *Journal of the History of Collections* 2, no. 1, 81–6.

Science and Art Department of the Committee of Council on Education, *Directory of the Industrial Museum of Scotland and of the Natural History Museum*, Edinburgh: George E. Eyre, 1858.

Scotland, James, *The History of Scottish Education: From the Beginning to 1872*, vol. 1, London: University of London Press, 1969.

Secord, Anne, 'Science in the pub: artisan botanists in early nineteenth-century Lancashire,' *History of Science* 32 (1994) 269–315.

Secord, James A., 'King of Siluria: Roderick Murchison and the imperial theme in nineteenth-century British geology,' *Victorian Studies* 25, no. 4 (June 1982) 413–42.

Secord, James A., *Controversy in Victorian Geology: The Cambrian–Silurian Debate*, Princeton: Princeton University Press, 1986.

Secord, James A., 'Dining in the iguanodon: the anatomy of a meal,' paper delivered at the Cambridge University Cabinet of Natural History, Department of History and Philosophy of Science, November 1992.

Secord, James A., 'Introduction' to Robert Chambers, *Vestiges of the Natural History of Creation and other Evolutionary Writings*, Chicago: University of Chicago Press, 1994.

Sellers, Charles, *Mr. Peale's Museum: Charles Willson Peale and the First Popular Museum of Natural Science and Art*, New York: W. W. Norton, 1980.

Sheets-Pyenson, Susan, *Cathedrals of Science: The Development of Colonial Natural History Museums during the Late Nineteenth Century*, Kingston and Montreal: McGill-Queens University Press, 1988.

Sheppard, F. H. W. (ed.) *Survey of London: The Museums Area of South Kensington*, vol. 38, London: Athlone, 1975.

Simcock, A. V., *The Ashmolean Museum and Oxford Science 1683–1983*, Oxford: Museum of the History of Science, 1984.

Stafford, Barbara, *Voyage into Substance: Art, Science, Nature and the Illustrated Travel Account*, Cambridge, MA: MIT Press, 1984.

Stafford, Barbara, *Good Looking: Essays on the Virtue of Images*, Cambridge, MA: MIT Press, 1996.

Stearn, William, *The Natural History Museum at South Kensington: A History of the British Museum (Natural History)*, London: Heinemann, 1981.

Stein, Richard L., 'Milk, mud, and mountain cottages: Ruskin's poetry of architecture,' *PMLA: Publications of the Modern Language Association of America* 100, no. 3 (May 1985) 328–41.

Stocking, George, *Victorian Anthropology*, New York: Free Press, 1987.

Stocking, George, *Objects and Others: Essays on Museums and Material Culture*, Madison, WI: University of Wisconsin Press, 1985.

Street, George Edmund, 'The true principles of architecture, and the possibility of development,' *Ecclesiologist* 13 (1852) 247–62.

Street, George Edmund, *An Urgent Plea for the Revival of the True Principles of Architecture in the Public Buildings at the University of Oxford*, Oxford and London: John Henry Parker, 1853.

Stroud, Dorothy, *George Dance: Architecture, 1741–1825*, London: Faber and Faber, 1971.

Tuckwell, William, *Reminiscences of Oxford*, London: Cassell, 1901.

Tyack, Geoffrey, *Sir James Pennethorne and the Making of Victorian London*, Cambridge: Cambridge University Press, 1992.

Van Eck, Caroline, *Organicism in Nineteenth-Century Architecture: An Inquiry into its Theoretical and Philosophical Background*, Amsterdam: Art and Natura Press, 1994.

Van Keuren, David K., 'Cabinets and culture: Victorian anthropology and the museum context,' *Journal of the History of the Behavioural Sciences* 25, no. 1 (January 1989) 26–39.

Vernon, Horace Middleton, and K. Dorothea Vernon, *A History of the Oxford Museum*, Oxford: Clarendon, 1909.

Wallach, Alan, *Exhibiting Contradiction: Essays on the Art Museum in the United States*, Amherst, MA: University of Massachusetts Press, 1998.

Watkin, David, *The Life and Work of C. R. Cockerell*, London: A. Zwemmer, 1974.

Watkin, David, 'Newly discovered drawings by C. R. Cockerell for Cambridge University Library,' *Architectural History* 26 (1983) 87–91.

Weale, John, *The Pictorial Handbook of London*, London: H. G. Bohn, 1854.

Weschler, Lawrence, *Mr. Wilson's Cabinet of Wonder: Pronged Ants, Horned Humans, Mice on Toast, and Other Marvels of Jurassic Technology*, New York: Vintage, 1995.

Whewell, William, *Architectural Notes on German Churches: A New Edition to which now is added Notes written during an Architectural Tour in Picardy and Normandy*, Cambridge: Pitt, 1835.

Whewell, William, 'The lamps of architecture,' *Fraser's Magazine for Town and Country* 41, no. 241 (February 1850) 151–9.

Whewell, William, 'Of certain analogies between architecture and the other fine arts,' *Royal Institute of British Architects Sessional Papers*, (1862) 175–85.

White, Adam, *Four Short Letters: The First and Fourth Addressed to the Late and to the Present Lord Provosts of Edinburgh, on the Subject of an Open Museum in the Scottish Capital*, Edinburgh: Edmonston and Douglas, 1850.

Wiener, Martin J., *English Culture and the Decline of the Industrial Spirit, 1850–1980*, Cambridge: Cambridge University Press, 1981.

Willis, Robert, and J. W. Clark, *An Architectural History of the University of Cambridge*, 4 vols, Cambridge: Cambridge University Press, 1886.

Wilson, George, *The Industrial Museum of Scotland and its Relation to Commercial Enterprise, A Lecture delivered at the Request of the Company of Merchants of the City of Edinburgh*, Edinburgh: R. & R. Clark, 1857.

Wilson, George, *On the Objects of Technology and Industrial Museums*, Edinburgh: R. & R. Clark, 1856.

Wilson, George, *On the Relation of Ornament to Industrial Art, A Lecture Delivered in the National Galleries at the Request of the Art-Manufacture Association*, Edinburgh: Edmonston and Douglas, 1857.

Winsor, Mary P., *Reading the Shape of Nature: Comparative Zoology at the Agassiz Museum*, Chicago and London: University of Chicago Press, 1991.

Winsor, Mary P., *Starfish, Jellyfish, and the Order of Life: Issues in Nineteenth-Century Science*, New Haven and London: Yale University Press, 1976.

Wonders, K. 'Exhibiting fauna – from spectacle to habitat group,' *Curator* 32, no. 2 (1990) 131–56.

Wonders, K. 'The illusory art of background painting in habitat dioramas,' *Curator* 33, no. 2 (1991) 90–118.

Wonders, K. *Habitat Dioramas: Illusions of Wilderness in Museums of Natural History*, Uppsala: Acta Universitatis Upsaliensis, 1993.

Wright, C. J., 'Holland House and the fashionable pursuit of science: a nineteenth-century cabinet of curiosities,' *Journal of the History of Collections* 1, no. 1 (1989) 97–102.

Yanni, Carla, *Building natural history: constructions of nature in British Victorian architecture and architectural theory*, PhD diss., University of Pennsylvania, 1994.

Yanni, Carla, 'Secular science or divine display: defining nature at the Natural History Museum in London,' *Journal of the Society of Architectural Historians* 55, no. 3 (September 1996) 276–299.

Yanni, Carla, 'On nature and nomenclature: William Whewell and the production of architectural knowledge in Victorian Britain,' *Architectural History* 40 (1997) 204–221.

Yeo, Richard R., *Defining Science: William Whewell, Natural Knowledge and the Public Debate in Early Victorian Britain*, Cambridge: Cambridge University Press, 1993.

Index